Biopolitical Screens

Leonardo

Roger F. Malina, Executive Editor

Sean Cubitt, Editor-in-Chief

The Visual Mind II, edited by Michele Emmer, 2005

CODE: Collaborative Ownership and the Digital Economy, edited by Rishab Aiyer Ghosh, 2005

The Global Genome: Biotechnology, Politics, and Culture, Eugene Thacker, 2005

Media Ecologies: Materialist Energies in Art and Technoculture, Matthew Fuller, 2005

New Media Poetics: Contexts, Technotexts, and Theories, edited by Adalaide Morris and Thomas Swiss, 2006

Aesthetic Computing, edited by Paul A. Fishwick, 2006

Digital Performance: A History of New Media in Theater, Dance, Performance Art, and Installation, Steve Dixon, 2006

MediaArtHistories, edited by Oliver Grau, 2006

From Technological to Virtual Art, Frank Popper, 2007

META/DATA: A Digital Poetics, Mark Amerika, 2007

Signs of Life: Bio Art and Beyond, Eduardo Kac, 2007

The Hidden Sense: Synesthesia in Art and Science, Cretien van Campen, 2007

Closer: Performance, Technologies, Phenomenology, Susan Kozel, 2007

Video: The Reflexive Medium, Yvonne Spielmann, 2007

Software Studies: A Lexicon, Matthew Fuller, 2008

Tactical Biopolitics: Art, Activism, and Technoscience, edited by Beatriz da Costa and Kavita Philip, 2008

White Heat Cold Logic: British Computer Art, 1960–1980, edited by Paul Brown, Charlie Gere, Nicholas Lambert, and Catherine Mason, 2008

Rethinking Curating: Art after New Media, Beryl Graham and Sarah Cook, 2010

Green Light: Toward an Art of Evolution, George Gessert, 2010

Enfoldment and Infinity: An Islamic Genealogy of New Media Art, Laura U. Marks, 2010

Synthetics: Aspects of Art and Technology in Australia, 1956–1975, Stephen Jones, 2011

Hybrid Culture: Japanese Media Arts in Dialogue with the West, Yvonne Spielmann, 2012

Walking and Mapping: Artists as Cartographers, Karen O'Rourke, 2013

The Fourth Dimension and Non-Euclidean Geometry in Modern Art, revised edition Linda Dalrymple Henderson, 2012

Illusions in Motion: Media Archaeology of the Moving Panorama and Related Spectacles Erkki Huhtamo, 2012

Relive: Media Art Histories, Sean Cubitt and Paul Thomas, 2013

Re-collection: New Media and Social Memory, Richard Rinehart and Jon Ippolito, 2013

Biopolitical Screens: Image, Power, and the Neoliberal Brain, Pasi Väliaho, 2014

See <http://mitpress.mit.edu> for a complete list of titles in this series.

Biopolitical Screens

Image, Power, and the Neoliberal Brain

Pasi Väliaho

The MIT Press
Cambridge, Massachusetts
London, England

MIT Press books may be purchased at special quantity discounts for business or sales promotional use. For information, please email special_sales@mitpress.mit.edu.

This book was set in Stone Sans and Stone Serif by Toppan Best-set Premedia Limited. Printed and bound in the United States of America.

Library of Congress Cataloging-in-Publication Data

Väliaho, Pasi.
Biopolitical screens : image, power, and the neoliberal brain / Pasi Väliaho.
pages cm. — (Leonardo)
Includes bibliographical references and index.
ISBN 978-0-262-02747-2 (hardcover : alk. paper) 1. Visual sociology. 2. Imagery (Psychology) 3. Art and society. 4. Art and technology. 5. Biopolitics. 6. Economics. I. Title.
HM500.V35 2014
306.46—dc23

2013044423

10 9 8 7 6 5 4 3 2 1

Contents

Leonardo/International Society for the Arts, Sciences, and Technology (ISAST)

Leonardo, the International Society for the Arts, Sciences, and Technology, and the affiliated French organization Association Leonardo have some very simple goals:

1. To document and make known the work of artists, researchers, and scholars interested in the ways that the contemporary arts interact with science and technology and

2. To create a forum and meeting places where artists, scientists, and engineers can meet, exchange ideas, and, where appropriate, collaborate.

3. To contribute, through the interaction of the arts and sciences, to the creation of the new culture that will be needed to transition to a sustainable planetary society.

When the journal *Leonardo* was started some forty years ago, these creative disciplines existed in segregated institutional and social networks, a situation dramatized at that time by the "Two Cultures" debates initiated by C. P. Snow. Today we live in a different time of cross-disciplinary ferment, collaboration, and intellectual confrontation enabled by new hybrid organizations, new funding sponsors, and the shared tools of computers and the Internet. Above all, new generations of artist-researchers and researcher-artists are now at work individually and in collaborative teams bridging the art, science, and technology disciplines. For some of the hard problems in our society, we have no choice but to find new ways to couple the arts and sciences. Perhaps in our lifetime we will see the emergence of "new Leonardos," creative individuals or teams that will not only develop a meaningful art for our times but also drive new agendas in science and stimulate technological innovation that addresses today's human needs.

For more information on the activities of the Leonardo organizations and networks, please visit our websites at <http://www.leonardo.info/> and <http://www.olats.org>.

Roger F. Malina
Executive Editor, Leonardo Publications

Preface

Biopolitical Screens attempts to chart and conceptualize the imagery that currently composes our affective and conceptual reality, producing and articulating our lived experience, as well as foreclosing alternative ways of inhabiting the world. It is meant to be a selective critical intervention into the power of images today, focusing on the modulations of feelings, gestures, and thinking that bear on how we structure existence and how we define social space. Thus, to examine the current "economy" of images—how sensations are made, distributed, and consumed in different registers, and how both material and temporal realities are administered within given contexts[1]—the following chapters plot the production and exchange of screen-based mediations within various settings, spanning popular entertainment, military applications, scientific imaginations, and contemporary art.

On a more personal note, this book has a twofold history. On the one hand, it continues the investigation of the aesthetics, politics, and technology of the moving image I began in *Mapping the Moving Image: Gesture, Thought, and Cinema circa 1900* (Amsterdam University Press, 2010), which analyzed the role of the new medium in scientific and philosophical rearticulations of both ourselves and our world in the late nineteenth and early twentieth centuries.[2] My concern there was the cinema as the "anthropological machine" of modernity, which delineated the design of bodies and thoughts. Some hundred years later, however, the key discourses of neuroscience are superseding those of experimental physiology and psychoanalysis in defining who we are, just as computer-generated animations are superseding photographic pictures, and the sociopolitical reality of life now follows the demands of neoliberalism. We have changed alongside the images that compose us. It looks like cinema's ontology and the view of the world it opens up have been supplemented by forces and practices we still find hard to comprehend.

On the other hand, *Biopolitical Screens* also emerges from another kind of feeling of things changing, of loss even. In the aftermath of the 2007–08 financial crisis, witnessing the gradual destruction of the pillars of the welfare state—and, more generally, of a sense of collectivity and sharing—in the United Kingdom, a country still heavily driven by imperialist military aspirations, has been the second impetus for this book. Everyday life became filled with distrust in existence, spurred by television news that arbitrarily juxtaposed reports about the global economic crisis and the need for "austerity" with reports of suicide bombings and war casualties in Iraq, Afghanistan, and elsewhere, alongside vague warnings about enemies lurking in the shadows. If the media present facts before which we recognize our powerlessness, as Giorgio Agamben observes,[3] they have also triggered a need to somehow make sense of what underpins those abrupt and even dadaistic montages, based on a mix of feelings of incapacity, frustration, and disagreement.

Though originating from that mix, this account is not about television or online news reports, nor about the representations—banal, stupefying, or otherwise—of wars, state power, and finance economy more generally. Its focus is instead on the aesthetics and politics of the forms and technologies that have emerged from within the military-entertainment-financial complex, a complex that defines our present and that machinates the political reality of our lives. Here "machinate" refers to the production and distribution of the sensible—"both 'what can be sensed' and 'what makes sense'"[4]—that envelops individuals in a certain texture of affectivity and imagination. From this perspective, *Biopolitical Screens* seeks to shed light on how images today plot the organization of our sensory apparatus, on the movements and interplay of the heterogeneous but often muddled audiovisual mediators that work to define both our individual and our social realities. To show what images can *do*, and how, it investigates the ways in which console game platforms, virtual reality technologies, personal computer screens, and the various kinds of images animated on them, capture human potential across the globe by plugging it into arrangements of finance, war, and the consumption of entertainment.

As it taps into the visual economy of these "screen captures," *Biopolitical Screens* goes beyond specific technical media (cinema, television, video games) and institutional contexts to approach the circulation and "life" of images across these boundaries. My main inspiration comes from recent developments in visual culture studies, starting with W. J. T. Mitchell's seminal work, which likens images to "living organisms ... best described as things that have desires (for example, appetites needs, demands, drives)" and that migrate from one medium to another at the same time they disseminate and define the feelings and values critical to a society's makeup.[5] Hans Belting has developed a similar concept of the image as a mediator between technologies and human bodies and minds and, by extension, between material reality and the private and public realms: "Images are exchanged between us and a pictorial medium in the double act of transmission and perception."[6] The politics of images, Belting explains, resides in the way their motions define the disposition of our bodies and minds, yoking the possible with the real and vice versa. My inspiration comes as well from Nicholas Mirzoeff's recent take on the notion of "visuality" to account for the orchestration and implementation of power through sets of relations "combining information, imagination, and insight into a rendition of physical and psychic space."[7] Mirzoeff sees images as entering into larger governmental frames of imagining and inhabiting, which produce social organization and shape an individual's psychic economy.

Drawing on these perspectives, I address the anthropology of our screen-based world, with "anthropology" understood in a quite general sense, following Tim Ingold, as "a sustained and disciplined inquiry into the conditions and potentials of human life."[8] My inquiry concerns the critical, perhaps even quasi-autonomous role that images play in our gestures, affections, and thoughts, as well as in the arrangements of power within which our life worlds are designed and apportioned. At stake are the conditions and potentials of doing and experiencing within contemporary visual economies, where the visible (pictures, screens, texts, bodies) and the invisible (images, imaginations, rationalities) are arranged and organized into particular patterns according to set codes and strategies—and where sayabilities and visibilities, sensations and desires, pasts and futures become particularly plotted.

Nowadays, very little remains of the daily sphere of existence that has not been in one way or another turned into an immanent object of political, scientific, or economic concern. This direct capture of our lives by the machinery of profitability is what Michel Foucault described as "biopolitics," a process historically rooted in the birth and dominance of liberalism. In the emergence of biopolitical modes of thinking and doing, Foucault observed, populations were for the first time considered "a sort of technical-political object of management and government."[9] As a result of this process, today's neoliberalism—broadly understood as an "apparatus" comprising different practices and modes of thought, spanning political agendas, governmental techniques, military operations, scientific rationalities, logics of finance, and the like—amounts to the instrumentalization and commercialization of virtually all domains of existence, from the personal to the social and from the biological to the mental. By means of scientific, governmental, and military administration, and under the market logic that promotes risk, competition, and crisis, life and the unknowability of life's becoming are turned into a source of value. It is in this sense, as Melinda Cooper points out, that life is "surplus" in the neoliberal era.[10]

Biopolitical Screens shows how current practices and strategies of capturing and taking charge of our lives feed on a variety of screen-based mediations. My concern is how images today proliferate and evolve in parallel with the production and promotion of the neoliberal way of life, with its notions of threat, contingency, and emergency. I examine how images participate in and give rise to the distributions of affects and actions as well as the sayabilities and visibilities through which the current political and economic order is reproduced at the level of subjectivation. For reasons that will become clear, I have dubbed the normative model of subjectivity studied in this book the "neoliberal brain," which refers to the key image by which we have come to understand and govern ourselves, and which is produced within diverse settings, spanning the neurosciences that dominate current discourses on the "human" but also other areas of reality such as psychotherapy and even video games. The "neoliberal brain" stands, in other words, for the dominant form of individuation that composes the circulation of various images and imaginations.

To understand the movement of images from the general anthropological perspective noted above, chapter 1 combines the concept of the image with the problematic of government, mirrored within the contemporary sociopolitical landscape in the West. Reviewing the theoretical and historical contexts of current screens and biopolitical modes of governance, it charts what matters most in the politics of life today, which revolves around a particular locus of mediation—the brain. The neurosciences, it points out, provide the central epistemic field of verification for neoliberal models of subjectivity. The ways we imagine ourselves are today characterized by a particular image of the "cerebral subject," which presents us not only as beings essentially tied to our biological materiality but also as emergent, adaptive, and plastic beings constantly open to novel challenges and modifications. The chapter shows how the brain has become the iconic subject-object of contemporary biopolitics and how screen-based mediations center on it as such in framing and shaping their beholders and thus distributing dominant models of sensibility and understanding.

Chapters 2–4 present more closely focused and detailed excursions into the current visual economy. Thus chapter 2 approaches the fabrication of experiences in first-person shooter games, a multibillion industry that capitalizes on the brain's capacities for arousal, anticipation, and imagination distributed and shared on the virtual playing grounds of television and personal computer screens across the globe. Tracing how this novel type of imagery has come to play a strategic role within the current arrangement of neuroscientific articulations, financial rationalities, and military perceptual regimes, the chapter unravels several thematic nodes and correspondences in networks of power. It articulates, first of all, how the visual-kinetic images of video games correlate with the neuroscientific episteme as coinciding models of individuation. These images exercise what has been called "neuropower," capturing the brain's capacity to simulate in order to teach the political reality of life today based on the management of risk and the securitization of the future, whether through military action, financial speculation, or other means.

Shifting from the securitization of the future to the administration of the recent traumatic pasts that neoliberal rulers wish to forget, chapter 3 charts contemporary zones of indistinction between entertainment and "operational images" prevalent in science and the military. It investigates the design and construction of virtual reality technologies used to treat the veterans of the wars in Iraq and Afghanistan (and potentially anywhere on the globe) who suffer from what is called "posttraumatic stress disorder" (PTSD). Expanding on the theme of the neuropower of images, the chapter plots the amalgamations of psychiatric knowledge, virtual reality screens, and therapeutic technologies that have emerged in the present-day military-scientific arrangement to modulate memory and affectivity. These screen-based mediations, which tap into the capacity of our brains to reshape themselves, are meant to produce and maintain psychological immunity based on the premise that life in its adaptive, emergent, and creative possibilities needs to be protected both from an ever-present and ever-expanding threat and ultimately from itself as the source of its own destruction.

In sum, chapters 2 and 3 map the movement of images related to finance, entertainment, science, and war so as to show how the possibilities of life are captured and shaped in today's networks of power. They point out the complexities involved in the government of subjects in capital's often violent expansion across the globe, analyzing how images work in training human beings to the apperceptions and reactions—mentalities and sensibilities—needed to deal with the current sociopolitical reality.[11] Yet they also point out the unruly capacity of images to mirror and critique themselves and thus to reorient the ways we are able to think about and imagine ourselves and the world around us.

Chapter 4 shifts the analytical framework to the fissures, cuts, and openings in the translations between images, technologies, science, and power within which our bodies and persons become subjects of a particular regime of truth. These demand another logic of interpretation, one that accounts for the ruptures and resistance whereby our bodies and minds can change their meaning. The chapter tracks three examples of contemporary video installation art that address the theme of biopolitical screens from diverging perspectives, ranging from the military-security complex to the techno-material underpinnings of the current screen culture. Through these works, the chapter develops the notions of montage, imagination, and what neuroscientists call the "reentry" of images so as to chart the power of images to reflect their own sociopolitical makeup and to generate points of rupture within the dominant regime of sensibility, to give rise to moments of what Jacques Rancière has called "dissensus," moments at which our habituated ways of making sense of the sensible are disrupted.[12]

In short, *Biopolitical Screens* creates a montage of the movements of images that partly compose our current visual economy and that plot the temporalities and rhythms of our existence. To that end, it provides snapshots of these movements that involve both domination and struggle. This inquiry is based on a rather broad notion of images, which refers at once to visual images and to imaginations, affectivities, and rationalities. Such images are both visible and sayable; they can be detected not only in various screen platforms (from video games to installation art) but also in scientific perceptions, theoretical ideas, bodily postures, and the like. Working with such diverse material, the chapters that follow aim to map and conceptualize the "diagram" that organizes our neoliberal present—as Gilles Deleuze called the expression of forces that shape the social field, in whole or part, actualized in the thoughts, gestures, emotions, and individuations performing the social at any given moment.[13] To detect the common logic or pattern by which heterogeneous areas of thinking and doing come together to form more or less consistent realities, such mapping involves making a montage of areas that may, at first glance, seem distant from one another. Thus, when combining neuroscientific articulations with video games imagery, for instance, the objective is not to explain the contemporary visual culture in any simple way. Instead, it is to map and analyze both scientific articulations and novel types of screen-based mediations as parallel and immanent expressions of the forces that at least in part compose the reality of our lives today.

This collection of snapshots has, of course, several limitations; most notably, it freezes and frames the movement of images and is, by definition, limited and partial. The epistemological value of such freezing and framing might be revealed in the way it reflects the social field within which it is inscribed and which in many ways dictates its conditions of production. In other words, the gesture of freezing and framing can itself be considered a symptom of the underlying movements of images that shape and feed it. Against this background, my hope is to shed light on how images currently make and unmake both themselves and our capacities to understand and to do.

Acknowledgments

I am most grateful to Jussi Parikka, Rachel Moore, and Sean Cubitt for their invaluable suggestions and encouragement. I also want to thank my colleagues at the Department of Media and Communications at Goldsmiths, University of London, for providing a stimulating and friendly working environment and my "Screen Cultures" students for being a sounding board for ideas developed in this book. Of my friends and colleagues, I would especially like to thank Chris Berry, Ryan Bishop, Lisa Blackman, Basil Chiasson, Mechthild Fend, Matthew Fuller, Olga Goriunova, Janet

Harbord, Julian Henriques, Ilona Hongisto, Eleni Ikoniadou, Matleena Kalajoki, Sarah Kember, Keisuke Kitano, Kaisa Kontturi, Kaisa Kurikka, Trond Lundemo, Laura Mulvey, Dorota Ostrowska, Volker Pantenburg, Jukka Sihvonen, Teemu Taira, Milla Tiainen, and Joanna Zylinska. I am very grateful to the anonymous reviewers at MIT Press for their valuable and critical advice, and to Doug Sery for his belief in and support of this project. Finally, a warm thank-you to my parents, Aino and Jukka Väliaho, for all their support and to Rebecca Birch for her affection, inspiration, and imagination.

1 Biopolitical Visual Economy: Image, Apparatus, a Cerebral Subject

What cultures do with pictures and how they capture the world in them leads straight to the center of their way of thinking.
—Hans Belting, *Florence and Baghdad*

Animations

When our eyes are closing in the darkness of night, between consciousness and sleep, images appear. These are endogenous apparitions, which revive events that happened earlier during the day as well as scenes buried deeper in memory, but which are also mixed with the stream of images we encounter when consuming the screen media that saturate our everyday lives—watching television, playing video games, surfing the Internet, and much more. Past and present, personal and social, psychic and corporeal, and real and fictive get effectively merged in the cerebral processes of cutting and composing this "movie-in-the-brain," as neuroscientists describe the continuous flow of sensations of the mind, the felt reality of both external and internal impressions.[1] In these apparitions, our interactions with screen technologies enter our psyches in the form of effects that can arouse, frighten, comfort, or reassure. Screens and the images they materialize echo and evoke both psychic and somatic events, weaving us and our inner visions into social fabrics of affectivity, desire, meaning, and behavior that we share with one another as collective beings.

Images act like vital entities situated at the intersection of mind and matter, undermining the distinction between appearances and the real world around us.[2] They are dynamic, as art historian Aby Warburg noted over a century ago; they mediate realms private and public and become the driving force of gestures, affections, and thoughts. This understanding dawned on Warburg when he witnessed the dance rituals of Pueblo Indians in New Mexico and Arizona in the 1890s, a pivotal reference point being the famous snake dance the Hopis practiced every August to evoke rain when drought threatened to destroy their crops.[3] With the figural correspondence between the snake's winding movements and the zigzags of lightning as its cognitive motive, the ritual was performed to turn living snakes into messengers that, upon their return to the newly freed souls of the dead, would call down rainstorms from the heavens. The snake thus became a "symbol of change and transformation" that were "causally inexplicable."[4] But the power of the performance lay in what Warburg called "incorporation," a process whereby performers expand their agency beyond the limits of the body and consciousness by means of a mimetic appropriation of things and beings. At the same time, the performers are themselves transformed, becoming something other than what they were. In the act of incorporation, Warburg wrote, "the subject is lost in the object in an intermediary state between manipulating and carrying, loss and affirmation. The human being is there kinetically but is completely subsumed by an inorganic extension of his ego."[5]

Incorporation points toward a twofold dynamic in which images are endowed with evocative powers to give birth to the real and, at the same time, to transform their makers and beholders. David Freedberg has mapped the different modalities of response and reaction—of affective and psychic investment—that we have had toward images across modern as well as premodern times. Although these range from sacralization to arousal and censorship, Freedberg sees a certain kind of animism as the most basic cross-cultural and cross-historical response to the pictures surrounding us—and as symptomatic of cognition.[6] Animism is considered here above all in the sense of investing images with lively powers, including the power to move us and to become a living part of our embodied realities. To this way of thinking, our engagement with images involves not only the animation and vitality we attribute to the pictures, sculptures, films, or video games we encounter daily but also the power of image-events to affect and animate us and to shape the ways we become as individuals and collectives.

Indeed, it is not only in the Hopi snake ritual that images have the power to evoke and suggest; contemporary governmental rationalities also seem to acknowledge their capacity to do so. The official government response to the killing of Osama bin Laden by U.S. Navy SEALs in Pakistan on May 2,

2011, is a case in point and serves to illustrate this, albeit somewhat indirectly. One of the controversies around the incident is why the world-dominating military and economic power decided not to release photographs of the dead body of its proclaimed archenemy, whom it had finally managed to locate and eliminate. "It's important for us to make sure," President Barack Obama explained in a television interview, "that very graphic photos of somebody who was shot in the head are not floating around as incitement to additional violence or as a propaganda tool."[7] Such prudence and precaution did not, however, prevent the White House from releasing graphic photos of other people killed in the same raid on bin Laden's compound. Indeed, images of dead bodies shot in the head, mutilated, and bathed in blood have become the common fare of media reports on what is called the "war on terror." Censoring the particular photographs of bin Laden was, in other words, not based on any moral or ethical imperative to ban images of violence that contemporary wars produce. Nor were these photographs said to contain any classified "information."

Instead, it looks like the Obama administration's decision was emotionally and strategically based on the felt political threat that the pictures of bin Laden's corpse would pose if they were to "float around" (like a spirit) on the Internet and in the media and thus in our bodies and minds as well. It seems that, in the Obama administration's eyes, images possess the capacity attributed to them since times immemorial to, in Freedman's words, "partake of the life of what they represent, or even of the life of things other than what they represent."[8] It is for this reason that the U.S. president's decision over the life and death of a particular person also entailed a decision over the life and death of the image of that person, whose face had become iconic of the otherwise shadowy enemy against which Western regimes have been fighting their "long wars." "Killing" the image of the dead bin Laden was necessary to enforce bin Laden's actual death. In this regard, the Obama administration's reasoning exemplifies a governmental logic that exercises power by preempting possible future actions and reactions through appearances—that, in other words, captures and administers potential movements of people by managing the movement and circulation of images. The war on terror is a war in which a "full spectrum" of future possibilities needs to be imagined in order to govern what happens in the present. Although the cognitive reality of that war is based on preemptive gestures legitimized by the felt reality of future threats, crucially, these future threats can reside nowhere else but in images as premonitory appearances. It is not a war against an enemy one can point out and locate, the very notion of "war on terror" being itself an oxymoron, much like a "war on fear."[9] In this war, rather, the enemy needs to be given life and death by means of a photograph, video, or other kind of picture.

The Obama administration's attitude suggests that we might think of images as forces operating intimately in our social and psychic organization, from instincts and drives to emotions and conceptual thought, thereby playing an ontogenetic role in our development as individuals and collectives. In this view, we should approach and critique the power of images with regard to not only their contents (ideological or otherwise) but also the passions and movements they might instigate. Images, Gilbert Simondon tells us, operate like microorganisms in our minds and bodies.[10] They are like subindividual and quasi-autonomous beings, which occupy an intermediary position between us and the world. "Containing to a certain extent the power of will, appetite and movement," Simondon writes, images "appear almost like secondary organisms within the thinking being: parasites or adjuvants, they are like secondary monads that at some moments inhabit the subject and leave it at others." As such, images are endowed with an "intense capacity of propagation."[11] The various kinds of groupings they can consolidate form the germ of our adaptation to the prevailing social reality and the object world. They are the force that binds individual bodies and persons with reality and collective ways of doing, making sense, and feeling.[12]

Simondon's conceptualization appears well attuned to the contemporary screen-based world, where various kinds of "visuals" can multiply themselves, propagate, and evolve almost instantaneously in digital networks and from one kind of technological platform to another, spanning cell phone screens, digital video, LCD displays, and so on. But only to a certain extent can the life of images be attributed to technical mediations. Hans Belting reminds us that images should not be reduced to mere artifacts of technology.[13] To be sure, technologies of production and distribution afford and inform their appearance and propagation. Movie, television, and computer screens are the material support on which the movements of images become actualized and shaped to such an extent that the concept of the image cannot today be meaningfully separated from the notion of the screen as the technical materialization that renders the image as phenomenologically real. Indeed, as Anne Friedberg points out, the screen functions as an "ontological cut" that transports us into spatiotemporal realms other than the here and now of everyday existence.[14] On the other hand, it is in our minds and bodies where images become actualized, independent of our persons. They live in our gestures, affections, perceptions, emotions, imaginations, and thoughts. They animate our bodies and minds and either fix or emancipate their dispositions. Belting suggests that our bodies and minds are the "living media" where images are materialized and enacted.[15] "We both own and produce images," he writes. "In each case, bodies (that is, brains) serve as a living medium that makes us perceive, project, or remember images and that also enables our imagination to censor or to transform them."[16] It is human bodies and minds, in addition to technological platforms, that carry images, reproducing them in gestures, clothes, thoughts, beliefs, politics, and rituals.

From such an anthropological perspective, this chapter aims to give readers a conceptual grasp of the power of images today—of their intimate work in the gestation of the social as well as individual reality of the contemporary world. To that end, it explores how images—and especially the groups of images that migrate back and forth between current screens and our brains—animate us as embodied observers and serve as part of larger sociotechnological networks that compose the world of appearances.

Visual Economy

If images are quasi-corporeal and even, to quote W. J. T. Mitchell, "parasitical" passengers that travel across time and space in their human mediators, where can we locate them conceptually?[17] Belting compellingly suggests that we can overcome the false dichotomy between internal (endogenous) and external (exogenous) images that threatens to reduce them to either mere phantoms or mere techniques by treating the triad image-medium-body as an indivisible whole.[18] Thus, by definition immaterial, images need a material host, a medium in which they can become embodied. Although technical media can help carry out this function, it is in our bodies that images are born, received, and transported. Thus, too, Belting tells us, a constant interchange takes place between the internal and the external: "When external pictures are re-embodied as our own images, we substitute for their fabricated medium our own body, which, when it serves in this capacity, turns into a living or natural medium."[19]

One way to conceptualize these continuous propagations and exchanges between images, bodies, and technological platforms is to model them as "visual economies" in the classic sense of "economy" as the management of lived realities. Although "economy" today refers, most of all, to the production and exchange of goods for profit, the management of resources and labor, and even to finance capitalism more generally, its older vocation, according to philosopher Marie-José Mondzain, is "to be the concept of management and administration of temporal realities, whether they be spiritual, intellectual, or material."[20] It is in terms of this earlier role—economy (*oikonomia*) as "living linkages," as sets of relations between the visible and the invisible—that the question of the image has occupied Western thought since the birth of Christianity.[21] The visible domain of pictures and screens evokes the invisible realm of visualizations, beliefs, and affective engagements, and it is at the intersection of these two—the visual economy—that power becomes established and that political rule over territories and the minds and bodies of people is implemented.

Focusing on the Byzantine Empire, Mondzain argues that "the attempt to rule over the whole earth by organizing an empire that derived its power and authority by linking together the visual and the imaginal was Christianity's true genius."[22] Through the production and circulation of images, in the form of portable icons, for example, temporal realities could be unified with celestial truths and the divine empire could maintain and expand its power without any apparent limits or boundaries. It was thus, she writes, that "the process of globalizing the image across the whole world" began.[23] Here the relevance of the concept of visual economy to the imaginal empires of our own, media-saturated times appears by way of analogy, even though today the government of life follows the dynamic logic of capital rather than divine truths.[24] Like the Byzantine world, ours is a world where power is instituted and claims wide-ranging authority through the production and circulation of images. It is managed within specific visual economies where pictures and screens feed the imaginations that both bind us to the object world and forge social relations.

The notion of visual economy encompasses the production and management of lived reality at the delicate threshold where internal and external, mental and physical images interact. To be sure, this interaction does not merely concern the single sense modality of sight but also other senses such as hearing, touch, and even awareness of where the parts of one's body are and how they move (kinesthesia). Although, in phenomenological terms, the interaction is a comprehensive process of embodiment, more importantly, it is also an issue of politics.[25] And, as we will see, in today's screen-based media environment, it is an issue of what can be called, after Michel Foucault, "biopolitics" in particular.

"Biopolitical" in this context refers, first of all, to a recent shift in the visual economies of modernity concerning the ways in which images express and take hold of the potentials of life. If, as several philosophical studies have asserted, the silver screen defined the frame of mind, bodily dispositions, memories, desires, and sense of self of the twentieth-century observer,[26] today's digital screens materialize a relatively unparalleled set of perceptions, imaginations, and capabilities for observers in the twenty-first century. Our cerebral movies are now meshed with images performed in online video game worlds, with viral videos that spread across the globe in an instant, and even with thanatographic images that heat up the reality of contemporary wars, to name just a few.[27] Many, if not all, of these images take the form of computer-generated animations, which arguably imply a perceptual reality different from that implied by their cinematic and photographic predecessors.[28] Furthermore, they are images that appear to be in several aspects distinguished by their action-oriented nature: images we interact with, play with, operate with; images that, like toys or instruments, require gestural manipulation and cognitive engagement based on anticipation and immersion rather than contemplation.

Despite the apparent novelty of these computer-generated images, there is nonetheless a lesson about them to be learned from the early critics of cinema who yearned to make sense of sociopolitical implications of the then new medium. Siegfried Kracauer, for instance, noted an intimate link between the visual culture of his times and the organization of social reality in capitalism.[29] Writing in the 1920s, Kracauer saw the spectacle of uniformly dancing girls in newsreels shown across the globe as reproducing a model of subjectivity based on the logic of Fordist production modes. In Kracauer's eyes, the medium of film gave expression to capitalist society's "will," merging the dancing legs of newsreel girls with the hand gestures of factory workers into a common social body. As he observed of the cinema, "the audience encounters itself; its own reality is revealed in the fragmented sequence of splendid sense impressions."[30] Likewise, Walter Benjamin, addressing modernity's massive technologies of speed, industrial production, and popular entertainment, argued that the most important function of film was "to train human beings in the apperceptions and reactions needed to deal with a vast apparatus, whose role in their lives is expanding almost daily."[31] With varying political consequences, film came to "establish equilibrium" between our senses and the imperatives of industrial capitalism. Benjamin imagined the cinema as a site of collective reception that, according to Miriam Hansen, "constituted a sensory-reflexive horizon in which the liberating as well as pathological effects of technological modernity could be articulated and engaged."[32] Borrowing from Jacques Rancière, one could say that both Kracauer and Benjamin envisaged cinema as implementing specific "distributions of the sensible" (*partages du sensible*), which gave rise to and disseminated common ways of seeing, feeling, saying, imagining, desiring, and doing vital to the life of their society.[33] The life of individuals and populations could not be separated from the life of images that animated themselves on the silver screen.

If the visual economy of cinema in the early twentieth century corresponded with modes of Fordist production and sensibility, one could say that postcinematic images correspond with post-Fordist production, neoliberal ideologies, and contemporary biopolitical ways of taking charge of the life of individuals and populations.[34] What these newer images describe is a reality where information and immaterial goods are at the center of production and consumption; where the imperative of investment-cost-profit circumscribes not only the realm of the economy proper but also the domains of the individual and the social; where subjects defined in terms of their biological, evolutionary, and emergent properties have entered the realms of both government and the production of wealth; and where wars are waged not to defend the state from external threats but to relentlessly expand free markets and the neoliberal way of life across the globe. A major social and political concern here is the waning of democracy in the face of contemporary amalgamations of military power, corporate power, and the state.[35]

This military-corporate-state complex is underpinned by networks of images that work toward reproducing and sustaining, albeit most often indirectly, the reigning affiliations of power. The codes and strategies by which the world today is made visible are embedded within processes by which bodies and persons become captured in the sensory fabrics of the global neoliberal order that has dominated our lived realities for more than thirty years. Thus, to take one example, video games such as *Grand Theft Auto IV* (Rockstar Games, 2008) make us experience North American urban life from an eastern European immigrant's perspective, letting us feel within our skin and play out what it means to live as an underclass in a present-day metropolis where individual entrepreneurial freedom thrives at the expense of law and order, and where contesting criminal forces wage a constant war against one another in a raw capitalist state of nature. Here we should note that the video game industry itself is modeled on contemporary post-Fordist production, which exploits the affective and cognitive capacities of its precarious workforce, whose members have ceased to differentiate between work and leisure and been stripped of traditional labor rights.[36] In a similar vein, novel video gaming platforms such as Nintendo's *Wii Fit* translate ideals of self-management and self-transformation (intrinsic to current neoliberal models of subjectivity, as we will see later in greater detail) into embodied experiences in front of a gestural interface that orders the movements of our limbs and the disposition of our muscles.

Moreover, and also in the form of video games, visual-kinetic images of warfare have invaded the television screens that cast their light on the walls of our living and bedrooms. These effectively reproduce in the sensory fabric of our lives the same imagery used to train and rehabilitate soldiers deployed in Iraq and Afghanistan (and elsewhere), and even the kind of imagery used in actual counterinsurgent operations executed remotely with unmanned aerial vehicles (UAVs)—drones—by means of screens and joysticks similar to those of video gamers. The main political task of this imagery is to train the brains of their observers to anticipate indefinite future military threats, especially within those parts of the earth which are rich in fossil fuels and other strategic raw materials. In a sense, what we are witnessing with warfare video game imagery is the militarization of the everyday, whereby the organization of the social body—which is to say, politics—appears to have become "the continuation of war by other means," to quote Foucault.[37]

Here we can already glimpse the visual economy of the neoliberal world. As distributions of the sensible, images act as vital links to join bodies and persons together into dominant social realities and to harness life and its potentialities into what James Der Derian has called the "military-industrial-media-entertainment-networks" that compose contemporary societies and that feed their violent efforts to expand without limits in space and time.[38] The video game imagery we consume in our everyday lives manufactures the kind of adaptive, supple, and plastic agency that is prepared for the exigencies of contemporary self-perpetuating wars and the neoliberal reality of competition, risk, and danger more generally.

To understand how our lives are being colonized by an overarching system of profit making and violence, we should pay close attention to how images are animated in our bodies and minds; how they circulate not only in technical pictures and material screens, but also in how we feel and become affected, how we act, and how we are able to think of and visualize the world and ourselves. As Mitchell tells us, we should pay attention to how images "live and move, how they evolve and mutate, and what sorts of needs, desires, and demands they embody, generating a field of affect and emotion that animates the structures of feeling that characterize our age."[39] In this view, shared by Kracauer and Benjamin, images form a "second nature," which, like the first nature, intimately intertwines with the collective organization of the affects, desires, and imaginations that we embody.

A variety of concepts has emerged in recent scholarship to critically chart the current work of screen-based media—spanning, for instance, notions such as software, code, and database, which all revolve around digital technologies and their implications in issues of power and the organization of the social.[40] But, if we are to decipher the grids of sensibility and intelligibility that determine both how today's world unfolds in perception and experience and how we position ourselves in this world, we need a theoretical framework that acknowledges the vital role of images in the production of the social. As David Rodowick points out, in the midst of new technological systems that have come to radically shape our perception and consumption of audiovisual media, "concepts of image, screen, time, space, and movement are as relevant to contemporary moving image theory as they were to classical film theory."[41]

Yet this conceptual framework implies a cross-medium approach to the movement of images. Mitchell has speculated that material media might serve as habitats or ecosystems where images come to live and evolve, much like microorganisms, in parallel with our body-minds.[42] In the age of digital networks, in particular, we need to think of media not as isolated objects, but rather as intermeshing systems that reiterate and remediate one another. Console games, for instance, are designed to be cinematic spectacles even as they demand novel forms of engagement from their players. Gameplay clips can be uploaded on YouTube and other video sharing websites, which in their malleable uses circulate traditional movie entertainment in low-quality digital versions while affording a new type of video blogging culture. What is labeled as "video installation art" often takes dominant forms of contemporary imagery as its critical object of reflection when transporting it into a different kind of experiential arrangement in the gallery or museum space, or in urban settings. Which is to say, the relationships between media elements overlap and differ in ways that force us to shift the analytical direction from objects to processes, or patterns of multiple connections, as Matthew Fuller sees them.[43]

Focusing on "visual economy" at the intersection of images, bodies, and screen-based media gives us the conceptual flexibility needed to detect such patterns. If we consider the *screen* to be quite simply a surface for animation (with its varying technical specificities of scale, size, location, portability, and so on),[44] we can then consider the *image* to be the critical operator that (to quote Rancière) "presents a relationship between the sayable and the visible."[45] The image can be visual or verbal, aural or tactile, or any combination of these, the main point being that it works, if not always subserviently, within networks of power and constitutes "the sensible system of self-evident facts of sense perception that simultaneously discloses the existence of something in common and the delimitations that define the respective parts and positions within it."[46] Images partition what is visible from what is not, what can be said from what cannot, and they tell us where and when. In doing so, they establish shared ways of sensing, feeling, and making sense; they weave the common fabric of sensibility that defines the social body with all its inclusions and exclusions.

The Biopolitical Apparatus

Underscoring, above all, how images administer, partition, and manage the distributions of the sensible—our affects and emotions, our desires and thoughts, our deeds and imaginations—visual economies are characterized by interconnections and reciprocal contacts as well as by cuts, jumps, and interceptions. The various "image-agents" act much like the neuronal tissue of our brains, which is in continual flux and whose millions of groups, as neuroscientists Gerald Edelman and Giulio Tononi explain, "are linked by a huge set of convergent or divergent, reciprocally organized connections that make them all hang together in a single, tight meshwork while they still maintain their local functional specificity."[47] Instead of drawing on the paradigms of reflection and refraction made prominent by the science and practice of perspectival pictures, we might make better sense of the propagation of images today by looking at the time-critical dynamism of synaptic connections and patterns about which neuroscience has much to say. Indeed, Patricia Pisters sees contemporary screen culture as nonlinearly organized, much like our brains, with images that mix and reorder "from all the previous image regimes, ungrounding and serializing according to a digital logic."[48] Which, for Pisters, means that we should call on recent insights of neuroscience into the workings of the brain to account for how we relate to screens and, more generally, to ourselves amid the "complexities and political realities of life in the twenty-first century."[49]

As will be addressed in greater detail in chapters 2 and 3, computer-generated interactive images such as the ones we encounter in video games and virtual reality applications seem to function less like optical processes and more like the affective-cognitive processes associated with hand-eye coordination and with the brain's capacity to simulate.[50] Whereas still pictures from paintings, drawings, and photographs, and sometimes even moving pictures from films, allow us to reflect from a distance and to visually grasp the whole, the flash flood of video game images makes only partial recognition possible, based as it mostly is on the brain's production of anticipatory images in reaction to constantly shifting screen events. These images exemplify a novel and curiously behavioristic dimension within contemporary image-body-medium circuits, one that relates to how screens draw on ever intensifying gestural and cerebral dynamics.[51] It is not merely the brain's representations but also its forces and intensities that become the material source of capital accumulation by the multibillion-dollar gaming industry—as well as the objects of direct modulation in the U.S. military's simulation training platforms.

The brain, and not the eye, becomes the primary locus of mediation and "capture" by which individual bodies and persons are woven into the political reality of contemporary life. In many ways, this organization of bodies, images, and screen technologies into particular kinds of arrangements echoes what philosophers Gilles Deleuze and Félix Guattari called the "apparatus of capture" (*appareil de capture*) when dealing with the problematic of power, state, and capitalism.[52] Deleuze and Guattari differentiated three major apparatuses of capture historically deployed in the accumulation of capital and the production of surplus: rent from land, profit from labor, and interest or tax from money. "Capture" is essentially a process of bringing together bodies and persons into specific arrangements or assemblages to capitalize on their productivity. Accumulation of capital thus implies the exploitation of living beings in circuits of production and consumption that impose on them a system of "self-evident" facts with standardized desires, ways of doing, and making sense.

The close and even organic relation of screen media to capitalism's processes of capture becomes evident in their genealogy. As Jonathan Crary has shown, visual forms, screen technologies, economic forces, and scientific statements were first mobilized in arrangements of individuation crucial to emerging commodity capitalism in the late nineteenth century. Essential to the rise of entertainment industry were, first of all, the transformation of images and sounds into measurable and distributable commodities and, second, the transformation of individuals into specialized units of consumption capable of constantly absorbing new audiovisual commodities as objects of attention.[53] The devices and technologies developed in Thomas Alva Edison's enterprise—the kinematograph (a forerunner of cinema), the gramophone, and the stock ticker in particular—sliced the sensory realm into abstracted and exchangeable bits of information that would circulate with ever greater speed and in ever greater numbers. This resulted in, to quote Crary, "a dramatic reordering of visuality, implying the new importance of models based on an economy of forces rather than an optics of representation."[54] Images, both popular and artistic, started to problematize subjectivity in terms of physiological and mental forces whose productivity would be systematized and maximized. In particular, this new visual economy gave rise to and distributed the sensibility of an observer suspended between attention and distraction, which is to say, an observer whose sensory apparatus and perceptual focus became the key force and source of value.

Accordingly, one can think of the biopolitical screens of our age as an economy of forces where images become shaped into abstracted streams of information whose consumption and exchange shape the social body. The power of images resides precisely in the embodied mediation and capture that shapes us into certain kinds of beings. It is less a question of ideologies than one of specific kinds of *dispositifs*, to utilize a concept that Michel Foucault developed in tandem with his genealogy of biopolitics. Instead of being anything primarily technological, *dispositif* (often translated as "apparatus") refers to the manufacture and distribution of certain kinds of capabilities (of action, perception, and thought). Foucault developed the notion while analyzing the liberalist and neoliberalist administration of self-regulating populations based on the "conduct of conduct" and the self-governance of desiring, doing, consuming, and committed individuals and populations according to ideals of what is good, healthy, righteous, and productive.[55] He defined *apparatus* quite loosely as a network or "ensemble" that, at a given historical moment, becomes established between heterogeneous elements such as discourses, institutions, architectural forms, laws, scientific formulas, philosophical and moral propositions, and even administrative statements.[56] According to Foucault, what makes the apparatus so distinctive a network of such heterogeneous and even discordant elements is that it has a "dominant strategic function" in relations of power, that is, in composing the dominant social field in a given historical situation and in manipulating forces of life in a desired direction, whether to block them or to stabilize and utilize them.

As such, apparatuses feed on images as mediators between bodies, minds, and the world. Deleuze characterized them as "skeins" (*écheveaux*) that bring together, transpose, and organize at least three different kinds of processes: forms of visuality and knowledge, formations of power, and processes of subjectivation.[57] According to Deleuze, an apparatus establishes and qualifies relations between power formations, individual minds and bodies, and images. It effects a particular kind of coming together and arrangement of sensibility, knowledge, power, and subjectivity in a given historical situation; in doing so, it channels and organizes the movements between bodies and persons, technologies, money, materials, and so on that compose the social. An apparatus constantly weaves together the three aspects of social production—images, power, subjectivity—and gives them a certain shape, quality, and direction. It could be considered a kind of editing machine that brings heterogeneous elements into operative constellations.

We can also perceive the idea of the social resulting from such dynamic montage making in Giorgio Agamben's recent interpretation of the apparatus, which Agamben defines as "literally anything that has in some way the capacity to capture, orient, determine, intercept, model, control, or secure the gestures, behaviors, opinions, or discourses of living beings."[58] Agamben highlights the etymological parallel between *dispositif* (deriving from the Latin *dispositio*) and *oikonomia*, especially in the sense of "divine economy," which the word acquired in Christian theological conceptualizations of divine rule on earth, and which closely corresponds to the notion of visual economy Mondzain has analyzed in Byzantine texts.[59] Without going into the details of Agamben's analysis, *dispositif* and *oikonomia* both find their semantic core in the notion of government, which is to say, in the sets of practices, measures, institutions, and bodies of knowledge used to organize and control the movements, behaviors, and actions of humans and other living beings. Agamben further argues that what we are witnessing in today's extreme phase of capitalist development is a "massive accumulation and proliferation of apparatuses," asserting that "today there is not even a single instant in which the life of individuals is not modeled, contaminated, or controlled by some apparatus."[60] He refers especially to screen-based media technologies from television to the mobile phone, which he proposes are essentially desubjectifying: instead of giving rise to subjects with individual identities (worker, bourgeois, feminist), the technologies render each as merely a numerical code, such as a mobile phone or credit card number, or as an abstract variable in the calculation of viewership ratings. Hence, according to Agamben, we are witnessing today "the most docile and cowardly social body that has ever existed in human history" and the triumph of *oikonomia*, which Agamben describes as "a pure activity of government that aims at nothing other than its own replication."[61]

Importantly, the notion of apparatus is intimately intertwined with the notion of visual economy as a specific distribution or montage of the sensible employed in organizing and controlling our movements, behaviors, and imaginations.[62] With this in mind, I will consider apparatuses in relation to governmental techniques that have recently emerged to capture and control the movements of human and other living beings and to capitalize on their productivity. In doing so, I will expand the scope of the Foucauldian notion of government (which broadly refers to techniques, rationalities, and methods used in directing the ways subjects perceive and act on themselves and the others around them) to encompass the work of images at the intersection of body-minds and technologies.[63] Government as a set of techniques that make reality something we can act on and think about is understood here in general terms as the management of life's capacities within particular visual economies. What is more, the notion of apparatus implies topological mapping of how images travel from one domain of reality to another—from the military and finance to politics and entertainment, for example. Although the process of mapping may change the form of these images, it does not change their key qualities and the general strategic role they play in producing the world as we experience and know it. Indeed, what constitutes critique in this sense is tracing and giving expression to (in a way resembling the cut-up technique) the continuities and gaps according to which the biopolitical apparatus keeps making montages of our lives.

Neoliberal Brainhood

As already implied above, critical to the biopolitical apparatus in charge of our lives today, and to the images it feeds on, is one particular material and embodied locus of mediation: the brain. If modernity's screen culture has historically been steeped in the capture of attention, one could argue that the focus has now moved from such psychological mediations to techniques and epistemologies more concerned with mapping our desires and deliberations on the brain and its neurochemistry. Contemporary visual economy and the bodily and mental dispositions it calls forth coincide with a shift in scientific self-perception, which neuroscientist Jean-Pierre Changeux encapsulated already in the early 1980s: "The impact of the discovery of the synapse and its functioning is comparable to that of the atom or DNA. A new world is emerging."[64] Today, the vast field of research called "neuroscience" has come to occupy a central position in explaining human reality in terms of the anatomy, physiology, and functioning of the central nervous system, seeking to find out how the activity of the brain's 100 billion nerve cells "give rise to the broad spectrum of abilities that we call consciousness, mind, and human nature."[65]

In particular, the "new world" of the brain has become apparent to what Joelle Abi-Rached and Nikolas Rose term the "neuromolecular gaze," which emerged in the 1960s and accompanied a new style of interdisciplinary, integrated thinking about the brain, mind, and behavior based on a "reductionist and predominantly molecular approach to the realm of the nervous system."[66] That gaze configures the image of *anthropos* in a new light. Today, "you are your synapses. They are who you are," as Joseph LeDoux famously said.[67] Articulations of this type have come to frame the normative understanding of ourselves as embodied beings, ranging from biological psychiatry and cognitive science to new areas such as neuroeconomics and neuroethics. These are predicated on the assumption that phenomena such as cognition, emotion, and action—in short, selfhood and agency—can and should be considered and explained with respect to their presumed cerebral substrata.[68] LeDoux argues that "your 'self,' the essence of who you are, reflects patterns of interconnectivity between neurons in your brain."[69] His statement echoes the underlying premise that subjectivity today is specified by what, following Fernando Vidal, can be called the property of "brainhood," that is, "the property or quality of being, rather than simply having, a brain."[70] According to Vidal, the ideology of the cosubstantiality of the brain and the self fuels (and legitimizes) the current neuroscientific field of verification, which attributes to the brain's evolutionarily modified functions the capacity to guide our behavior, whereas basic biological needs are seen to regulate our perceptions, and even human sociability is explained in terms of the neural underpinnings of key emotions such as empathy.

This shift from "selfhood" to "brainhood" can be considered an instance of the workings of the contemporary biopolitical apparatus, which interweaves development of scientific techniques and discourses with the political rationalities of our times. LeDoux's "synaptic self," like Changeux's "neuronal man," both implement a model of subjectivity that seeks to apply political power to virtually every aspect of human life and that conceptualizes and defines the "human" as, first and foremost, a productive entity rooted in biology and, more precisely, in the brain, which contains "in its neurons and synapses, representations of the world around us."[71]

The neurobiologization of the self thus exemplifies in general terms what Foucault meant by the notion of biopolitics, referring especially to more recent changes in the way political subjectivity and agency are conceived.[72] Instead of being concerned only negatively with its subjects in the form of the power to kill or let live, biopolitics seeks to positively promote the productive capacities of bodies and populations. In it, life enters directly into the mechanisms of government.[73] Foucault clarified that, by "biopolitics," he "meant the attempt, starting from the eighteenth century, to rationalize the problems posed to governmental practice by phenomena characteristic of a set of living beings forming a population: health, hygiene, birthrate, life expectancy, race."[74] For him, "a threshold of modernity" was reached in the nineteenth century at the latest, when life became abstracted from singular individuals into an independent and measurable entity as well as into a collective factor that did not depend on individual experience.[75] A normative political reason emerged that started to govern on the level of self-regulating populations, of multiplicities of "individuals who are and fundamentally and essentially only exist biologically bound to the materiality within which they live."[76] Also relevant to our contemporary concerns were two specific domains where this materiality became studied, conceptualized, and administered.[77] First, the science of political economy, which had developed in the eighteenth and nineteenth centuries, inaugurated the notion of production as the indispensable source of value. The origin of wealth became lodged in biological life, in the productive capacities of the breathing, moving, and doing living being, in the time-based physiological processes of force, labor, and fatigue. And, second, scientific disciplines such as statistics, epidemiology, experimental physiology, and evolutionary biology, developed at the same time, scrutinized life in the biological materiality of its emergent, evolutionary, and reproductive capacities with the objectives of normalization, correction, exclusion, and optimization. "In the nineteenth century," Melinda Cooper explains, "the economy begins to grow for the first time, just as life comes to be understood as a process of evolution and ontogenetic development."[78]

We can thus understand biopolitics as the entry of life as an evolutionary, productive, and emergent force into the fields of knowledge and power, spanning the domains of state control, economy, and science, and their development in modernity. For Foucault, the emergence of biopolitics aligned closely with the appearance of liberalist and neoliberalist thinking about the market, society, and the individual. The problems of governance concerning health, hygiene, birthrate, and so on, he wrote, "were inseparable from the framework of political rationality within which they appeared and took on their intensity. This means 'liberalism,' since it was in relation to liberalism that they assumed the form of a challenge."[79] In the liberal context, old or new, the politics of life is considered in terms of populations governing and regulating themselves according to the rationalities of the free market and trade as well as entrepreneurial freedom. Yet, whereas liberalist thought confined itself to the economic sphere in this respect, neoliberalist thinking—promoted originally by the Mont Pelerin Society, formed around the Austrian political philosopher Friedrich von Hayek, and by the Chicago School of economics after the Second World War—regarded economic rationalities as almost universally normative and applied them to the organization of the state and governmental bodies, to political culture, and to models of subjectivity in addition to the economy proper.[80] In his critique of neoliberalism, Foucault noted how neoliberal thinking extended the rationality of the market with its analytic and decision-making criteria into the domains of the family and the birthrate as well as delinquency and penal policy.[81] More recently, Wendy Brown has suggested that "neo-liberalism carries a social analysis which, when deployed as a form of governmentality, reaches from the soul of the citizen-subject to education policy to practices of empire. Neo-liberal rationality, while foregrounding the market, is not only or even primarily focused on the economy; rather it involves *extending and disseminating market values to all institutions and social action*, even as the market itself remains a distinctive player."[82]

In neoliberalism, the ideals of economic competition, efficiency, profitability, satisfaction, benefit, and success are fundamentally generalized into the domain of life itself.[83] Neoliberal political rationality, Cooper tells us, seeks to "efface the boundaries between the spheres of production and reproduction, labor and life, the market and living tissue."[84] Indeed, it seeks to subject the life of individuals and populations to the dynamics of competition, where the free movement of capital between regions and countries across the globe is paramount, and where the market rationality of investment-cost-profit is seen as something that needs to be developed and disseminated across all dimensions of life.[85] As Foucault observed, neoliberalism makes economic rationality the "model of social relations and of existence itself, a form of relationship of the individual to himself, time, those around him, the group, and the family."[86] According to this model, the individual becomes molded into *Homo economicus*, "an entrepreneur of himself, being for himself his own capital, being for himself his own producer, being for himself the source of [his] earnings."[87] Neoliberal political rationality sees human life in terms of "human capital" that needs to be maximized, and individuals as "ability machines" in constant competition with one another, machines that implement this imperative in their actions, beliefs, and thoughts. In neoliberal biopolitics, the subjects of government and social organization thus shift from being law-abiding "men of rights" to being dynamic multiplicities of autonomous, competitive, speculating, entrepreneurial, and consuming individuals who fundamentally lack political consciousness and an idea of collective action.

Neoliberalism's instrumentalization of human existence works to undermine the Enlightenment ideal of self-constituting, rational, and morally autonomous political subjects who come together to form social bonds through informed communication and mutual recognition. What becomes normative in the making of *Homo economicus* is the so-called freedom to optimize and maximize the accumulation of capital, both physical and human, through calculation, competition, and speculation. Neoliberal subjects are controlled *through* their freedom.[88] They are fundamentally obliged to be free—free to govern and enhance themselves (go to the gym to conform to a physical norm of healthiness, consume video games for personal satisfaction) in a world full of possibilities and, consequently, contingencies and risks. Exercising freedom means becoming atomized units of production and consumption and being constantly exposed to uncertainty and danger.[89] Political scientist Sheldon Wolin points out that the neoliberal system, which downplays the idea of collectivity, "thrives on disaggregation, on a citizenry who, ideally, are self-reliant, competitive, certified by standard testing, but equally fearful of an economy subject to sudden downturns and of terrorists who strike without warning."[90]

Whether as calculating, fearful, or atomistic, *Homo economicus* is a being whose personal actions and behavior are constantly subject to manipulation and administration, and whose forms of behavior can be artificially created and modulated by modifying and shaping their environmental conditions and variables.[91] Crucially, this individualistic notion of behavioral manipulation also entails a specific conception of the body as the source and locus of capital accumulation and biopolitical normalization. This takes us back to the neurobiologization of the self and the brain as the key locus of mediation in the neoliberal present. *Homo economicus* and the cerebral subject indeed appear as conceptually homologous, as Vidal notes: "The individualism characteristic of western and westernized societies, the supreme value given to the individual as autonomous agent of choice and initiative, and the corresponding emphasis on interiority at the expense of social bonds and contexts, are sustained by the brainhood ideology and reproduced by neurocultural discourses."[92]

Catherine Malabou has further explored how the brain as an image of thought has come to occupy a central position in the contemporary scientific mapping of the human, a mapping that converges with and corresponds to neoliberalism's demands. The brain Malabou tells us, is "the essential thing, the biological, the sensible, and critical locus of our time, through which pass, one way or another, the political evolutions and revolutions that began in the eighties and opened the twenty-first century."[93] According to Malabou, the primary basis for equating neoliberalism with the current scientific understanding of the brain is neoliberalism's nonhierarchical and flexible organization. Just as the brain is currently thought to be "organized according to multiple interconnected functional spaces, always in movement and susceptible to self-modification," so neoliberalism "rests on a redistribution of centers and a major relaxation of hierarchies"[94]

Indeed, one could argue that the cerebral subject is where neoliberal political rationality finds its scientific legitimization. The brain appears today as a dynamic and self-organizing system whose underlying neural activity drives individual and mental responses.[95] Furthermore, although an outcome of selective processes of evolution, the brain has been found to be plastic and self-modifying, its development being to a large extent stochastic and epigenetic, which is to say, subject to environmental contingency.[96] As such, the brain defines the human as ready, in Malabou's words, "to adapt to everything, to be ready for all adjustments."[97] It provides material provenance to *Homo economicus* as a dynamic, autonomous, flexible, and adaptable agent. Above all, the brain's morphological plasticity underwrites the neoliberal demand that we take responsibility for our abilities and for the "freedom" to modify ourselves according to future demands, risks, and contingencies.

The neuroscientific rationality that proclaims the neural underpinnings of virtually every form of human activity has found a variety of instantiations in the contemporary socioeconomic realm. Pharmaceutical industries accumulate capital and govern souls through advances in neurochemistry and the medicalization of the psychological sciences. Criminology employs neurobiology in studying criminal behavior and assessing how likely individuals are to engage in such behavior.[98] Psychology deploys novel neurofeedback technologies in its treatment of patients, even as the military uses neuropsychiatric screen-based technologies to train and rehabilitate its personnel.[99] All these are instances of how brainhood has become the subject-object of biopolitical capture today, indeed, the source and locus of capital accumulation and government.

The cerebral subject is, at bottom, a biopolitical being, whose potential can be harnessed by modifying and modulating the brain's blood flow and neural tissue. Rooted in modernity's accumulation of knowledge about the central nervous system, brainhood has developed into a governmental problem in the neoliberal era. It assumes an image of subjects who experience themselves as, first and foremost, biological beings, and whose existence in all its vitality is inseparable from the brain's dense material texture of nerves and synaptic transmissions.

With regard to the manufacture of this image, we should take particular note of neuroimaging, which has meant a decisive (however uncertain and questionable) change of approach in the production of neuroscientific knowledge, even as it has become commonplace in popular imaginations of ourselves. Visualizations of the brain in vivo through techniques such as functional magnetic resonance imaging (fMRI) and positron emission tomography (PET) are believed to unlock our inner space.[100] Carried out in artificial laboratory settings where we are induced to perform various tasks within the confines of the scanner, measurements of the activity or structure of brain cells are meant to provide "readouts" of our actions, thoughts, and perceptions, thus reducing the complexity of what goes on in our minds at any given moment to visualizations that seek to approximate the neural processes corresponding to an event. The pictures produced by these scans reveal "neural correlates," visually materializing on their surfaces how, within the concept of the cerebral subject, biological interiority has replaced the age-old metaphysical interiority of the self.[101]

It is worth noting that these mappings of the brain's morphology and dynamics are not as direct and self-evident as they might seem to a lay observer, going well beyond the optical and the photographic. The most widely used current technique of fMRI, for instance, involves a complex process of transformation and modification whereby data on particular subjects are mapped onto standardized magnetic resonance atlases of the typical brain.[102] Furthermore, what fMRI images actually reflect are changes in blood flow (more precisely, changes in magnetic signals generated by protons in blood and tissue); the causal relation of such changes to the activity of brain cells is itself something inferred by neuroscientists.[103] Thus we find ourselves within a realm of computer-generated animations produced to give a visible appearance to something that itself falls outside the realm of visibility. And the epistemological weight assigned to these animations rests on a series of inferences, from the brain's chemistry to neural activity, from neural activity to mental events, from the experimental laboratory setting to the world outside, and so on.

As such, visualizations of the brain can be seen as strategic distributions of the sayable and the visible that use our bodies and, by implication, minds as "host media," to quote Belting, which they shape and redistribute to make them amenable within a certain logic of truth.[104] The visualizations are instruments of capture and intervention that affect how we perceive ourselves as doing, thinking, and speaking beings.[105] Congruently with the model of *Homo economicus*, which posits flexibility, adaptability, and openness to constant intervention and optimization, animations of brain activity in vivo exhibit the powers of control and modification. In some accounts, these visualizations not only accumulate data of the brain's functioning in view of neural correlates of action, but even predict behavior by assessing "processes that are introspectively opaque."[106] Such accounts hold that tracing the neural correlates of stimulus and response can reveal and anticipate a person's future deeds and decisions, based on the assumption that, as neuroscientist Chris Frith puts it, "we are not aware of the action we are about to perform until the brain has made an unconscious choice about what that action should be."[107] Some scientists in other words believe that, with brain imaging, they can detect the unconscious neurological processes thought to determine future behavior.

What we are witnessing here is the production of visual truths about who we are or should become within the current biopolitical apparatus, which deploys these images in its logics of capture, drawing on their powers of demonstration and even on their alleged capacity to perform the future in the present. Based on this imagery, there might be a more general lesson to be learned about today's biopolitical imagination. If governmentality concerns the "conduct of conduct," as Foucault has argued, what characterizes the political ontology of neoliberalism, first and foremost, is the attempt to rule the whole world by joining together visuality and the anticipated future, a theme chapter 2 will pursue in greater detail. In several aspects, the current biopolitical apparatus works through prediction and preemption. The cerebral subject it manufactures is a being that "naturally" anticipates opportunity in a world of risks and dangers.[108] The logic governing this being converges closely with that of finance capitalism, which has adopted preemptive methods of risk management, deploying new financial instruments such as derivatives, to deal with the uncertainty of unknowable contingencies.[109] The world of finance appears as the outcome of conjuring and speculation, where the future needs first to be successfully imagined before it can become reality.[110] Following the same logic of invoking and acting on the future—of securitization against future disaster—the current biopolitical apparatus seeks through preemptive and self-perpetuating wars waged in Iraq, Afghanistan, and elsewhere to eradicate potential threats to the evolution and expansion of the free market and the neoliberal way of life more generally.[111]

This is precisely the setting in which the work of contemporary screens becomes paramount. As particular threads in the biopolitical apparatus' skein, they come to administer our temporal realities accordingly. In so doing, they compose a regime of sensibility that differs from the cinematic one we have been accustomed to. Contemporary visual economy hinges on, to use Richard Grusin's term, "premediations" of the future rather than on renderings of the immediate, on images that mediate possible future events as affective facts in the present.[112] Brain scan images exemplify such premediation in the scientific context, but, in more general terms, images today speak of the reality of what has not yet happened, of what our brains simulate and what we in our gestures mime will happen. From video games beating the rhythms of actual wars and virtual realities of past contingencies to stock market speculations and risk assessments, the internal and external cause of these images is not in the present but in the future—and its "living" host medium, the brain. Images incorporate the future in the present; they make the future a fact lived here and now in our bodies. In doing so, they reiterate the key logics of biopolitics today, logics based on the management of future possibilities, on the ontogenetic effectiveness of appearances to conjure up what has not yet happened but will happen.[113] The politics of images today seems to be particularly concerned with the future anterior: something nonexistent, a mere imagination,

which nonetheless is effective in triggering actions, provoking affects, and animating collectives, if not whole populations.

We might better think of images as self-determining rather than as playing an externally assigned part in the course of events. This is not, of course, to suggest that images act by themselves. Instead, it means that they work as mediators, which feed off and shape our affective and cognitive worlds, and which are "vital" in the sense that they connect, capture, transport, exchange, modulate, shape, and govern. In doing so, they generate the reality we can sense and make sense of, taking our bodies and minds as the host media where the dramas of existence that result from this economy of captures and exchanges are played out. Insofar as images have the capacity to capture bodies and persons in an arrangement of power and capital accumulation, scholars of governmentality should be mindful of how groups of images come to administer the disposition of our emotions, gestures, and thoughts. Arrangements of power do not become operative without the desires, fears, beliefs, thoughts, and actions that images animate. They depend on visual economies where subjectivities are produced and managed at the threshold of internal and external images. This dynamic of the internal and the external is an issue of politics. As such, however, it is not simply a question of determination, but rather one of tensions, ruptures, and struggles as much as it is one of intervention, modulation, and control.

Because images do not act alone, their workings and politics become meaningful only when considered part of larger arrangements that configure the social field at any given moment. The actions and animations of images are always embedded within a network of various other types of expressions and only become intelligible and describable as such. Approaching the present-day visual culture from an interdisciplinary perspective, the following chapters will focus on contemporary forms of individuation and the production of neoliberal brainhood in terms of the montages of images, experiences, discourses, and rationalities from within which these emerge.

2 Future Perfect: First-Person Shooters, Neuropower Preemption

The brain is a biological forecasting machine.
—Alain Berthoz, *The Brain's Sense of Movement*

Immersion

"Round one. Fight," a male voice announces to a throbbing disco beat, followed by shouts, growls, and the sound of blows, as a girl stares intensely ahead, her mouth twisting and her face contorting as her torso and shoulders move in time with the blows. Thus begins Robbie Cooper's video installation *Immersion* (2008), which documents the faces and gestures of children playing action video games on a console platform. We hear the sounds of the game environments, explosions and gunfire of a first-person shooter war game, splashes and growls of a kickboxing game, and even Russian rap from *Grand Theft Auto IV* (Rockstar Games, 2008). The camera carefully documents the children's reactions, but it does not show us what they themselves are seeing. The children seem to be looking at us even as they gaze at their game screens (figures 2.1 and 2.2),[1] but they take no note of our presence.[2] In the absence of any dialogue of gazes, what we see are eyes that reveal a consciousness lost in virtual worlds, shoulders and necks tensed up, facial muscles twisting in response to events that excite and arouse, gestures that mime the rapid and jolty visual-kinetic images flashing on the screens. One child is crying, whilst another one cheers vividly. Cooper's piece is like a physiognomic study of what happens in the psyches of the video game players or, rather, between the body-minds of the players and the console technology. It traces the energetic dynamics on the surface of their bodies and in the signs the players unconsciously give out of their intimate, even secret relationship with the game.

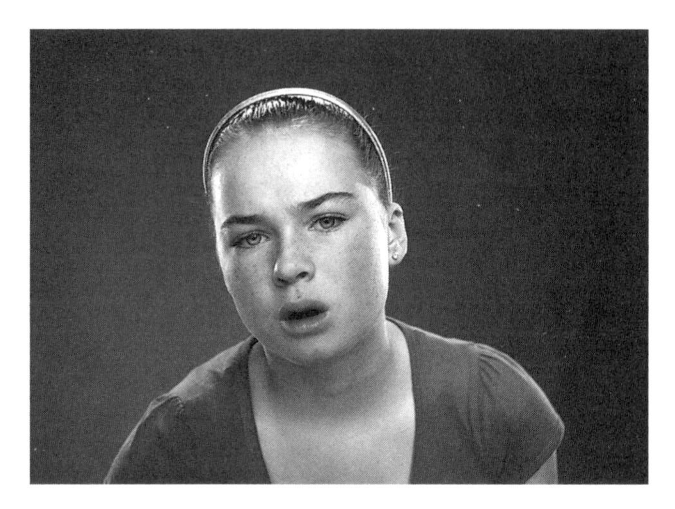

Figure 2.1
Young video game player in *Immersion* (2008). Courtesy of Robbie Cooper.

Figure 2.2
Young video game player in *Immersion* (2008). Courtesy of Robbie Cooper.

Art history knows of numerous pictures of people looking at pictures, of observers investing images with the qualities of life and consequently responding to them as if they were real living beings, confounding signifier with signified, inanimate with animate. As David Freedberg suggests, "there is a cognitive relation between looking and enlivening; and between looking hard, not turning away, concentrating and enjoying on the one hand, and possession and arousal on the other."[3] Such a cognitive relation between the children and a video game screen that we cannot see is evident in Cooper's video. It portrays spectatorial engagement that is at once vitalizing and engulfing or, as the video's title suggests, "immersive." Immersion, Oliver Grau argues, can be considered "mentally absorbing and a process, a change, a passage from one mental state to another," and "characterized by diminishing critical distance to what is shown and increasing emotional involvement in what is happening."[4] In such a broad sense, "immersion" designates rhythmically intertwined processes of arousal, affectivity, and motor response by which we animate images, rendering them as real and living in perception—but, just as important, we invest these images with the power to animate us and to become part of the intimate material of our subjective realities.

This chapter is about the ways video game imagery is bodily embraced and cognitively assumed by us and comes alive in our gestures and in other types of our cognitive and somatic activity, whose surface effects *Immersion* so meticulously traces. As the central feature in the video installation, the signs of life the children express—cheers, tears, smiles, grimaces, and frowns—indicate the bodily rhythms of the players' vital engagement with and immersion in the screen. These signs show how the screen's animations resonate within the intimate interior of the gamers' bodies, which go through several passages simultaneously, from nervous intensities and reactions of extremely short duration to episodes of consciousness lasting a few seconds, spanning bodily affections as well as more elaborate apperceptions and emotions from one mental and corporeal register to another.

These rhythmic resonances result in the performance of actions. Cooper's video emphasizes the obvious but easily forgotten fact that, as Alexander Galloway observes, "people move their hands, bodies, eyes, and mouths when they play video games."[5] The children's reactions show how video game imagery possesses the power to literally make us move by evoking fundamental feelings of arousal and kinesthesia at the heart of self-experience. Indeed, it is this investment of kinetic vitality that materializes video games in the first place. Galloway notes that video games are, first and foremost, an action-based medium; it is human actions that breathe life into them.[6] Without the gestural feedback and bodily performance of their players, and without the very basic gesture of switching on the devices that execute their software, video games would remain no more than static computer codes and abstract sets of rules. By functional necessity, the images a console machine such as PlayStation makes from the electronic signals dancing on LCD video screens need to be animated by the gestures of players; they cannot simply be enjoyed from a cognitive distance. Video game images come into being only when players enact them: their becoming visible and apprehensible rests on our bodily performance rather than on our gaze.

Although the visual economy of video games draws primarily on rhythmic and gestural incorporation, we should also note, as Galloway does, that "machines also act."[7] Thus the computers or console machines of video game players not only perform algorithmic operations in response to the players' actions; they can also act independently, communicating automatically with other devices in a network. Independent computational processes, of which players are ordinarily unaware, effectively play their part in defining the phenomenology of gameplay. Referring to regular interactions between computers in a network, Claus Pias even asserts that the video game player "is an embodiment of a particular kind of communication between devices. Losing consciousness ... is simply the moment of success in becoming a peripheral device and thus the possibility condition of a computer game."[8] The kinds of experiences that immersion designates require smooth but largely repetitive interactions between the players' body-minds and their machines, as well as between the machines themselves, with more or less continuous rhythmic and gestural feedback loops between game screens and players.

Every gaming experience has a pulse, a beat. But because computers are largely machines of periodic oscillation and bare repetition, it falls to their human operators to generate variation and contingency. Rhythmicity, that is to say, entails differences within repetition.[9] Video game players introduce not only style and learned skills but also imperfection, interruption, and randomness to the otherwise predictable, functional, and self-repetitive universe of computer codes and rules—a universe whose possibilities are predetermined until the players bodily enact them.[10]

Insofar as they demand what would appear to be inconsequential bodily engagement and require the learning of a variety of sensorimotor and cognitive skills, video games could be characterized, to quote Clifford Geertz, as "sentimental education." Geertz studied the seemingly trivial activity of staging cockfights as metasocial commentary in the Balinese culture. These fights made ordinary, everyday experience comprehensible by presenting it through acts and objects stripped of their everyday consequences, and, in doing so, they served to put Balinese society itself on display.[11] The same might be said of the activity of gameplay. As Ian Shaw and Barney Warf put it, "like a roller coaster, the player experiences the thrill ... without the risks: a premeditated adrenaline."[12] The ostensibly inconsequential but viscerally compelling and rhythmically immersive activity of beating up a virtual adversary, killing virtual aliens, or stealing virtual cars may tell us something significant about what kinds of beings our society needs us to be. Critical here is the way in which video games facilitate affectively intensive play with contingency and crisis, detached from real-world consequences.

This chapter approaches video games as an embodied practice that, at once, teaches about, reinforces, and contributes to the separations and qualifications that determine individuation in contemporary societies. It focuses on the political nature of gameplay—"political" understood here to refer to the shaping and reshaping of corporeal capacities and textures of experience that characterize contemporary society in terms of sensations and sensibilities rather than representations.[13] Thus it considers video games from a rather specific and narrow perspective, exploring the ways this novel type of action-based imagery teaches us how to move our bodies, be affected, and manipulate and live both with the material world and with others around us. The chapter will show how video games establish rhythmic and even behavioristic roller coaster–like visual economies within which they pattern and capture our sensations and gestures through the interactions between screens and our body-minds, and how video game imagery is emblematic of a more general anthropology of subjectivity today, which chapter 1 described in terms of the epistemology and politics of the "neoliberal brain." And, in tracing how video game images operate as particular nodes or threads in the biopolitical apparatus, it will show how they resonate and coincide with other key practices and imaginations defining the political reality of life today, from scientific formulas to military (ir)rationalities and economic pursuits.

Arousal and Affect

Let us start with a paradigmatic example: the first-person shooter war game *Call of Duty: Modern Warfare 3* (Activision, 2011), which soon after its release became the fastest selling entertainment product in recent history, with $1 billion in sales in sixteen days.[14] In singling out this particular kind of video game, my aim is not to generalize about the properties of a genre or medium, but rather to reason analogously between different areas of contemporary political reality, moving by way of montage from one aspect and dimension of the biopolitical apparatus to another.[15]

Call of Duty: Modern Warfare 3 transports players to the year 2016, when World War 3 has devastated the West. As perhaps its main purpose, this very near future apocalyptic scenario allows players to experience in its virtual world today's high-technology, network-centric warfare, which emphasizes both instantaneous communications to achieve greater synchronization, flexibility, and speed and the use of unconventional weapons such as unmanned vehicles on the ground and in the air. The game deploys a plethora of military robots, drones, and satellites, as well as technologies such as "intelligent" CCTV and thermal vision, making these integral elements of online battles, where hundreds of thousands of brains become repetitively entrained into synchronized rhythms. Though set in the near future, *Modern Warfare 3* seems to render the reality of contemporary wars as an embodied virtual experience in households across the developed world, thereby reifying and reinforcing the militarization of civilian life.[16]

In this regard, more critical than the game's story are the hectic rhythms that its players incorporate in patterns of movement, affectivity, and arousal. The online multiplayer version in particular seeks to emphasize contingency based on random, which is to say, unprogrammed interactions between players in the gaming environment. Leaving narrative development aside, it is structured around periodic oscillations between the manipulation of the game settings and episodes of combat with friendlies and adversaries where points are earned that will take players to the next skill level. These repetitive matches take place within clearly demarcated

Figure 2.3
The game kicks off. Screen grab from *Call of Duty: Modern Warfare* 3 (Activision, 2011).

settings or "maps," as they are called, which are hermetic virtual locations that range from the devastated city centers of London, Paris, and New York to the Bakaara Market in Mogadishu and an abandoned ghost town in Russia.

The match begins. With my fellow teammates, I start running to occupy the operational area and to search for enemies. The first step in playing *Modern Warfare 3* online is setting out along a path of movement, which feeds on bodily engagement with the screen (figure 2.3).[17] Pushing the joystick on the left side of my PlayStation controller with my left thumb lets me move the viewpoint forward, while rotating the joystick on the right side with my right thumb lets me move the viewpoint up and down and side to side. My awareness is completely engaged by the operational area, or what Galloway terms "fully rendered actionable space," where new situations develop millisecond by millisecond.[18] Because the gaming experience is, first and foremost, based on moving around in and exploring a virtual environment, a crucial and fundamental requirement is that the player's viewpoint also be moving and free. Players perceive their game environment as a stream of constantly changing rhythmic stimuli that elicit their motor behavior. Indeed, their perceptions cannot be separated from moving about, probing, and interacting with their virtual surroundings. Walls and other solid objects give cover. Open spaces should be crossed as quickly as possible because a player can never tell if there is a sniper hiding somewhere. A mere glimpse of an adversary triggers the learned gestures of raising the sights, aiming, and shooting.

The kinds of images that fill the gaming experience of those who play first-person shooter games such as *Modern Warfare 3* are, first of all, visuomotor: in them, eye merges with hand, vision with gesture, calling to mind recent discussions in cognitive neuroscience and philosophy on the nature of vision as a process that depends on interactions between viewer and environment. Indeed, in his enactive theory of perception—where perceiving cannot be separated from doing—Alva Noë contends that perceptual experience "is an activity of exploring the environment drawing on knowledge of sensorimotor dependencies and thought."[19] The perceiver, Noë's main argument goes, should not be taken as a "brain-photoreceptor system" that decodes inputs and encodes outputs, but as embodied and "situated in the environment, free to move around and explore."[20] The contents of perception are something we enact when probing the world with our sensorimotor capacities and skills.

Noë's approach draws on the ecological theory of perception developed by James J. Gibson, whose starting point was the world as it is "seen from now here," from the perceiver's point of observation (figure 2.3), which always entails movement: perception is based on motility and constant interactions between observer and material environment.[21] Gibson argued that perception is fundamentally direct, rather than mediated by representations, categories, schemata, or computational processes; it emerges in interaction. We perceive the world not in terms of abstractions, such as time and space, but as surfaces, which mark the physical qualities of objects in our environment (texture, shape, size, color) and as events, which embody the changes those surfaces undergo (deformation, transition, destruction, emergence). To the perceiver, these surfaces and events come across as action possibilities or, in Gibson's terminology, "affordances" for different kinds of behavior.

According to Gibson's theory, the directness of perceiving also holds for what he called "virtual objects"—photographs, paintings, films, and here we should also add video games.[22] In effect, these virtual objects come to us as firsthand experiences of the real world, which is to say, as directly present to our perception and as something we enact with gestures. Barbara

Maria Stafford concludes from Gibson's theory that "images are mental objects, and they belong back in mind—not as secondary perceptions or mediated representations, but as performances crucially involved in first-hand awareness of both actual and imaginary or nonexistent things."[23]

In *Modern Warfare 3*, the visual-kinetic surfaces players perceive and interact with furnish the video game's virtual world with its immediately embodied materiality: what appears to be hard metal in that world can be used as cover, whereas bullets can penetrate what appears to be the shaky wooden walls of huts, behind which players feel their vulnerability. The video game is very much about the changes that various surfaces undergo: cars blow up, windows are smashed, things are constantly appearing and being destroyed. Most crucially, this rich rhythmic sensory stream of transformations comes as a dynamic of action possibilities. Players are constantly seeking different ways of inhabiting and acting in the environment, and what they perceive as space varies according to their mobile and enactive viewpoint, with new surfaces and events unfolding in their field of vision moment by moment. According to Gibson's theory, in first-person shooter video games such as *Modern Warfare 3*, "instead of geometrical points and lines, we have points of observation and lines of locomotion."[24] From the moment these games kick off, we need to perceive so we can move, but also to move so we can perceive (figure 2.3). Indeed, a signal feature of video games' visual economy is that their images belong in our mind-brains as motor performances, drawing on the way these are, above all, geared toward the prediction and production of movement through action simulations.[25]

In the visual economy of the first-person shooter, the directness of perception is coupled with affective immediacy: killing our adversaries gives us pleasure; being killed by them teaches us through pain. The virtual worlds of video games are colored in particular with danger and anxiety related to the constant awareness of potential threat. Enemies lurk around corners waiting to kill us while we try to keep one step ahead of them; we can never tell if there is an enemy sniper hiding somewhere; the threat of death is imminent. This affective embodiment is based on rhythms that reify our primal need to survive and that are part of what psychologist Daniel Stern calls "dynamic forms of vitality." Essential to the coupling of individual with milieu, these forms compose a domain of intense bodily dynamics described with words like "exploding," "surging," "accelerating," "fading,"

Figure 2.4
Action-reaction circuit. Screen grab from *Call of Duty: Modern Warfare* 3 (Activision, 2011).

"fleeting," "powerful," "pulsing," and "rushing."[26] Most basically and crucially when it comes to conceptualizing gameplay, Stern holds that "the experience of vitality is inherent in the act of movement. Movement, and its proprioception, is the primary manifestation of being animate and provides the primary sense of aliveness."[27]

Gameplay is filled with the coming and going, surging and fading, of such intense experiences of vitality.[28] The sight of an enemy makes our hearts beat faster and causes us to tighten our grip on the controller (figure 2.4), whereas hiding behind a corner gives us a brief moment of relaxation. Images here have a powerful hold on our material nervous dynamics. The flow of vitality in gameplay feeds on our different levels of arousal, which Stern characterizes as "the 'fundamental force' for all bodily and mental activity."[29] Deeply embedded in the ancient part of the basal forebrain called the "amygdala," arousal systems are seen as essential to all aspects of animal life, from basic movements to emotions and perceptions. In our central nervous system, neuroscientist Donald Pfaff writes, "beneath all of our specific mental functions and particular emotional dispositions, a primitive neuronal system throbs in the brainstem, activating our brains and behaviors."[30] Evolutionarily ancient and most significant when it comes to behavioral responses, arousal is what triggers our responsivity to the environment. It elicits our emotions, makes us alert, focuses our attention, and initiates our movements. "Arousal," Stern argues, "determines when we do what we do, and the dynamic manner of doing it."[31]

Thus, according to this neuropsychological model, we need to be aroused and feel alive in order to move and act in the first place. Gestures arise when we feel animated for whatever reason; when neurons fire in our brains and we begin to focus our attention, we feel willing to act. Sensory contingencies such as explosions and gunfire in *Modern Warfare 3* are precisely meant to elicit this very basic dimension of experience: change, uncertainty, and unpredictability promote arousal, whereas the lack of these decreases it.[32] In their attempts to capture, control, and captivate video game players, first-person shooter images come across as distinctly behavioristic. They draw on perceptual automatisms that tag changes in our field of vision; a mere anticipatory glimpse of an enemy triggers defensive action, and we pound repeatedly on the fire button. Arousal systems germane to feelings of vitality are commonly thought to be prenoetic, operating before conscious recognition has even time to emerge.[33] We can therefore surmise that first-person shooter images pass directly through our arousal systems before becoming part of our phenomenal experience and objects of recognition. In the pace of the video game, constantly changing visual stimuli modulate amplitudes of arousal and related affect states, which shift, in a split second, from creeping anxiety and sometimes even outright fear to the explosive pleasure of killing an enemy.

Zombies

Much of gameplay happens on levels that words cannot reach. When we play *Modern Warfare 3*, embodiment takes place on the level of our bodies' intense dynamics, beyond self-awareness. The video game images seek to frame us as basically affective and aroused beings, who are constantly reacting to shifting, contingent screen events. And in this type of affective capture lie the thrill and power of the game.

To find the scientific discourses that shed most light on such behavioristic sensory thrills, we should look primarily not at those concerned with the embodied subject's introspective capabilities, but rather at those which strive to establish normative models of individuation by assimilating our ontology, as first-person shooter video games do, to its natural dimension.

Given that the biopolitical apparatus is, to quote Gilles Deleuze, "a machine that is almost blind and mute, even though it makes others see and speak,"[34] it is the neuroscientific way of seeing and speaking about the subject that best explains the logic according to which video games assume and position the persons who play them. Considering the larger economy of images and imaginations within which the potentials of contemporary life become an issue of government, first-person shooter imagery resonates with and relates to the move from the speaking to the cerebral subject so important to the psychiatric and life sciences today.[35]

Indeed, recent fMRI-based research into brain activity during gameplay associates video game imagery with the basic, even primal processes of reward, addiction, and autonomous arousal.[36] It couples this imagery with what Antonio Damasio calls the "primordial feelings" of pleasure and pain that are linked with arousal systems and the motivation of behavior.[37] Damasio argues that reward and punishment, pleasure and pain, motivate exploration based on value, which is integral to the maintenance and regulation of homeostasis, that is, to the biological need to adapt at the basis of life. In this view, the behavioristic nature of video game images—how they feed on elementary biological functions of reward and homeostatic regulation, and thus directly modulate the ways players feel pleasure and pain and thus evaluate experience—is fundamental to their very makeup.[38] Even if they only scratch the surface of the myriad rhythmic electrochemical processes that take place within the brains of video game players, brain imaging–based studies suggest how the stream of visual, auditory, and kinetic stimuli of video game imagery comes to us as a powerful experience embodied below our conscious minds.

In line with current neuroscientific reasoning, we should note how the visual economy of the first-person shooter coincides with that of the cerebral subject: both are driven and shaped by the brain's learned or genetic automatisms—or "zombies," as Vilayanur S. Ramachandran calls them—which work below conscious awareness and control.[39] In his study of perceptual illusions, Ramachandran showed how much unconscious and "automatic" brain processes structure and direct our perception and behavior, echoing a common and decisive theme in neuroscientific thought, which considers agency with respect to a neurological unconscious to be at the origin of self-awareness. According to Gerald Edelman, it is "underlying neural activity" that "drives individual and mental responses,"[40] and that, as Hermann von Helmholtz proposed in the mid-nineteenth century, gives rise to conscious awareness through a host of unconscious inferences.[41]

Neuroscientists see the cerebral subject as an emergent, moving, and doing being who arises out of complex interactions with a basically chaotic and originally unlabeled environment, and who is molded by the accidents, challenges, threats, and dangers of that environment. Thus the individual human is an evolutionarily qualified and ontologically uncertain being, whose composition is constantly subject to contingent transformations and emergence. This view, Michael Dillon and Luis Lobo-Guerrero tell us, reflects a particular biopolitical imaginary that informs contemporary societies, one within which contingency is considered "*the* property of life as emergence, both its ontological condition and its adaptive, epistemic, challenge."[42] Indeed, since the molecular and digital revolutions in the biological and information sciences, contingency has become the "epistemic object of rule" by which networks of power are established and capital accumulated. And, one should add, it has also become an object of "sentimental education" in the culture of gaming. As we have seen, the simulation of contingency is a key feature of the virtual environments in *Modern Warfare 3* and other video games of its kind. Indeed, Thomas Malaby suggests that such games are "distinctive in their achievement of a generative balance between the open-endedness of contingencies and the reproducibility of conditions for action."[43]

For its part, the biopolitical imaginary of contingency and adaptation becomes particularly manifest in the way neuroscience emphasizes the brain's vital power of creative interaction with the world as fundamental to its workings.[44] A signal feature of the brain is its plasticity: the synapses and neurons of the brain are constantly subject to degeneration, regeneration, and growth. Synaptic connections respond to environmental changes, and neurons renew and repair themselves in what is called "secondary neurogenesis"; both processes are seen as fundamental to behavioral modifiability. Critical to the brain-milieu coupling is thus the brain's capacity not only to maintain homeostatic equilibrium against environmental influence but also to regenerate itself and to impose its own organization on the world. The brain's dense patchwork of neurons and synapses is connective, dynamic, and self-organizing; its responses are therefore not simply reactive but autopoetic as well. The brain, in short, "can develop strategies of its own. It anticipates coming events and elaborates its own programs."[45]

Edelman, for one, has stressed how action and pattern recognition play a central and essential role in the growth of the brain's structure and dynamics. Sensory and motor systems, he argues, are necessary for perception, learning, and sense making.[46] Others, like György Buzsáki, propose that it is the rhythmic, oscillatory patterns of our brains' neural activity that enable us to come up with our own image of reality in negotiation with the environment, that produce both our sense of time and our intuition of space.[47] Buzsáki argues that the primary task of the brain is to anticipate and predict environmental events, quoting François Jacob: "One of the deepest, one of the most general functions of living organisms is to look ahead."[48]

Here, in a key anthropological assumption of contemporary neuroscience, the human brain is considered innovative and productive, self-organizing and pattern forming: instead of merely illustrating, copying, or calculating, it fills in, hypothesizes, predicts, and simulates.[49] The brain's main duty is to anticipate the future by simulating what will occur next. Indeed, it is the very ability to anticipate actions and events to come that defines the brain and its rhythms, and that neuroscientists see as intrinsic to the adaptive and emergent qualities of human beings. As Rodolfo Llinás put it, the self is the "seat of prediction."[50]

Thus, the cerebral subject is, by definition, constantly looking ahead. Which takes us back to the first-person shooter experience. The way that *Modern Warfare 3*, especially in its online multiplayer mode, draws players into a constantly transforming web of actions and reactions, much like those of predators hunting prey (figure 2.4), reflects how games of its kind present movement and contingency as an adaptive challenge. In doing so, they underwrite in their own fashion the present-day biopolitical imaginary. Their images draw players into complex rhythms organized and processed below conscious awareness; these images require engagement that is anticipatory and preemptive by nature, tapping into how "the brain is used to predict the future, to anticipate the consequences of action (its own or that of the others), and to save time."[51] New to video game imagery is the extent to which the images of *Modern Warfare 3* and its kind draw on our proactive capacities to manage novelty and chance, to anticipate at each moment what will happen next. Players are called on to forefeel the looming threat, to foresee the adversary's position and movements, and to preempt the adversary's capacity to act. *Modern Warfare 3*'s online gameplay is based on a rhythmic relationality in which the brain conjures up the world to come with the objective of acting preemptively on the perceptions, actions, and conditions of other beings. In this way, its video game screen aims to enlist each player's brain as "an inventive simulator that forecasts future events."[52]

In short, first-person shooter imagery defies critical distance, triggering a primal need to be constantly foreseeing dangers: there is no time to think about what is in the image, no time to reflect. Fast-paced rhythmic entanglements draw on the brain's processing of the visual field through the affective anticipation of threats and the production of motor responses to preempt those threats. Although such a description of the immersive embodiment of video games like *Modern Warfare 3* says nothing about the role of players' "higher-level" consciousness in gameplay, the primary activities of tracking down or evading the enemy, of predicting what lurks around the corner engage, first and foremost, the unconscious processing of actions, or prereflective "motor cognition."[53] Because it responds to our actions in one way or another, video game imagery is something we relate to proactively. In a sense, we do not embody such images as something occurring here and now but as something that is to come, something we automatically foresee. For players, then, the screen exists as a simulated future, capturing our bodily rhythms and prenoetic adjustments through which the affective and predictive functions of the brain merge with the video game screen and vice versa.

Neuropower

If images have the power to induce a bodily response from those who view them, the power that video game images have over the behavior of players encompasses somatic processes that fall within the domain of neurological "zombies." In this way, games like *Modern Warfare 3* promote a process of individuation that serves contemporary biopolitics with its imaginary of emergent, material, and self-organizing living beings struggling for existence in an utterly contingent world of survival, threats, and risks. This process of individuation, in turn, becomes an epistemic object of rule within contemporary neuroscientific conceptualizations and visualizations of the cerebral subject. However unexpected such a juxtaposition might seem, it nonetheless points out a particular immanent logic to the machinations of life in our neoliberal age that both the realm of entertainment and the realm of science express: a "diagram," to echo Deleuze, of contingency, threat, and, as we will see, crisis.

The contemporary strategies of governing life thus differ somewhat from the ones Michel Foucault outlined in terms of two forms of power over life that emerged in the West starting in the seventeenth century—"two poles of development linked together by a whole intermediary cluster of relations."[54] At one pole, the "anatomopolitics of the body" viewed individual bodies as types of machines whose capabilities and performance needed to be optimized, economized, and controlled to maximize their productivity. At the other pole, the "biopolitics of populations" viewed humanity in terms of "births and mortality, the level of health, life expectancy and longevity, with all the conditions that can cause these to vary."[55] It sought to capture and enhance life processes on the level of populations by means of statistical knowledge, biological engineering, and regulatory policies, among other things.

Although certainly containing traces of both of these ways of administering the living, the contemporary biopolitical apparatus exerts through its imaginary a kind of neuropower that is not immediately disciplinary or regulatory but is instead based on the indirect modulation of the brain's adaptive and autopoietic capacities germane to the feelings, values, and imaginations that inform our minds and behavior. This power shapes the ways in which the brain's homeostatic system regulates our responses and value systems, our feelings and perceptual continuity, in short, the emergence of our minds. With regard to video game images, neuropower refers in particular to the capacity of these images to engage the brain's self-organizing powers to simulate the world as an object of preemptive perception, concerning futurity as the outcome of action.

Here I am using the concept of neuropower in much the same way as Warren Neidich, who developed it to account for what Neidich calls a "new focus of sovereignty: that of neural plasticity itself and its potential as a generator of fields of difference."[56] According to Neidich, contemporary forms of power administer "the pluripotential of neuroplasticity in the *curating* of a homogeneous people both in the present and future."[57] Neuropower, for Neidich, involves "the production of people in the future," that is, the management of what individuals can become.[58] The same can be argued about the first-person shooter screen's capacity to "curate" or educate the gamer. Its action-oriented images can be considered epigenetic and developmental, functioning as environmental conditions in response to which the brain adjusts and modifies itself.

A detail in *Modern Warfare 3*'s interface exemplifies this type of curating of minds. Notably, what adds an extra cognitive and affective dimension to the first-person shooter video game is the two-dimensional minimap of where the battles take place, visible in the upper left corner of the screen (e.g., figure 2.3). Typical of the aesthetics of most action-based video games, the map is "live" rather than static: it shows the movements and positions of teammates as green triangles and those of enemies as throbbing red dots, once a "killstreak" named "Spy Drone" is deployed. The map mimics an omniscient eye hovering over the virtual battlegrounds; by supplementing the first-person perspective of the shooter with a third-person bird's-eye view, it further develops the screen as a rhythmic surface of preemptive action. More important, the map assumes a cognitive interface, one that binds situated, embodied perception seeking to act on things and the actions of others (motor cognition) to synoptic perception seeking to locate, track, and position (spatial imagination). Here "binds" is used in the neuroscientific sense to reflect how the screen demands perceptual grouping of heterogeneous visual processes into an apprehensible and meaningful unity—a connection-seeking and relation-forming sensorimotor activity that synchronizes varying rhythms to achieve spatiotemporal coherence and coordination.[59]

The tiny live map possesses a compact cognitive power. Welding together two disparate viewpoints (first- and third-person), it lets players locate and anticipate the movements of others and position themselves strategically in space. It allows multiple action-oriented brains to cohere in a mutually reflective pattern of movements, functioning as a cue for spatial awareness. But, above all, the map creates (to quote Christian Jacob) "a space of anticipation, of predictability, of omniscience tied to the very fact of the synoptic gaze,"[60] enabling players to engage in anticipatory rhythm analysis of the movements of friends and foes, and emphasizing the critical role that the domination of visibility has in gameplay.

The binding dynamic of *Modern Warfare 3*'s interface thus establishes a perceptual order within which the subjective, embodied first-person viewpoint finds its bearings and is interlinked with an objective, global third-person viewpoint, and the more or less coherent contours of the operational area are drawn. This process of perceptual ordering and cognizance is exactly what neuroscientists call "mapping," which, in the neuroscientific sense, refers to dynamic, rhythmic, and transient interconnections formed between series of neuronal groups.[61] According to Damasio, these patterns of interconnection make up the neural basis of embodiment: they represent things and events in the external world or in the body as well as the brain's processing of them.[62] Maps become subjectively experienced as images, which is to say, as the rich sensory mix of sights, sounds, touches, movements, and emotions that fills existence from one moment to the next. In other words, neural maps underlie what emerges in our mind-brains as an emotionally imbued and perceptually coherent and sensible picture of the world.

The stream of images composing the mind is seen to rest on the brain's constant work of mapping. Like the minimap in *Modern Warfare 3*, brain maps are dynamic, "not static like those of classical cartography," Damasio explains. "Brain maps are mercurial, changing from moment to moment, to reflect the changes that are happening in the neurons that feed them, which in turn reflect the changes in the interior of our body and in the world around us. The changes in brain maps also reflect the fact we ourselves are in constant motion."[63] Brain maps are constantly drawn and redrawn as the organism interacts with the environment; tied to the succession of events in the here and now, they relate to changes in the body's internal structure and state (interoceptive maps), to changes in the position and work of joints and muscles (proprioceptive maps), or to changes in the immediate sensory realm (exteroceptive maps). Indeed, formed as the organism learns to move about, brain maps are "signs of future possibilities," which tie our bodies to our surroundings.[64]

The brain's work of mapping is not only embodied, temporal, and dynamic but also selective and imaginative, discriminatory and categorizing, that is, it not only represents; it also creates, based on value. According to Damasio, "the images in our minds are given more or less saliency in the mental stream according to their value for the individual," whereas value "comes from the original set of dispositions that originate our life regulation" and "from the valuations that all images we have gradually acquired in our experience have been accorded."[65] For Damasio, value systems (relating, most fundamentally, to the biological need to maintain and regulate homeostasis) selectively cut and compose the mind's imagery, whether consciously or unconsciously experienced, working much like film editors. In a similar vein, Edelman holds that value systems (salience, reward and punishment) constrain the perceptual categorization of patterns out of the multiplicity of varying signals from the world: they regulate how we feel the world, how we simulate in perception, and how we selectively discriminate "an object or event from other objects or events for adaptive purposes."[66] Value, Edelman argues, "is a *precondition* for arriving at a perceptual or behavioral response."[67]

It is important to note that neuroscientists see value systems as modifiable rather than fixed.[68] Against this backdrop, and given the extent to which the action-oriented images of video games can shape the players' basic affective experiences, we can surmise that they both externalize and coordinate the brain's mapping activity. From this perspective, the images serve as maps of the maps the brain makes. Thus video games like *Modern Warfare 3* instantiate not merely the mind-brain's enacted content and the direct manipulation of behavior, but also the selective environmental conditions of perception and performance. The first-person shooter screen edits the movies running in our minds as it regulates the pleasures and pains according to which our brains develop their maps and we discriminate and navigate our world. Accordingly, mapping can be seen as an ontological and epistemological practice that integrates the microcosm of the brain with the macrocosm of the world—a practice of regulating and systematizing autopoietic mental constructs based on perceptual categorization through which reality gets captured as a site of ordering, prediction, and action. Here the video game screen is a "screen" in the double sense of the word: both a material instantiation of the images it displays and a sort of sieve that selects what kinds of images will emerge in our cognitive reality.

Just as the neuroscientific episteme describes our behavioral and perceptual capacities to self-organize with respect to the contingencies of our surroundings, so the visual economy of *Modern Warfare 3* administers our perceptual and motor capacities, through our brains' autopoietic adjustment, to respond to the game's intentionally random environmental screen effects. It is here that the neuropower of the video game images is located—and exerted, above all, over the conditions for perception, rather than over perceptions themselves. We should note that video game screens are not simply normative mechanisms according to which gamers must mold themselves mentally or even physically, nor are gamers "machinically enslaved" beings.[69] Instead, video game screens converge with what Foucault in his genealogy of neoliberal biopolitics called "environmental intervention," a mode of power that seeks to modulate and regulate the conduct of individuals, not through mental subjugation, but rather by modifying their adaptive and self-organizing capacities and conditions.[70]

Drawing especially on Gary Becker's writings, Foucault dealt with the constitution of the famous *Homo economicus* of neoliberal thought as, above all, a free, moving, doing, and enterprising being that pursues and calculates its own interest, and whose needs, deeds, and activities should not be directly interfered with, but that, though free to choose, pursue its goals, calculate gains and losses, and seek pleasure, is also involuntarily subject to the contingencies and, above all, accidents of its environment. Outstripped by effects it cannot directly influence, the neoliberal subject is—like the Darwinian species-being, or the video game player—embedded in a dynamic of change and itself becomes changed through its adaptive and innovative responses based most notably on the calculation of interest and the maximization of value. *Homo economicus* is, in Foucault's words, "someone who responds systematically to systematic modifications artificially introduced into the environment," someone "eminently governable" through the environmental effects that shape the dynamics of action.[71] The neoliberal model of the ideal economic agent thus serves the biopolitical imaginary of contingency's essential role in life and the administration of individual freedoms.

Aside from superficial similarities between the video game player and *Homo economicus* (concerning the ways in which both calculate gains and losses and make choices egoistically pursuing their benefit), what links the two conceptually is that both are beings whose behavioral and, more generally, mental capacities are a matter of administration and regulation by indirect means. The point here is not to propose that gamers be considered rational economic actors, but to argue that what weaves together the individuating conditions of video games and those of contemporary biopolitics is the way both operate on the level of the milieu. Both seek to administer a random field of action and survival—be that virtual battlefields, fluctuating markets, or financialized social security systems—where the individual is made, as Foucault put it, to try to maintain a "sort of homeostasis," that is, to survive.[72] Not surprisingly, environmental modifiability is also a fundamental feature of the cerebral subject conceptualized within the neuroscientific episteme, which, as noted, emphasizes the self-organizing capacities of living organisms to adapt to constantly new conditions and to simultaneously maintain their compositional integrity.

The Preemptive Brain

We can see how the blind and mute system machinating the political reality of life today makes us see ourselves as flexible and affective cerebral beings constantly anticipating and adapting to the world's randomness, while manufacturing, in video games, visual forms that reproduce this mode of being in embodied reactions and adjustments. To what extent do the technovisual animations of these games, and the gamers' experiences of them, coincide with the general models of affectivity and cognition that define contemporary societies? How, in other words, should we describe the sociopolitical momentum of video game imagery in the present?

It is precisely because of its preemptive visuality and temporal patterns that *Modern Warfare 3* and other games of its kind can be seen to capture their players within the larger complexes of standardized desires, ways of doing, and making sense that shape our societies today. The catchword "preemption" crystallizes much of what is happening within the realms of both politics and the economy. Since 9/11, it has come to define how the West responds to perceived threats at home and abroad: by waging "small" but "long" wars in the global South and by introducing increasingly stringent measures of control for the "security" of populations in our so-called democratic societies. These "overseas counterinsurgent operations," as the Obama administration calls today's wars,[73] are being waged in defense, not of the state, but of the neoliberal way of life, so that it might expand and come to dominate the world. In the words of Colonel Daniel S. Roper, director of the U.S. Army and Marine Corps Counterinsurgency Center: "The U.S. strategic goal in the Long War is to preserve and promote the way of life of free and open societies based on the rule of law, defeat terrorist extremism, and create a global environment inhospitable to extremists."[74] Viewed in biopolitical terms, the strategic imperative of the "wars on terror" is to promote both the "free" (entrepreneurial) way of life by preempting threats and dangers to it across the globe and environments in which this way of life can flourish and expand, at the expense of all others.

Admittedly, the presence of unceasing terrorist threats has made neoliberal governance embrace a state of exception and perpetual war. Interlinked with the logic of warfare and control is how preemption also defines the temporal logic of contemporary finance capitalism, which is based on trading with future promises and the production of debt through securitization. Financial instruments such as derivatives are meant to colonize the future by managing the amount of risk involved in investment and by turning time as the uncertain difference between the now and the not yet (between current and future exchange rates, for example) into a commodity. In doing so, Randy Martin tells us, "preemption acts to turn a presumed certainty about the future into a present suddenly made uncertain and therefore open to opportunity."[75] The "rationality" of finance capitalism lies in its efforts to master randomness, to translate future expectations into expected futures and thus tame the forces of time.[76]

Preemption, then, crystallizes the parallel logics according to which wars are fought and capital accumulated in our neoliberal present, logics according to which "contingencies of the future are to be lived out in the present, blurring the distinction between the not-yet and the now."[77] Military dominance and finance capitalism—in addition to being all too material practices that ravage the natural environment and decimate populations—are also mental constructs in the sense of specific temporally oriented emotional and perceptual categorizations. Characteristic of neoliberalism in this respect is the cognitive, political, and economic value assigned to "securitization," in the extended sense of hedging against future threats by military, financial, or other means. Intrinsic to securitization is the affective anticipation of constant and indefinite future threats that shapes neoliberalism's emotional landscape. In this mental landscape, following Brian Massumi, threat is "ubiquitously generic."[78] Threats and dangers often translate into the feeling of fear, which Massumi describes as "the anticipatory reality in the present of a threatening future," that is, "the felt reality of the nonexistent, loomingly present as the *affective fact* of the matter."[79] On the other hand, the landscape of future threats constantly forefelt in the present is experienced, not as fear in the normal, specific sense, but as continuing anxiety. The distinction here is significant because fear and anxiety—or "unresolved fear," as Joseph LeDoux describes it[80]—can lead to different outcomes: corrective action taken in fear of a specific danger often allays the feeling of fear, whereas action taken in anxiety about an ever impending but indefinite danger most often has no such effect.[81]

Neoliberal brainhood thus organizes itself specifically around the felt reality of threats, risks, and insecurities, which are the key values that constrain how we simulate and act on the world. The neoliberal brain, to use Richard Grusin's term, "premediates"—affectively forefeels—future possibilities in the present with an eye toward anticipatory responses, especially when fear or anxiety about future threats or danger is involved.[82] Against this backdrop, it is not surprising that neuroscience conceptualizes fear and anxiety as fundamental and intrinsic to life. Indeed, it regards the fear system deployed by the brain to detect dangers and organize defensive behavior as a genetically programmed module operating outside conscious control.[83] According to this model, sensory cues of a potential threat strongly impel the organism to take aggressive, preemptive action to deal with that threat and thus maintain homeostatic balance; the affects of fear and anxiety are naturalized as key biological conditions of existence. Thus neuroscience underwrites contemporary endeavors to make individuals, in Foucault's words, "experience their situation, their life, their present, and their future as containing danger."[84] Or, to put it another way, such neuroscientific conceptualizations reflect what Roberto Esposito has called the "immunitary logic" of biopolitics, a logic (dealt with in greater detail in chapter 3) according to which self and nonself, inside and outside are in an endless conflict with each other, and external influence must be violently suppressed to preserve and prolong the life of the organism.[85]

Something like this type of affective naturalization of danger is also what happens at *Modern Warfare 3*'s interface. Anxiety is admittedly one of the defining affects of the video game's psychosomatic environment, with its looming and persistent threats. The repetitive and seemingly meaningless activity of virtual killing, dying, "respawning," killing, and dying again amounts to a reemerging and never-ending crisis. In this recursive action-reaction circuit, the moving margin between self and nonself constantly reemerges as a site of struggle, and the ubiquitous presence of varying dangers requires a continued and unresolved state of alertness based on anxiety and stress that trigger the impulse not to escape, but to violently defend oneself.

An obvious node of contact and intersection for such video game images is the U.S. military and the preemptive visuality that informs the contemporary wars it is waging. Video game development has historically close ties with the U.S. military when it comes to the design of interactive three-dimensional virtual environments, artificial intelligence, and distributed network systems, with the purpose of modeling and simulating realistic and imminent future combats.[86] Above all, as we will see in greater detail in chapter 3, the military-entertainment complex has embraced video game images as vehicles for training and therapy, from the visual-kinetic interfaces of first-person shooter video games to advanced artificial intelligence systems employed to teach "counterinsurgents" how to navigate the intricate sociocultural environments they encounter.[87] Moreover, the history of video game technology parallels that of cybernetics, the art of governing time-critical processes by technical means. Thus, Patrick Crogan tells us, "the first-person shooter enacts a powerful technocultural desire to encounter the future in the form of anticipated, controllable contingencies"—a desire embodied in the "AA predictor," an antiaircraft system developed by Norbert Wiener in the 1940s to calculate the future flight paths of targeted aircraft several seconds in advance.[88]

But in addition to industrial or technological linkages between gaming and warfare, the two effectively coincide under the rubric of the neoliberal view of the world and its attendant perceptual and cognitive models. Contemporary wars, Nicholas Mirzoeff points out, are perceptually challenging visual "complexes" based on managing chaos and interminable states of emergency and crisis.[89] No longer is the battlefield clearly and vividly visible to the commander's sovereign eye, which, in the words of Carl von Clausewitz, "easily grasps and dismisses a thousand remote possibilities."[90] The present-day wars on terror are much messier. The enemy, we are told, is not distinctly visible and identifiable but rather spectral and networked, emerging at one moment and disappearing at another. The battlefield itself has expanded indefinitely because the eventual location, extent, and timing of an anticipated terrorist attack are undefined and uncertain. Instead of being about one sovereign will fighting against another, as von Clausewitz imagined them, global wars today are fundamentally about sovereign wills preemptively imagining whatever future attacks the enemy might make, or whatever vulnerabilities the enemy might have, and acting accordingly.

The preemptive fight for world governance—to make the future certain—makes the present ever more uncertain, however, as Massumi explains:

For one thing, the epistemology [of preemption] is unabashedly one of *uncertainty*, and not due to simple lack of knowledge. There is uncertainty because the threat has not only not yet fully formed but ... it has *not yet even emerged*. In other words, the threat is still indeterminately in potential. This is an ontological premise: the nature of threat cannot be specified. It might in some circumstances involve weapons of mass destruction, but in others it will not. It might come in the form of a strange white powder, or then again it might be an improvised explosive device.[91]

Preemptive war is thus proactive; instead of reacting to actual facts, it operates by simulating future potentialities, which are brought to bear on the present. And this futurity made present—the perceptual production of indistinct forms of threat and fear—is the motor of its actions.

The military strategies implemented in recent wars in Iraq and Afghanistan directly encapsulate this logic. Indeed, the preemptive administration of behavior informs the counterinsurgency (COIN) doctrine employed as a principal strategy in fighting for global governance.[92] Counterinsurgency seeks to militarize the government of populations; it views the domains of "culture" and "popular support" as the means and object of warfare and takes a "learn and adapt" approach toward them.[93] Counterinsurgency operates in an environment where, as one of its prominent theorists David Kilcullen writes, "all sides engage in an extremely rapid, complex, and continuous process of competitive adaptation."[94] The world as counterinsurgency doctrine pictures it closely resembles the Darwinian milieu of struggle for survival, or the contingent fluctuating circumstances of finance capitalism, or indeed the "maps" of first-person shooters—a world premised on "adaptability in the face of a rapidly evolving insurgent threat and a changing environment."[95] The doctrine sees the enemy as a self-organizing system that depends on flows of matter and energy from the environment in order to maintain stability and structure, and that (like any organic system) exhibits emergent behavior that cannot be predicted by analyzing its component parts. Consequently, the way to suppress such an enemy is not to eliminate every "element" (person) within its system but rather to change the enemy's "pattern of interaction" into a "stable and peaceful 'system state.'"[96]

To that end, counterinsurgency strategy is to clear, hold, and build: to remove insurgents by lethal force and to establish neoliberal governance in the space thus opened up, by supplying the basic means of living and by building infrastructure, for example.[97] But there is another, more ominous side to this militarized way of government: it relies on the constant tracking and monitoring of the movements of populations with the objective of detecting and eliminating insurgent threats *before* they can emerge. Its imperative is thus to act on what is potential, to colonize future actions either by promoting life or by managing death. Counterinsurgency doctrine subscribes to a particular imperialism of time. Based on adapting to constantly changing surroundings, counterinsurgency's biopolitical imaginary sees the entire planet as a potential battleground, where recurrent insurgent emergencies need to be foreseen before they actually arise and eliminated with network-centric "precision operations" that cut out "cancerous tissue while keeping other vital organs,"[98] and thus "allow the [targeted] country's indigenous immune system to be restored."[99]

The guiding image of counterinsurgency in this violent and lethal sense is the ground control system of unmanned aerial vehicles (UAVs; figure 2.5), or drones. One of the central tactics emphasized by the U.S. military and security forces in their legally questionable administration of the changing environments of counterinsurgency operations has focused on

Figure 2.5
Predator UAV remote control station, Balad Air Base, Iraq (2004). U.S. Air Force photo by Cohen A. Young.

developing and deploying drones such as MQ-9 Reapers and Predators for remote surveillance and killing. These drones are robot aircraft operated via satellite video feed by pilots in ground control stations on U.S. soil, such as the Creech Air Force Base in Nevada. The drone control crew is in contact through an extended communication network with troops on the battleground and with intelligence analysts and commanders in various other locations.

What animates the development of this form of aerial warfare is the desire for both omniscience and omnipotence—the desire to treat foreign territory like the "fully actionable space" of video games, to transform it into a theater of self-perpetuating crises, and to impose on it what Jonathan Crary calls "a permanent state of fearfulness."[100] In point of fact, the remote controls of UAVs have much in common with the interface of a first-person shooter video game. Two television screens are placed one on top of the other: the one above presents a digital map pinpointing the position of the drone; the one below shows video feed from the drone's nose. The screens seem to require the same kind of cognitive binding between two different perspectives that we encounter in *Modern Warfare 3*, binding that enables the pilot/player to position, track, and locate an object of preemptive action. Moreover, as Mirzoeff observes, drones are coordinated with "a joystick familiar to video game players."[101] Unlike first-person shooter screens, however, UAV screens translate their perceptual disposition into actual control of life and death. The tireless and unblinking eyes of UAVs are meant to facilitate the "synoptic coverage of an area and the capability to zoom in on and track and follow multiple activities or actors, cue and tip other sensors, and build an integrated understanding of an area's 'pattern of life.'"[102] Drone cameras record footage of human interactions and transactions, footage that ideally allows the pilots, military intelligence analysts, and computer algorithms, by engaging in a constant rhythm analysis of people living in a particular location, to establish the patterns of their daily activities and habits.[103] The objective is to separate the uneventful from the eventful, to eliminate contingency by singling out abnormal behavior that might signal a potential insurgent emergency—and to eliminate that emergency preemptively with precision operations in which drones play a crucial role as hunter-killers.

The patterns of life that UAVs track thus enable anticipatory perceptual discriminations that pinpoint "cancerous" elements to be cut out as threats to the advancement of the neoliberal way of life. In other words, they allow the U.S. military and security forces to discriminate between behavior that should be positively promoted in support of neoliberalism's "system state" and aberrant behavior that should be eliminated—in service to a "necropolitics," to use Achille Mbembe's term, that generalizes and instrumentalizes the sovereign decision of who shall live and who shall die into an organized system of violence and destruction.[104]

As a key part of that system, UAV screens dehumanize people into mere living things to be monitored, tracked, located, and killed in the crosshairs of their synoptic and potent focus. In this respect, a critical attribute of the necropolitical visuality of UAVs is that it implements perception as anticipatory action. Reported incidents where drone pilots have mistakenly identified civilians as insurgents serve as gruesome cases in point. To briefly summarize one such case: on February 21, 2010, a group of Afghan travelers set out on a trip in three vehicles and happened to cross the area into which U.S. special operations soldiers had been dropped to root out insurgents.[105] One of the Afghan cars flashed its headlights, which when spotted by the crew of a ground attack plane protecting the ground troops was interpreted as signaling. The travelers became targets of suspicion. A Predator drone surveying the area started to track their movements, looking for signs of suspicious behavior, its two-man team—a pilot and a camera operator—aided by a team of video analysis experts, or "screeners," as they are called, sitting in front of high-definition television screens in Florida, which displayed live feeds from drones operating in Afghanistan. At one point, the drone pilot thought he spotted something that resembled a rifle inside one of the cars, but the camera operator could not verify it. Soon the convoy stopped and someone got out of one of the cars. When the drone camera zoomed in, it looked like the targeted person was carrying something—a rifle, the camera operator now assumed, which the pilot then affirmed. Images were fuzzy and the video feed briefly intermittent. One of the screeners in Florida reported spotting one or more children in the group. Despite this observation, and acting on some equally ambiguous additional information, Army commanders ordered an attack. Subsequent reports counted at least twenty-three people killed and more than a dozen wounded, all civilians, including children.

Drone screens, one could argue, bring the distant affectively very near, and in doing so materialize images that afford the instrumentalization of death. They become enacted as future-invocative perceptions that are at least somewhat affected by a "strong desire" to find weapons, as a U.S. Air Force investigation of the incident above concluded.[106] The reasons for the impulse to exaggerate the level of threat are of course open to interpretation, one of them quite likely being, as Derek Gregory suggests, the drone operators' strong empathic identification with the ground troops within a psychic space distinguished by enforced differentiations between self and other, us and them.[107] In this sense, one could also argue that the incident instantiated an immunitary logic, which seeks to aggressively assimilate and suppress improvised outside dangers. Given that the self, as neuroscience teaches us, is a seat of prediction that seeks to maintain homeostasis against what is identified as external influence, one could consider the drone pilot's actions as instantiating the brain's automatic anticipatory, projective functions, which seek to eliminate ambiguity by means of hidden assumptions—assumptions that can sometimes turn into hallucinations.[108]

According to Massumi, preemptive cognition simulates signs of future threats before action is committed and the event actually takes place.[109] Rather than calculate probabilities, it affectively forefeels what might happen, and discriminates and acts on the world accordingly. For the preemptive brain, it is, above all, threat that delineates what kinds of images emerge in the mind. The felt presence and degree of threat serve as what Damasio calls a "somatic marker" for the relative importance of the image, a marker that directs how the brain will select among the images the mind presents it with.[110] As LeDoux points out, it is the fear system, anatomically structured around the amygdala, that processes defensive responses to threatening stimuli.[111] Furthermore, recent studies in neuroscience have shown how even subtle and uncertain signs of potential threat promote arousal and trigger what is sometimes called the brain's "security motivation system,"[112] defined by one study as "a reasonably independent module or system in the brain, which evolved in response to the adaptive problems posed by rare, potentially catastrophic risks."[113] The security motivation system is thought to manage the organism's response to potential dangers that are by nature "hidden" or "not yet present," its "central motive state" being anxiety rather than fear. In its responses, it relies on "robust, precautionary" behavior rather than on escape and avoidance. Once this system identifies a potential threat, it remains on alert until "corrective action" is executed, meaning that it impels the organism to act preemptively on the presumed source of danger.[114]

Here the threat comes fundamentally from within, and if hidden cues of a not yet present threat have such a strong affective pull, it is not surprising that perceptual discriminations can shift from one category to another under the impulse for preemptive maneuvers—suddenly, the flashing of headlights looks like a secret signal, a fuzzy object looks like a rifle, and children look like adolescents. For, as so many of us fear and as President George W. Bush famously put it, "the smoking gun ... could come in the form of a mushroom cloud."[115] Indeed, the current, neoliberal wars of counterinsurgency are premised on the accumulation of potentially catastrophic threats and feed on the continuous (re)production of apparent chaos, which serves as the precondition for emergent order.[116] The point of these wars, Mirzoeff argues, "is less to win than to keep playing, permanently moving to the next level in the ultimate massively multiplayer environment."[117] Following Massumi, one could say that it is characteristic of the political physiology of preemption to "countermimic" the accident[118]—to activate and modulate the brain's security motivation systems that make the subject anticipate the world in terms of looming threats and seek to preemptively control the future in all its unknowability.[119]

One could also say about the political physiology of video games that players enact the game images in affects of anxiety related to the constant forefeeling of an impending attack, in amplified levels of arousal, and in rhythmic performance directed by preemptive motor cognition trying to defend the organism against never-ending danger. Thus we can see how both video game and UAV screens, through converging bodily dispositions and requirements, materialize and reinforce neoliberal brainhood, conditioning their viewers to accept catastrophic contingencies as the weight of future. The aim here is not to argue that the action-oriented images materialized on UAV screens induce any kind of playstation mentality toward killing or that they turn warfare into a disembodied spectacle; rather, it is only to acknowledge the convergent cerebral modulations that UAV and video game screens give rise to. It therefore comes as no surprise that several critics have associated gameplay with the militarization of everyday life in the West. Focusing on the first-person shooter game *Full Spectrum Warrior*, originally developed as a military training simulation and released commercially in 2004, Nick Dyer-Witheford and Greig de Peuter, for instance, assert that such action-based mediations induce in players a "consciousness of a collective military entity," thereby "habituating" civilians to perpetual war.[120]

Yet claims that video games are militarizing our consciousness are at best dubious generalizations. Rather, the ways in which the games are cognitively and affectively attuned to the demands of the biopolitical system seem less obvious and a bit more complicated. One should add that these ways are shared by finance capitalism, which is also predicated on a temporal logic of preemption, and where preemption creates and feeds on its own catastrophic realities, as the economic meltdown of 2008 so powerfully brought home. Of particular note is the extent to which finance capitalism, or the debt economy, has now permeated the societies of the West, bringing its logic of systemic risk and securitization to bear on daily life. As Melinda Cooper observes, "market-related events on a more or less catastrophic scale have become so endemic to the workings of capitalist relations today that it is no longer possible to dismiss them as a surface effect of underlying or real economic forces."[121] In the personal and domestic sphere, Randy Martin points out, pensions, consumer loans, home mortgages, and the like are caught up in the turbulent flow of global capital: debts are bundled together and turned into tradable securities, and equities are combined into derivatives to hedge risks involved in fluctuating currency or interest rates.[122] These securities and derivatives are then repackaged and traded on the futures market, where everyday lives are entwined in them and displaced in anticipation of future but fundamentally unpredictable gain. Cooper explains that the crux of finance capitalism lies in how the flow of capital has been desubstantialized and abstracted to the point where the creation of surplus from debt "is magnified many times over," so that "what is being exchanged is not simply a future claim to a given commodity, asset or risk category but a future claim to an expansive network of fluidly interlinked futures."[123] There is no anchor, no equilibrium reference point to calculate value. Instead, promise itself becomes "the means and ends of [capital] accumulation."[124] And, as a direct result, the economy becomes increasingly fragile, with local events, investor confidence, and subjective expectations threatening to disrupt the whole financial network. Which is to say, securitization, by countermimicking future catastrophe, actually brings it about and even hastens it.

At the heart of finance capitalism lies a model of neoliberal brainhood that is centered on imaginative mappings of future possibilities and preemptive measures—on the transformation of a dissimilar future into a similar present.[125] The biopolitics of finance concerns how daily life becomes subjected to the small and large potential crises that finance capitalism entails. We should bear in mind that it is in the living rooms and bedrooms of households swept up in the volatile and contingent fluctuations of capital that the action-oriented, future-invocative images of games like *Modern Warfare 3* are consumed on video game screens. Although the movement and life of these images in global networks may seem inconsequential and irrelevant to the worldwide financial regime (which depends on this same technological network infrastructure for the real-time circulation of information at the speed of light), one cannot help but think of the images' role as "sentimental education," binding the players in the sensory fabric of the neoliberal present. As we have seen, these images teach affective and cognitive engagement with contingency, randomness, (in)security, and crisis; they animate preemptive perceptions and gestures that seek to act on the future. But, in doing so, they also affirm the absence of equilibrium and the potentiality of catastrophic events in the present. In many ways, they embody and disseminate the kind of "extreme internal sensitivity to disruptive events" that, according to Melinda Cooper, lies at the core of the current financial system's claim on events yet to come.[126]

If images represent not the actual world, but what the world could be, within the visual economy of video games, they operate as propositions of what one might call "future perfects." We have seen how the type of individuation at play in video games like *Modern Warfare 3* is intrinsic to contemporary societies. Video game imagery reveals and crystallizes a vital dimension of the current Western world and its models of subjectivity, subscribing to parallel logics with contemporary neuroscientific articulations, military strategies, and the (ir)rationalities of finance capitalism. Neuroscience has shown us how the self-organizing affective and cognitive capacities of the cerebral subject hinge on and coevolve with contingent events in the environment as a site of struggle, risk, and survival. We have seen how today's biopolitics of preemption likewise conceptualizes the West's campaign for world governance as taking place in a milieu of threats and risks, within which the military works as an adaptive, self-organizing system fighting against other equally adaptive systems in protecting and prolonging the neoliberal way of life. And, finally, we have seen how finance capitalism has turned the global flow of capital into a desubstantialized and turbulent system, where the future's potentially catastrophic contingencies have become a source of dynamic innovation and capital accumulation.

Insofar as video games materialize and distribute the kinds of action-based images we encounter in *Modern Warfare 3*, they adhere to this social reality as technologies of neuropower, modulating and administering our affective and cognitive capacities. Video games, in other words, provide the imagery through which the biopolitical system reproduces itself on the level of embodiment. This, however, does not rule out alternative embodiments. Far from an exhaustive account of the culture and aesthetics of video games, this chapter has not taken into account, among other things, creative acts of "counterplay" that can potentially challenge and overturn neoliberalism's normative models of experience.[127] For instance, in a project called "dead-in-iraq" begun in March 2006, Joseph DeLappe entered *America's Army*, the online multiplayer first-person shooter recruiting game of the U.S. Army, and typed in at the chat interface the name, age, service branch, and date of death of each service person who had died in the Iraq war.[128] By December 2011, when the last U.S. troops officially withdrew from Iraq and the project was completed, DeLappe had recorded a total of 4,484 names. This unusual act of protest brought the consequences of actual death to bear on the Army's virtual playing ground and the avatars populating it. It functioned as an unwanted, traumatic reminder of the messy reality that surrounds the secured simulation environment and its curating of minds.

For its part, this chapter has shown how, within and beneath large-scale political, economic, and scientific processes and developments, specific kinds of images, however mundane and insignificant in appearance, operate as embodied adjustments to serve the demands of today's biopolitical reality. In doing so, these video game images reinforce and expand the current "system state" by reducing the randomness of individual and collective responses. Within the neuroscientific episteme, and drawing on Brian Sutton-Smith's neuropsychological theory of play, one might say that video games operate as sociocultural extensions of the brain's plasticity, actualizing in their players novel cerebral connections that have not yet become the subject of real-life accommodation.[129] Immersing ourselves in the virtual battlegrounds of games like *Modern Warfare 3* thus means learning to cope with the demands of the biopolitical system. More precisely, it means ascertaining in our perceptions and affections potentially catastrophic contingencies as the weight of this system's impoverished future.

3 Contingent Pasts: Affectivity, Memory, and the Vir Reality of War

Either biopolitics produces subjectivity or it produces death.
—Roberto Esposito, *Bíos*

Operational Screens

On the left, a black screen reflects its observer's intrigued gaze; on the right, another screen displays a computer-generated environment resembling a marketplace in the Middle East. As the first-person viewpoint moves forward, we see a man standing in front of a booth, greeting the viewer politely; a woman walks in front. Suddenly, there is an explosion and several people fall to the ground while others run away. This is followed by the title sequence, after which the right screen goes black and a person appears on the left one, looking and gesticulating toward the screen beside him:

> Now we have some ... a little ambient background sound. In a second, you'll hear some gunfire ... the person will then run into the alley here, then call in for a helicopter. Over time, we expanded the environment a little bit, made it so that you could adjust time of day, the weather conditions, sandstorms, night vision, building interiors that you could navigate through ... this is from the city.

Suddenly, the left screen also goes black, and a rooftop view of the computer-generated marketplace appears on the right screen. We see a military helicopter flying overhead, and we hear the person say: "There's rooftops that you could get onto now." There seem to be two different sensibilities, or realities even: on the one hand, the orderly actual realm of real reallocations and professional discourse gathering images into its signifying regime; on the other, the anarchic virtual realm of computer-generated gunfire, explosions, and fighter helicopters.

This describes the first two minutes of German artist Harun Farocki's dual-channel video installation *Serious Games III: Immersion* (2009). The person on the left screen is Albert "Skip" Rizzo, a psychologist at the University of Southern California's Institute of Creative Technologies; the computer animations on the right screen come from a new "psychotechnology" called "Virtual Iraq" that Rizzo and his colleagues have developed in a project partly funded by U.S. Office of Naval Research: an experimental virtual reality (VR) technology for the treatment of combat-related posttraumatic stress disorder (PTSD) among soldiers of the wars in Iraq, Afghanistan, and anywhere else in principle. Originally recycling the graphic assets developed by the U.S. Navy for a tactical simulation training platform (released as the commercial video game *Full Spectrum Warrior* in 2004), Virtual Iraq presents a multisensory environment created with three-dimensional audio and visual effects (through head-mounted virtual reality display) and sometimes with olfactory and vibrotactile effects as well. Combining generic views such as driving across the desert in a Humvee or being in an Iraqi city market square, it produces individually tailored scenarios that re-create the settings where the patients' traumatic events originally occurred. The therapeutic assumption is that reliving traumatic experiences in the virtual world will help patients significantly reduce if not banish the flashbacks, hallucinations, and dreams of the experiences that torment them and that give rise to fears, anxieties, and stress in their present-day lives.

In Farocki's *Immersion*, we see the workshop where Rizzo demonstrated the Virtual Iraq technology to a group of U.S. Army psychologists at Madigan Army Medical Center, Fort Lewis, Washington, in January 2009. Right after the helicopter flies over the market square, we see Rizzo again on the left screen, while the right screen now shows the interface meant for use by the therapist (called by developers the "Wizard of Oz"). Rizzo operates a window showing the view visible to the patient and rows of buttons with which the therapist can manipulate the virtual environment (figure 3.1). "Location change," says Rizzo, "this is a new feature."

> We can now start off in different places. So … you're now up near where there's a palm tree grove, where there's an ambush that you can select. You can jump ahead to a relatively safe zone … where there's … where there's friendlies parked by the side of the road. Up here is a start of the city ambush, up here is where the bridge ambush can occur, and over here is the checkpoint, and there's some stuff that can go on over there as well. So you can move the person around.

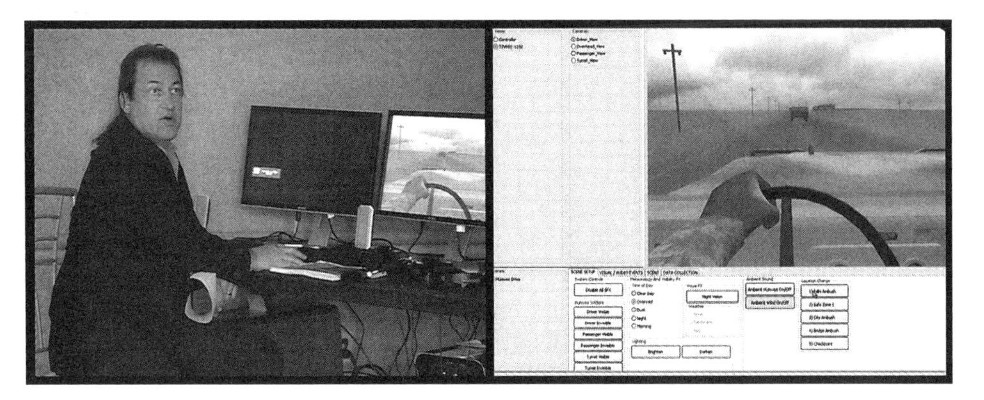

Figure 3.1
Albert Rizzo operates Virtual Iraq (left); the "Wizard of Oz" interface (right). *Serious Games III: Immersion* © Harun Farocki 2009.

Thus the basic message of the workshop presentation seems to be that, with computer-generated animations simulating the traumatic imagery from which soldiers diagnosed with PTSD suffer, virtual worlds can be conjured up in which patients can be "moved around" not only in re-creations of the traumatizing events but also in the folds and depths of the traumatic memories themselves.

The two different sensibilities that Farocki's *Immersion* distributes on its surfaces embody, on the one hand, the reality of a traumatized psyche and, on the other, the reality of the therapeutic techniques, discourses, images, and rationalities surrounding treatment of that psyche, which is to say, the invisible inside and visible outside worlds of psychic trauma. Farocki's work maps the unparalleled visual economy that has emerged in the biopolitical taking charge of the psyches of soldiers. Whereas in Robbie Cooper's *Immersion*, feeding off preemptive motor cognitions, the video game screens transport the children (figures 2.1 and 2.2) to an outside world of future possibilities, in Farocki's *Immersion*, virtual reality goggles transport patients to the inside world of their past traumas (figure 3.2). In this context, the involuntary recurrence of time by means of images becomes critical. When immersed in Virtual Iraq, patients feel and see what their psyches do not want them to remember: the technology insistently re-creates the affects and memories they have repressed from their conscious minds. Its images are intended to facilitate the therapist's direct action on memories of the

Figure 3.2
Inside Virtual Iraq: driving a Humvee in the desert (left); VR goggles turn the gaze inward (right). *Serious Games III: Immersion* © Harun Farocki 2009.

past. Thus, where chapter 2 showed how computer-generated animations are mobilized to evoke and administer the future, Virtual Iraq compels us to think of how they are being mobilized to administer the past—with the aim of rehabilitating subjects amenable to its catastrophic realities.

We should note that Farocki's *Immersion* is part of his ongoing critical investigation into images that today circulate, unnoticed by and even concealed from the public, in settings such as closed-circuit television (CCTV) systems, which can track the movements of supermarket customers and prison inmates alike (*I Thought I Was Seeing Convicts*, 2000), image-processing robotics, and high-precision weapons systems (*Eye-Machine I–III*, 2001–03). These images do not conform to what is traditionally expected of them, whether in education, art, politics, or entertainment.[1] They are defined not by their capacity to instruct, to give aesthetic pleasure, to entertain, or even to serve as propaganda, but by their operational functions. As Farocki characterizes them, rather than portraying a process, they are part of that process, being instrumental to the execution of a technical, industrial, or military operation, such as calculating and predicting the average paths of consumers or recognizing patterns on assembly lines or in so-called smart bombs. In this sense, operational images take up the work of tools, more precisely, tools of power that impose a grid through which the world becomes visualized, intelligible, and, crucially, an object of manipulation.

Operational images present themselves as objective statements of the real world, statements that filter the ways we can act on things and events. Farocki's interest has, most of all, been in problematizing how contemporary screens—of CCTV, weapons systems, and security checking devices, among other things—work toward making people's lives predictable and eliminating elements of chance and contingency.[2] As we saw in chapter 2, these screens are deployed in the current counterinsurgency wars, most notably, in the remote control systems of drones. They serve either to make the human observer ubiquitous and omnipotent, extending neoliberalism's field of anticipatory perception and action across the globe, or to render the observer as inessential, when, working autonomously, they are not even meant to be seen by human eyes.

Furthermore, such operational images have increasingly gained importance in the training of soldiers. Deployed in video games, they now teach recruits how to kill. Computer-generated animations are used, first of all, to train motor skills, including almost reflex-like shoot or no-shoot decisions occurring at the thresholds of consciousness, decisions critical in urban warfare, where civilians also populate the battlefields. Second, through intensive repetition, the simulations are used to desensitize soldiers to danger and fear and to diminish their empathic identification with the enemy ("someone who could have been me") and hence also their reluctance to kill. As John Protevi points out, "because [computer-generated] images are so lifelike, they activate the protoempathic identification present in most. In other words, the simulation-trained soldiers of today have already *virtually* experienced killing before *actually* having to kill."[3] Even if this argument calls for a more elaborate understanding of how these video game images exactly activate and desensitize emotional reactions and emphatic identification, we can see how the military uses screen technologies to produce and manage specific kind of affectively qualified subjectivity. Training screens are deployed to optimize the soldier's ability to function as a killing machine. Virtual Iraq, on the other hand, comes into the picture when this killing agent, overburdened with fears, anxieties, and feelings of guilt, becomes psychologically dysfunctional and needs to be readapted and recapacitated to the realities of war and its continuous state of emergency.

In the contexts of both training and therapy, what we are witnessing is a military version of the screen-based fabrication of neoliberal brainhood, as discussed in chapters 1 and 2—a model of an adaptive, emergent, and contingent being characterized by its capacity to experience and manage stress and fear in particular. In mapping those instances where the model being breaks down, this chapter will focus on the production of traumatic brainhood that has emerged from the wars Western regimes wage to expand their hegemony worldwide, and that directly relates to the lethal dimensions of nurturing the neoliberal way of life.

Posttraumatic stress disorder is fundamentally a disease of time and affectivity.[4] A key pathology of our neoliberal age, it was codified in the *Diagnostic and Statistical Manual of Mental Disorders* (published by the American Psychiatric Society) to account for impaired emotional processing of memories that recur in flashbacks, hallucinations, and dreams where traumatic past events relentlessly repeat themselves. Those who suffer from PTSD remain in an affective state of emergency, where exaggerated feelings of fear and danger overwhelm their sense of reality and normal action is suspended. As Judith Herman explains: "Traumatic reactions occur when action is of no avail. When neither resistance nor escape is possible, then the human system of self-defense becomes overwhelmed and disorganized. Each component of the ordinary response to danger, having lost its utility, tends to persist in an altered and exaggerated state long after the danger is over."[5]

Restoring the "system of self-defense" is the principal therapeutic goal in treating PTSD. And this is precisely the purpose for which Virtual Iraq was developed. Rizzo described his technology as "a nice merger between game development, computer graphics, psychology and all of the engineering technology that goes into creating virtual environments."[6] Yet, more important, Virtual Iraq represents a "nice merger" between computer-generated animations, biological psychology, and the management of affectivity and memory. Because affective responses and behavioral patterns are seen to be interiorized in the organism's neurophysiological circuits, they appear, to quote Allan Young, as "reviseable only through evolutionary mechanisms."[7] Accordingly, Virtual Iraq crystallizes a rather particular visual economy, one where images are enclosed within the organism's internal milieu, folding perception back into the subject's endogenous apparitions instead of extending perception outside itself. Such images treat brain functions and their plasticity as their sole field of operations. Within this economy, the traumatic realities of war become a matter of affective habituation and the modulation of memory and, as such, of the organism's internal functioning; the reality of images in this process becomes a matter of biology and the evolution of the species. Moreover, this reality comes to involve the production and maintenance of (psychological) immunity that Roberto Esposito has identified as the inherent logic of biopolitics—a logic that views the living being as an emergent "war zone" where a constant battle is fought against destructive forces, both external and internal.

Evocative Images: A Genealogy

In 1980, mainly in response to pressure from Vietnam veterans' advocacy groups, posttraumatic stress disorder was included in the third edition of *The Diagnostic and Statistical Manual of Mental Disorders* (*DSM-III*) and has since become widely diagnosed and intensively researched.[8] Although we should bear in mind that diagnosis of this and other mental disorders is based on shifting definitions, and that most critical, etiological, and therapeutic discussions about PTSD revolve around elusive anthropological concepts such as memory and selfhood, the third edition of the diagnostic manual cited four essential diagnostic criteria for the disorder: an etiological event, recurrent encounters with memories of this event, symptomatic avoidance and numbing, and autonomic arousal.[9] Whereas the first three of these criteria deal with a patient's traumatic experiences and with the patient's personal stories of, and attitude toward, what can be called "mental memory," the fourth criterion—autonomic arousal, evidenced as irritability, a tendency to explosive violence, and hypervigilance, among other symptoms—reflects the biological and constitutive materiality of the trauma. This "bodily memory," Allan Young tells us, does not involve biographical inscriptions but instead recalls "the evolutionary story that the patient shares with all human beings."[10] In conceptual terms, it derives from the nineteenth-century neurologist Herbert Spencer's concept of phylogenetic memory which positioned basic emotions such as fear and anxiety within autonomic functions of the nervous system beyond cognitive control. The distinguishing feature of posttraumatic stress disorder is that the body acts autonomously in a state of chronic hyperarousal—a psychological state of emergency—and overresponds to stimuli coming from the environment. A patient's own physiology thus becomes the source of the patient's fears.[11]

Virtual Iraq is designed to capture and modulate this bodily memory. As noted above, its operational purpose is to modulate affect and to pattern behavior or, in more general terms, to produce, manage, and channel psychic and somatic flows. The technology allows therapists to conduct virtual reality exposure therapy (VRET), where, in the words of Virtual Iraq's developers, Thomas Parsons and Albert Rizzo,

> users are immersed within a computer-generated simulation or virtual environment (VE), that updates in a natural way to the user's head and/or body motion. [I] mmersed in a VE, [the user] can be systematically exposed to specific feared stimuli within a contextually relevant setting. VRET comports well with the emotion-processing model, which holds that the fear network must be activated through confrontation with threatening stimuli and that new, incompatible information must be added into the emotional network.[12]

Based on this account, putting on VR goggles and dropping into the simulation of past events almost immediately opens up the PTSD patient's pathogenic affects for modification. Advocates of virtual reality–based therapies are quick to point out a key therapeutic advantage of the technology: because it "does not rely upon individual imagery ability or even the ability of the patient to verbalize his or her experiences,"[13] the virtual reality interface impedes patients' more or less conscious efforts to obstruct the reorganization of their "fear networks" and indeed overwhelms their resistance to therapy. The technology's efficacy is most often described in terms of how it helps patients become affectively immersed in or synchronized with their virtual environments, at the same time that it gives therapists external control over their patients' heightened arousal.[14]

Images flood into the patients' minds and back out again whether they want them to or not. Inside a head-mounted display, their sense of the external world becomes muted, their only contact outside their simulated surroundings being with the therapist (figure 3.3). A handheld controller, such as a fully weighted model of an M-16 rifle with toggle switches and buttons, allows them to move their "weapon" about realistically within the isolated environment. Biofeedback equipment facilitates the constant monitoring of the patients' blood pressure, heart rate, respiration, and perspiration. The distinguishing feature of Virtual Iraq is its Wizard of Oz Clinical Interface, designed to let the therapist control the content of the simulation and monitor the patient's physical response to it, which is

Figure 3.3
Virtual Iraq in use at Andrews Air Force Base, Maryland, June 25, 2009. U.S. Air Force photo by Renae Kleckner.

"essential for fostering the anxiety modulation needed for therapeutic habituation."[15]

Therapists exposed a 29-year-old male combat engineer suffering from "intrusive recollections" of an attack on his desert convoy to virtual reality in three 90-minute sessions. "During the first VRE session," their case report reads, "simply being in the Humvee and feeling the vibration, and moving ahead along the road lined with telephone poles, triggered the identified trauma."[16] In subsequent sessions, the traumatic experience was re-created over and over again, with the gradual addition of auditory "cues" ranging from background radio chatter and a helicopter flyover to explosions and gunfire. The patient's expression of affect remained "relatively strong" over the course of the treatment, but, more important, "the valence shifted over repetitions from horror, grief, and guilt to include feelings of admiration and pride around the resourcefulness and bravery of fellow soldiers, and acceptance around actions taken in time of war."[17] The treatment thus drew on the technology's remarkable ability to modulate patients' affective lives and to transform the nature of intense emotions attached to their traumatic memories—in this case, transforming grief and guilt to acceptance and even admiration.[18]

These discourses and governmental practices are rooted in the currently influential psychobiological view of trauma. Drawing on contemporary neuroscience and the early twentieth-century findings of French psychologist Pierre Janet on traumatic memory and dissociation, Bessel van der Kolk asserts that the intense affectivity of PTSD patients results in large part from impairment of the "declarative" or "explicit" memory system, which processes experiences in words and symbols and underlies conscious awareness of a fact or event.[19] Impairment of this system revives remembrances engraved in the "nondeclarative" memory system, which controls conditioned responses, emotional intensities, and reflexive actions, as well as skills and habits related to an experience. This "implicit" bodily memory system processes emotions on a sensorimotor and iconic level, involving visceral sensations, behavioral enactments, nightmares, and flashbacks. "Memories of trauma," van der Kolk argues, "may have no verbal (explicit) component whatsoever. Instead, the memories may have been organized on an implicit or perceptual level, without any accompanying narrative about what happened."[20] Deprived of the process of symbolization or narration, traumatic memories are experienced "as fragments of the sensory components of the event: as visual images; olfactory, auditory, or kinesthetic sensations; or intense waves of feelings."[21] Furthermore, because traumatic memories are dissociated from conscious awareness and the ego, they are often reproduced in involuntary actions.

In therapeutic terms, the definition of traumatic memory as a nonsymbolic, somatosensory "imprint" implies that pathogenic images or memories may be accessible and modifiable only by methods that operate on the same (nonverbal) level as the implicit memory system.[22] "The realization that insight and understanding are usually not enough to keep traumatized people from regularly feeling and acting as if they are traumatized all over again," van der Kolk explains, "forced clinicians to explore techniques that offer the possibility of reprogramming these automatic physical responses."[23] It is this idea of reprogramming that informs Virtual Iraq. Rather than serving as elements in narrative constructions, images animated on the VR platform operate instead as "evocative media," to borrow a concept from Edna Foa and Michel Kozak's classic article on the emotional processing of fear.[24]

Foa and Kozak asserted that fear and affects more generally are represented in memory structures that serve as blueprints for certain kinds of behavioral patterns. In the therapeutic session, an affective memory must first be activated and then modified by replacing it with a new such memory.

In Virtual Iraq, images both evoke and modify traumatic memories. In creating immersive experiences that teach the patient "mastery over cognitive, affective, and physiological arousal,"[25] it is the affective and emotional charges related to traumatic events, rather than conscious memories of the events, that are significant. By embodying these charges, Virtual Iraq's images make patients "relive" the events in sensorimotor terms. The images generated in the therapeutic setting evoke and animate the bodily memory, and because they do so repeatedly, they are meant to trigger "habituation" and the extinction of the fear response—the notion of habituation deriving from Pavlovian conditioning, which interiorizes the source of affects within the organism's nervous system and conditioned actions.[26]

Although this affective and largely involuntary evocation and revision of the traumatic past appears to be an altogether novel type of therapeutic intervention, it can be traced to a far older technique, hypnosis, used in the treatment of traumas since the late nineteenth century. "Like hypnosis, virtual environments may allow the mind access to memories that are out of conscious awareness," one study of VR therapy observes.[27] The association of virtual reality with hypnosis, a major tool in experimenting on memory and the unconscious when modern conceptions of the psyche were being formed, has a crucial bearing on the aporias of affectivity, memory, and dissociation that posttraumatic stress disorder inherits from the past. It was in the late nineteenth century that an epistemic shift occurred in psychiatric thinking about the nature of the self, trauma, and memory, the consequences of which we are still experiencing today, even if the names of disorders and their diagnostic criteria have been in constant flux since that time.[28] It was then that a particular discourse of remembering and forgetting emerged, which was organized around concealed memories and traumatic affects, and around specific codes and procedures for deciphering these. At stake was a new way of speaking of and positing the question of individuality. The influential French psychologist Théodule-Armand Ribot conceived of the self as inseparable from memory, which he saw as an organic process of conservation and reproduction, something that could not be isolated as a separate entity but continued to both grow and diminish in the course of our lives.[29] Memory became malleable, dynamic, and essentially based on forgetting. Ribot's conception of the self had a significant influence on later psychologists, notably Pierre Janet, who considered traumatic memories as affective elements that are dissociated from the ego and lead an autonomous life in the "subconscious." In Janet's conception of psychotherapy, based on the notion of fundamental forgetting, curing psychological traumas meant removing dissociated recollections or "fixed ideas," as he called them, from the memory. For Janet, hypnotic suggestion, by providing direct access to those parts of the psyche split off from consciousness, was the key mnemotechnology in the manipulation of pathogenic psychic material.

In this regard, Janet's thinking reflected the general psychological episteme of the late nineteenth century, in which hypnosis became a technology of subjectivation that yielded new ways of experiencing the self and new ways of knowing what the self means. Those attending the First International Congress on Experimental and Therapeutic Hypnotism, held in Paris in 1889, included notables such as Jean-Martin Charcot, Hippolyte Bernheim, William James, and Sigmund Freud. A commonly shared view among attendees was that hypnosis presented "the most effective entryway into previously inaccessible territories and processes of human psychic life."[30] Although delegates to the congress may have differed quite significantly in their understanding of how and to what extent hypnosis was able to explore and master these territories, and even of what these territories actually were, they did not question the importance of hypnosis in mapping novel terrains of subjectivity. In the writings of Charcot, Bernheim, Freud, and James, among others, an image of the subject emerged that was fundamentally split and shaped by phenomena antithetical to Western rationality—influence without logical foundation, engulfment of self by its outside, mental contagion, and production of illusory relations with the world. The individual became seen as fundamentally relational and distributed—a node within a network of forces and intensities—and as having an unconscious and fundamentally bodily and affective affinity with the material flows of its environment.[31]

Understood as both a mental state or disposition and a technique for inducing a particular mental state, hypnosis circumscribed what Michel Foucault would later call an "economy of souls," a way of conducting subjects through their self-knowledge and self-perception.[32] This especially applies to the evocation and modulation of repressed memories and the psychic imagery that may involuntarily emerge in perception. Hypnosis appears as a technology for the government of souls through those forces the conscious ego cannot command. It is thus not surprising that the use of hypnosis as a therapeutic technique culminated in the treatment of "shell-shocked" patients during and after the First World War, that is, in the management of the traumas of the first global war of industrialized destruction.[33] In 1918, another prominent psychologist influenced by Ribot, Sigmund Freud, addressed war neuroses at the Fifth Psychoanalytic Congress precisely in terms of an affective conflict splitting the ego.[34] Furthermore, it was here that Freud, learning of the positive experiences his colleague and follower Ernst Simmel had had with hypnosis in the cure of traumatized soldiers, was compelled to change his view of hypnotic suggestion, which he had exorcized from the psychoanalytic episteme in the 1890s.

Simmel told delegates to the congress how, by means of "analytical-cathartic hypnosis," he was able to render "the patient in the same state of consciousness as that in which during the war he had acquired the origin of illness."[35] In Simmel's hands, hypnosis became a decisive tool in evoking pathogenic material inscribed in the depths of the unconscious and in "abreacting" the affects of terror, anger, rage, and guilt that resulted in destructive compulsive behavior, recurring nightmares, and the like. Hypnosis thus became an experimental technology for restaging traumatic events and reviving the attached affects, a kind of time machine that possessed the power of making the scene reappear and the patient relive it anew:

> During hypnosis the soldier relates, or once again lives through, all the things that he had experienced in former circumstances only unconsciously. We learn of distressing pains of which, when he was buried, he never became conscious. In such a hypnosis, we see his anxiety displayed, his anger arise, feelings which at the moment of the excitation were benumbed and like lightning were dragged violently into the unconscious.[36]

Simmel emphasized that, under hypnosis, the freeing of traumatic memory takes place in sensorimotor terms, in the bodily acting out of the traumatic event: "An abreaction by means of words is mostly insufficient in this compressed form of treatment. The soldier is under the suggestion of the deed 'an eye for an eye, a tooth for a tooth.' His overburdened subconscious now is freed by means of an *acted* abreaction."[37]

Simmel compared the hypnotic recovery of traumatic memories to the experience of watching a film: "The [traumatic] experience can be repeated. The 'film' is made to roll once again; the patient dreams the whole thing one more time."[38] Yet one should note that there is a difference between filmic images and the ones evoked in hypnosis, a difference rooted in the different visual economies of the two technologies. Whereas cinematic images can direct perception to a world outside the limits of the viewer's mind, hypnotic images effectively originate and stay within the patient's psyche. On the other hand, Simmel's hypnocathartic therapy closely parallels virtual reality exposure therapy using Virtual Iraq. With virtual reality technology, as with the technology of hypnosis, patients are drawn back to their unconscious memories and images become simulations of traumatic past events as well as the subjectively lived affective charges related to them. Thus we might well consider hypnotic therapy to be the primary psychotechnological precursor of virtual reality exposure therapy. The images conjured up by both hypnosis and Virtual Iraq embody pathogenic mnemic and affective material, their source being fundamentally endogenous. Rather than representations in the usual sense of mediators between inner and outer worlds, the images induced by both technologies are at once sensory, affective, and motor evocations of the traumatic past.

What indeed distinguishes virtual reality from previous image technologies such as photography and cinema is its phenomenology, more precisely, the way in which VR almost completely abolishes distinctions between internal and external worlds, between perception and image. The VR interface, Mark Hansen argues, "serves to couple [users] directly and immediately with [their] own physiological states" and hence accomplishes a passage from "interactivity to dynamics, from image perception to body-brain simulation."[39] In virtual reality, images become simulations of the brain's power of imaging the world—or the "movie-in-the-brain," to use Antonio Damasio's expression—instead of disclosing a world outside their frame or eliciting critical reflection on their surfaces. Hansen sees virtual reality as an all-encompassing and fundamentally frameless visual field, one that calls for an understanding of perceptual immanence. In the somatosensory coupling experienced within virtual reality—a coupling that precedes separations between subject and object, individual and environment—subjects intuit themselves as dynamic forms immanent to their surroundings. Indeed, Hansen asserts, there is no distinction in virtual reality between screens and how subjects intuit themselves in space as dynamic, kinetic, affective beings; no distinction, to put it in neuroscientific terms, between the image and the brain's simulation of its surroundings. In the VR experience, screen events coincide exactly with subjects' physiological states, whence the impossibility of distinguishing between the intuitive "here" of first-person perspective and the "there" of the object world. In virtual reality, the brain's self-affections and actions cannot be separated from the technical operations of the VR screens. The VR technology–observer interface thus parallels hallucination, understood as the mind's creation of what it sees. Moreover, the lack of distance between perceiver and virtual environment in this machine-human interface also means that the observer has no cognitive mastery over the screen but is rather caught in bodily self-affection: "By placing us into 'direct coupling' with information, this technical extension not only dissolves the mediating (framing) function of the image, but it renders perception itself secondary in relation to the primary affective experience of self-enjoyment."[40]

Here we should note that the erasure of distinctions between screens and observers' brain processes that the VR interface brings about serves as a means by which power invests in the body in the neoliberal age. The VR interface is a biopolitical technology of capture through which individuals and their lived pasts can be harnessed to the contemporary reality of never-ending wars. More precisely, Virtual Iraq exemplifies a governmental rationality that takes charge of processes of subjectivation by modulating the brain's capacity to configure the world as it appears in affective memory. In this respect, the genealogy of virtual reality technology extends back to the economy of souls as practiced with hypnosis in the late nineteenth and early twentieth centuries, when memories, emotions, and selfhood became seen as having no clear-cut boundaries, but as fundamentally malleable and subject to modulation and transformation by media technologies.

Reptilian Cinema

Although hypnotic therapy and virtual reality exposure therapy converge in situating traumatic memories within patients' unconscious and its affective textures, they diverge in their understanding of subjectivity. Whereas hypnotic therapy views patients as individual persons, VRET, proceeding from an evolutionary perspective, views them as expressions of biological traits distributed across the human and even other species.[41] For his part, van der Kolk sees the traumatized individual as possessed by emotional memories based in the subcortical regions of the brain, influenced by the brain's evolutionary functions as much as—and even more than—the individual's personal experiences.[42] Likewise, Parsons and Rizzo position themselves directly within the psychobiological episteme when they claim that, "anxiety and fear are concentrated emotional experiences that serve critical functions in organizing necessary survival responses," which is to say, autonomic fight-or-flight actions performed by the nervous system.[43]

These statements echo the evolutionary view of emotions first articulated by Charles Darwin and developed, after a hundred years of near silence about emotional life in the natural sciences, from extensive neurobiological research into the "emotional brain" in the 1990s, spurred by new neuroimaging technologies and funded in large part by the U.S. government. Emotions, Darwin was the first to argue, evolve through natural selection and play a crucial role in the organism's survival and adaptation. Following Darwin's lead, recent neuroscientific research views emotions as rooted in evolutionarily ancient parts of the brain. Jaak Panksepp, for instance, divides the neurobiology of the human brain into various "basic emotional systems"—"affect programs" or "emotional circuits"—which range from fear, seeking, panic, and rage to lust, care, and play, and which "appear to rapidly instigate and coordinate the dynamic forms of brain organization that, in the course of evolution, proved highly effective in meeting various primal survival needs and thereby helped animals pass on their genes to future generations."[44] In this view, the most critical role emotions play is to influence and shape our actions and behavior, from moving, exploring, attacking, and escaping to socializing, sexual arousal, and maternal care. Most fundamentally, they energize and guide survival mechanisms that, according to Panksepp, "arise from the activities of ancient brain processes that we have inherited from ancestral species."[45] Another key scientist in this area, Joseph LeDoux, defines emotions as "biological functions of the nervous system" and considers the brain systems that generate affective behavior a matter of conservation "through many levels of evolutionary history."[46] For LeDoux, too, emotions are associated with basic survival needs and involve brain mechanisms that operate largely below the threshold of awareness.

In the contemporary neuroscientific episteme, it is the emotional brain that provides a passage from the materiality of cerebral functions and structures to the complexes of the soul.[47] The emotional brain in many ways crystallizes the truth about what it means to be a subject today. The psychobiological view of posttraumatic stress disorder quite vividly demonstrates this. Panksepp sees psychological stress and trauma as originating in the brain's evolutionary past, and therefore as falling under its ancient, subcortical rather than higher cognitive functions. For Panksepp, "chronic psychological stress" appears as something that takes place below the cortex, which is to say, outside functions such as awareness, language, and thought.[48] For Antonio Damasio, among others, emotions "are curious adaptations that are part and parcel of the machinery with which organisms regulate survival."[49] They form a part of what Damasio calls the "homeostasis machine," composed of multiple automated processes to maintain equilibrium, spanning metabolic regulation (controlling the balance of internal chemistries), basic reflexes, the immune system, pain and pleasure behaviors, drives and motivations, and finally "emotions-proper" (such as joy, fear, sorrow).[50] Emotions, in other words, work toward self-preservation; from this perspective, PTSD can be seen as a dysfunctional, persistent state of emergency in the homeostatic system.

By separating emotions from the realm of cognition and communication and situating them in evolutionarily ancient functions of the brain, current neuroscience relocates agency from the individual subject to impersonal affect programs, that is, to preprogrammed and autonomic behavioral modules. A crucial figure behind the epistemic shift to the neurobiological theorizing of emotions was Paul MacLean, who in the 1950s divided the human forebrain—thought to control the display of emotions, among other things—into

> three basic evolutionary formations that reflect an ancestral relationship to reptiles, early mammals, and recent mammals. Radically different in chemistry and structure and in an evolutionary sense countless generations apart, the three neural assemblies constitute a hierarchy of three-brains-in-one, a triune brain. Based on these features alone, it might be surmised that psychological and behavioral functions depend on the interplay of three quite different mentalities. ... [Each formation] has its own special intelligence, its own subjectivity, its own sense of time and space, and its own memory, motor, and other functions.[51]

The "reptilian formation," according to MacLean, involves not only rudimentary bodily movements but also other kinds of behavioral functions such as the struggle for power, adherence to routine, and imitation. The "paleomammalian formation," or limbic system, which developed with the emergence of mammals, organizes maternal care, audiovocal communication, and play, and plays a notable role in the generation and regulation of affectivity and the emotional motivation of behavior. And the "neomammalian formation," which has developed most recently among the primates, "appears to be primarily oriented toward the external world," and in humans it provides the neural substrate for verbal communication.[52] MacLean's triune model is remarkable in going beyond a conventional structure of rigid functional hierarchies to posit the existence of twists, folds, and reticulations between the three formations. "There are ongoing communications [between] the triune assemblages," Elizabeth Wilson explains, "MacLean understands them to be 'intermeshing' and cofunctioning systems."[53] The course of brain operations and their development is not simply directed from the "lower" to the "higher"—rather, the triune brain model implies repetitions, temporal folds, and recurrences in which more primitive formations constantly influence the functioning of the more complex ones.

Drawing on MacLean's model, both Panksepp and LeDoux theorize that affectivity operates on the temporal folds of evolutionary stratification between formations. Our basic capacity to have emotions returns us on the phylogenetic continuum to the reflexive behavioral patterns of reptiles, to fear mechanisms whose primary function is defense against danger, "perhaps an organism's number one priority," according to Le Doux.[54] These fear mechanisms "seem to have been established eons ago, probably at least since the dinosaurs ruled the earth, and to have been maintained through diverse branches of evolutionary development."[55] Detecting and responding to danger thus takes us back to our reptilian ancestors: "In some ways, we are emotional lizards."[56] So, too, the imagery that fear mechanisms produce in humans dates back to the prehistoric reptiles. Our brains, Panksepp argues, are "full of ancestral memories and processes that guide our actions and dreams," although these memories "rarely emerge unadulterated by corticocultural influences during our everyday activities." As he later observes, many of the feelings and behavioral tendencies that characterize the basic emotions reflect, more than anything else, the intrinsic, genetically prepared properties of brain organization. Although the underlying emotional circuits influence and guide learning, their initial adaptive functions were to *initiate*, *synchronize*, and *energize* sets of coherent physiological, behavioral, and psychological changes that are primal instinctive solutions to various archetypal life-challenging situations.[57]

On the other hand, in psychic disorders such as PTSD, these "archetypal situations" become revived. According to Panksepp, the hyperemotional state of PTSD originates in "deep subcortical networks" that operate independently of "higher cognitive faculties."[58] Regarding the onset of the trauma, it is not so much the content of the external situation that matters but rather the involuntary, self-generated imagery of fear and anxiety, which recapitulates the evolutionary past of the human animal. Likewise, for LeDoux, "a fairly standard view of the way the amygdala mediates conditioned fear provides a plausible account of [PTSD]."[59] Even if the stimulus for the hyperaroused state of posttraumatic stress disorder is external, the affective disorder is fundamentally due to the brain veering off course on autopilot. It may even be that the brain itself generates the traumatic images. Contemporary neuroscience holds that the brain functions autopoietically, not only in disordered states but in general, and that it is a closed, self-referential, and self-activating system geared toward generating intrinsic images instead of faithfully "representing" the external world.[60] The brain "emulates" reality instead of acting as a simple translator. The significance of sensory experience lies not in its informational content but rather in how it corresponds to internal states that reflect ancestral circuits acquired through evolution and the intrinsic images that these contain.

Crucial to Virtual Iraq is the way it taps into the brain's endogenous production of images. The tailored scenarios that the therapist conjures up have less to do with working on patients' personal memories, that is, exposing autobiographical-symbolic mnemic content, than with experimenting on and directing the foldings, recurrences, and stratifications of neural circuits. Images here concern the capture and government of behavior and emotions originating in the brain's ancestral affect programs. Indeed, whereas affects in cinema and visual studies are often aligned with issues of embodiment and the phenomenology of the sensing, breathing, and moving subject, in VR technologies such as Virtual Iraq, they play a decisive role in governmental strategies that invest power in the subject's body by managing its forces on the collective biological level.[61] John Protevi sees current biopolitics as conceptually organized more around the distribution of affective cognitive traits in a population than around the emotional textures of personal life.[62] The subject from this biopolitical perspective is a being shaped and governed at the level of biological properties ranging from behavioral patterns to emotional disposition. As noted, it was Darwin who stressed the centrality of affectivity in the contingencies of animal life. Emotions are essential to the organism and its survival in detecting the dangers of the environment. Fear, above all, is the generative principle of a human being that, Foucault argued, has come to be seen, no longer as part of "mankind" (*le genre humain*), but as part of "the human species" (*l'espèce humaine*).[63]

In this respect, VR technology differs very little from ordinary video games, which Barbara Maria Stafford calls "autopoietic devices," that is, from screen media that evoke and modulate the autonomic functions of affectivity and wake up the "emotional lizard" within us by producing generic environments of survival to which we respond most often with a mixture of rage and fear.[64] By "autopoietic," Stafford refers to how these games trigger stereotypical affective and motor responses based on the nervous system's drive for self-preservation. Such automatism-based interaction between screen and player leads rather straightforwardly to the concept of "fixed action patterns" (FAPs), which refers to sets of motor patterns—or "ready-made motor tapes," as Rodolfo Llinás calls them[65]—that are switched on to produce coordinated movements such as escaping, walking, running, and swallowing. Llinás explains that these patterns of motor activity are called "fixed" because they are more or less the same in all individuals within a species, although they can adapt and are open to modification through repetition and practice.

First-person shooter video games seem designed to modify and adapt our (species-specific) fixed action patterns through repetitive gestures performed in shifting virtual environments. If the brain, as Llinás argues, generates "a seamless, dreamlike movie" by "anticipating or looking ahead,"[66] then first-person shooter games emulate the way the brain acts as a reality emulator, especially when it comes to directing emergency (fight-or-flight) responses and related affective states. Seen in this light, that marines coming in from patrol would often play combat video games such as *Call of Duty* does not seem very surprising.[67] We can surmise that the video game enabled the modulation of emotions through repeated exposure to experiences of danger and threat—becoming a sort of "stress inoculation training" to preempt posttraumatic stress.[68]

The imagery of first-person shooter games thus reflects the general thanatographic nature of our biopolitical screens—"thanatographic" referring, in Protevi's words, to "representations of violence provoking physiological changes, analogous to the provocation of physiological change through pornography,"[69] and hence to the modulation of behavioral patterns distributed across a population. First-person shooter games and virtual reality environments, as prime examples of such visuality, are designed to produce archetypal defense-against-danger situations and to modulate subpersonal processes of threat perception. In a sense, then, the reality of the wars the soldiers now wage does not originate in the brain's orientation toward and interpretation of the external world but, rather, in the regulation of basic action and affect programs by media technologies and in the endogenous imagery they produce.

This applies to Virtual Iraq in particular and to virtual reality exposure therapy in general. In this context, images of explosions, attacks, and death teach adaptation to catastrophic contingencies and a permanent state of crisis by "reprogramming" affects related to painful memories, by modulating those "reptilian" aspects of brain activity having virtually no connection to phenomena such as insight, understanding, or planning for the future. There is no mention of the "moral of the story," no questioning of what the patient saw or did—such issues are deemed irrelevant or even incomprehensible. The therapeutic operation follows no a priori code except the promotion of life's emergence and becoming through the affective administration of death. This coincides with Brian Massumi's argument that, in contemporary society, the norm according to which subjectivity is shaped "comes to be intrinsic to the biological processes of the human-species population and its innovatory evolution."[70] Quite tellingly, Parsons and Rizzo couch their assessment of the outcomes of VRET in neuroscientific language: "Systematic and controlled therapeutic exposure to phobic stimuli may enhance emotional regulation through adjustments of inhibitory processes on the amygdala by the medial prefrontal cortex during exposure and structural changes in the hippocampus after successful therapy."[71] They describe PTSD patients in terms of cerebral functions whose self-organization needs to be redirected and whose relative equilibrium needs to be maintained. Such individuals are neither "normal" nor "pathological" but, in the words of another study, display "a normal response to an abnormal situation."[72]

Thus, with the computer animations of Virtual Iraq and commercial video games, we have moved far from the subject-object structures and gaze dialectics that characterize the conventional functions of images into situations of neural adaptation and reemergence. As another aspect of the neuropower of contemporary screens, the meaning of what is seen or, more generally, experienced counts very little in comparison with the general operational goal of the images. The frameless virtual reality interface evokes the experience of self-affecting embodied interiority, with no reference to a world external to this coupling of screen and observer, which, in Hansen's analysis, corresponds to contemporary neuroscience's internalist view of the brain as the producer of endogenous movies.[73] Within the visual economy of VR technologies, images become functions of affective stratification, or "habituation," and hence of the brain's self-organization, in particular situations. What Virtual Iraq focuses our attention on is how VR screen technology, and media screen technology more generally, is meant to generate imagery primarily linked to the ancestral cerebral folds and stratifications of our brains and to the neurological rewiring of our phylogenetic past.

Brain Plasticity and Immunopolitics

Virtual Iraq captures the brain's evolutionary strata with the aim of modifying traces of the past and reprogramming the biopolitical subject to the contingencies of the future. It is designed to evoke and edit the movies emerging from the amygdala—a reptilian cinema that contains the cross-species imagery that defines us as affective agents. In doing so, its screen becomes a kind of self-organizing environment on which our neural mechanisms codepend and with which they coevolve in service to the demands of neoliberalism.

Above all, Virtual Iraq taps into the brain's plasticity—the ability of our brains to re-create themselves and to constantly modify, modulate, and renew their synaptic organization through experience. Our neural circuits develop and change, not only according to genetic programs, but also in response to environmental events (which include screens and the images animated on them). Catherine Malabou distinguishes between three aspects of the brain's plasticity, as the concept is used in neuroscience: (1) the newborn brain's capacity to establish synaptic connections and to model and reorganize those connections under the influence of its surroundings; (2) the capacity of established synaptic connections to self-organize in response to external events; and (3) the brain's capacity to renew and repair itself anatomically.[74] At the start, the brain's morphological development is determined by genetics, but this gradually becomes less the case as information received from the environment grows in importance. In the second aspect of the brain's plasticity, established cerebral networks self-organize: the synapses of these networks adjust their "efficacy" and modulate the force of their interconnections in response to external events. On this functional level, our neural circuits are constantly reorganizing themselves as they respond to our individual patterns of repetition, memory, and learning, in particular, which either "potentiate" or "depress" synaptic efficacy. Although controversial, the third aspect of the brain's plasticity refers to secondary neurogenesis, whereby the brain produces new nerve cells in at least some of its regions that have been damaged. In sum, Malabou notes, far from being fixed and mechanical, the brain is extraordinarily supple; the multilayered concept of neural plasticity is an attempt to capture the brain's remarkable capacities to adapt, self-organize, and become. "In fact," she writes, "plasticity is the dominant concept of the neurosciences. Today it constitutes their common point of interest, their dominant motif, and their privileged operating model, to the extent that it allows them to think about and describe the brain as at once an unprecedented dynamic, structure, and organization."[75]

Malabou shows how the contemporary conception of the brain as self-organizing and self-reparative networks closely corresponds to the economic order of present-day societies and the neoliberal rationalities sustaining them, most especially, to the current managerial strategies of decentralization and openness and to the material organization of work premised on constant adaptability, connectedness, and flexibility.[76] As Luc Boltanski and Eve Chiapello point out, today's workers must be at once "*adaptable* and *flexible*, able to switch from one situation to a very different one, and adjust to it; and *versatile*, capable of changing activity or tools, depending on the nature of the relationship entered into with others or with objects."[77] Malabou goes on to say that "the phenomenon called 'brain plasticity' is in reality more often described in terms of an economic flexibility. Indeed, the process of potentiation, which is the very basis of plasticity, is often presented simply as the possibility of increasing or decreasing performance."[78] As such, plasticity feeds into the neoliberal understanding of the subject as *Homo economicus*, ever ready to take on new forms and identities generated by socioeconomic imperatives, ever supple and docile vis-à-vis the exigencies and risks of the competitive environment.

Not surprisingly, brain plasticity also informs our current understanding of posttraumatic stress disorder, which is thought to involve both structural and functional changes in key areas of the brain (amygdala, hippocampus, and prefrontal cortex) as well as modifications in the plasticity of neurons and synapses.[79] Accordingly, virtual reality therapies developed for treatment of the disorder draw on the brain's ability to modify and re-create itself so as to make the traumatized neural circuits of PTSD patients structurally and functionally operative again. VR technologies furnish environments where the plasticity of the traumatized circuits, neurons, and synapses can be constantly decoded and recoded for the psychological management of never-ending crises in self-perpetuating wars.

Crucially, the traumatized PTSD patient represents the other side of the moving, adapting, and calculating biopolitical subject, *Homo economicus*. Indeed, because traumatic experiences entail change, deformation, and reformation, they are paradoxically emblematic of the adaptive, flexible, and constantly transforming individual. As the fundamental marker of indetermination, trauma crystallizes the basic neoliberal imperative that the subject always be ready to become something other than it was. It is important to note here that the brain's plasticity—its ability to constantly re-create itself, to become, and to adapt to new situations—entails not only modification or reparation, but also the destruction of form or identity. Underlying the neuroscientific model of plasticity, Malabou points out, is the assumption that there is no permanent memory trace, no fundamental core of identity in the brain; indeed, no pattern that cannot be erased or eradicated.[80] By extension, underpinning neoliberalism's cerebral subject are the forces of metamorphosis, destruction—and death.

A traumatic event, such as a catastrophe, violent shock, war, or rape, can completely transform a subject's personality. Malabou calls this "destructive plasticity," which she describes as something akin to a "death-like break,"[81] the obsessive and self-destructive reenactment of traumatic events in flashbacks, hallucinations, and dreams that interrupts the psyche's normal functioning. An affective disorder in which the brain simulates the world as a place where traumatic memories and reactions keep on reproducing themselves and threaten to destroy the affected individual, posttraumatic stress disorder stands between two polar extremes: the constant regeneration of form and the production of subjectivity, on the one hand, and the complete destruction of form, in essence, death, on the other. In this light, PTSD effectively crystallizes what it means to be a person in the neoliberal era—a subject in a self-perpetuating state of crisis.

To better describe the paradoxes of neoliberal subjectivity, there is another concept we should consider along with neural plasticity, the concept of immunity. It is no coincidence that the psychobiological model of posttraumatic stress disorder harks back to the metaphors of infection, defense, and resistance in describing the trauma, viewing its resultant flashbacks and dreams as akin to immune responses to foreign bodies.[82] Here the psyche becomes a war zone, in which the brain fights against pathogens from the traumatic past, echoing the modern biomedical notion of immunity, which views the organism itself as a war zone, where the immune system constantly battles against outside threats to the organism's identity and integrity.[83]

In addressing the self-destructive logic of contemporary biopolitics, Roberto Esposito invokes the aporia of immunity that characterizes the modern view of life as something adaptive, emergent, plastic, and creative that needs to constantly protect itself from ever-present and ever-expanding threats. In his genealogy of the concept of immunity in modern political thought from Thomas Hobbes to Carl Schmitt, Esposito argues that biopolitics "makes of individual self-preservation the presupposition of all other political categories, from sovereignty to liberty."[84] In this context, "immunity" can be understood as the power to preserve the form and integrity—the inside—of the individual or collective organism by defensively incorporating the outside. Quite in line with the vital and destructive impulses that characterize neural plasticity, however, Esposito points out that in the notion of immunity, life's power to preserve itself is often articulated with life's power of life to destroy itself, which is to say, autoimmunity.

Here the correspondence between the immunitary logic of self-preservation and the therapeutic logic of the virtualization of war, on the one hand, and the political and economic logic of contemporary wars, on the other, becomes apparent. Just as, in the epistemo-politics of PTSD, virtual reality therapies such as Virtual Iraq see the psyche as a war zone, where defense against threats to it becomes priority number one, and where images are evoked for the sake of self-preservation, to fight against pathogenic memories and to make patients operative and flexible again, so Western societies see the globe as a war zone, where they fight to defend and expand the neoliberal way of life against threats to it, incorporating the outside under their rule. Thus virtual reality images, on one level, and current wars, on another, both positively promote the neoliberal way of life and its impulse to adapt and expand by incorporating the outside to the point where inside and outside become indistinguishable. Thus, too, "self-defense" in the age of the preemptive "war on terror" comes to mean expansion through destruction of all threats to the collective organism.

At the same time, however, posttraumatic stress disorder reveals an inherent and fundamental paradox in this notion of life's emergence and self-protection. That contemporary wars, in attempting to protect and promote life by administering death, produce as their effective outcome the traumatic body of PTSD in constant crisis runs directly counter to immunitary logic, turning self-preservation into self-destruction. In the traumatic body, certain memories integral to the organism are identified as foreign to it, as something the organism can get rid of only by destroying itself: seeing itself as a foreign body, the species-being attacks itself. This persistent state of emergency, according to Esposito, embodies the autoimmunitary crisis of wars waged after 9/11, a crisis within the immunity system of the collective organism, whereby the imperative of protecting and promoting life is pursued so aggressively that it turns against itself:

> War is no longer the always possible inverse of global coexistence, but the only effective reality, where what matters isn't only the specular reality that is determined between adversaries ... but ... the exponential multiplication of the same risks that would like to be avoided, or at least reduced, through instruments that are instead destined to reproduce them more intensely.[85]

Thus the immunitary paradigm of protecting life from what threatens it is inverted, and the preservation of life becomes its destruction, a suicidal project. In contemporary wars, as the problematic of PTSD demonstrates, the promotion of the neoliberal way of life with advanced military technological power produces traumatic events and endogenous simulations destructive of this very way of life. In this respect, the self-destructive tendencies of PTSD, as currently understood and treated, closely correspond to the self-destructive tendencies that emerge in the excessive pursuit of the biopolitical imperative to protect and promote life.[86]

The forces that define life in our current world are the very ones that seek to erase it, whence the impossibility of making clear distinctions between the active and the passive, or between the promotion of life and its destruction, that characterizes the traumatic body in particular and neoliberal subjectivity in general. Posttraumatic stress disorder and biopsychiatric efforts to treat it crystallize the logic of contemporary biopolitics, according to which "it is no longer only death that lies in wait for life, but life itself that constitutes the most lethal instrument of death."[87] Thus Virtual Iraq can be seen to implement the suicidal logic of biopolitics, repeatedly reproducing the trauma of PTSD patients and accelerating the fears that animate it, which is to say, turning the organism further against itself by presenting it with constant flight-or-fight situations, colored by ever-growing fear that finds no relief because fear is seen as essential to the very life of the organism. It may well be that, in attempting to immunize the psyche by turning the world into the brain's endogenous apparition, the images circulating on military, virtual reality, and video game screens end up triggering the psyche's potential for self-destruction, producing, instead of salvation from trauma, the world as a never-ending nightmare.

A whole network of psychobiological rationalities, traumatic bodies and minds, military training and rehabilitation strategies, screen technologies, and actual "overseas contingency operations" surrounds the images produced on the Virtual Iraq platform we started this chapter with. Alongside discourses, institutions, scientific statements, and technological materialities, simple computer-generated animations, like the one of driving a Humvee on a desolate road in the desert under the evening sky (see figure 3.2), function as important operational tools with which bodies and persons are captured in ever-expanding and self-perpetuating wars. The virtual reality and video game images used in training, therapy, and entertainment serve to produce agency that is prepared for the exigencies of hostile combat environments specifically and for the neoliberal reality of competition, risk, and danger more generally.

That agency is at once distributed, affective, and plastic. First, the mental and bodily dispositions of the biopolitical subject, considered as a member of the human species rather than as a psychological individual, are distributed across the evolutionary folds of the brains of the entire species. Second, this subject is fundamentally an affective being whose motivations boil down to a few "basic emotions" crucial to the survival of the organism. Third, and most important, the brain of the biopolitical subject is plastic and amenable to modulation by media technologies. Virtual reality video game images, by erasing distinctions between themselves and the body-brains of their observers, predispose those observers to the ready modification of their cerebral circuits, especially in the name of self-preservation and immunity.

However, the visual economy we encounter on Virtual Iraq produces subjects immune not only to their outside but also to themselves, subjects that experience the past as an alien force operating from within them. And this conflation of life with death, emergence with destruction may well be symptomatic of the more general autoimmunitary crisis that characterizes the thanatographic images we consume on our game consoles and computer screens. The power of these violent images lies not so much in what they show as in how they animate the reptilian cinema of basic affectivity that runs deep in the ancestral folds of our brains, and that makes us want to violently defend ourselves against any threat—even when *we* are the threat.

The opening of Farocki's *Immersion* points to at least one significant way we can counter the destructive power invested in these images. As the black left screen reflects back on its observer, the video installation asks us to ask ourselves: What exactly are the images we are about to see? What are the forces that bind them together and in binding them shape how we think and act? The images themselves become objects of questioning and evaluation. This kind of "double exposure" generates a "cut" into the prevailing models of sensation and perception, giving rise to another level of (re)cognition, one that can critically reflect on the production of our perceptions and mappings of the world. Such cuts and double exposures will be the focus of chapter 4.

4 Emergent Present: Imagination, Montage, Critique

Life lurks in the interstices of each living cell, and in the interstices of the brain.
—Alfred North Whitehead, *Process and Reality*

Politics and Aesthetics

Images manifest their power over life in their recursive movement between the interstices of our mind-brains and the object world.[1] Concrete, material images work and shape the ways we map constantly shifting perceptual scenes, both internal and external, real and fictive.[2] In other words, material images fix mental ones and vice versa, which, as we have seen, involves a complex interplay between the somatic, the personal, and the social.

Chapters 2 and 3 dealt with how images become alive on video game and virtual reality screens, on the one hand, and with how they provoke specific kinds of affective and cognitive engagement, on the other. At issue in both instances is how the biopolitical apparatus weaves a fabric of sensibility and individuation from images actualized in various types of materials, spanning screen technologies, scientific rationalities, cerebral modulations, and the like, thus tying us to the future it seeks to create for itself and "liberating" us from the painful realities of its past. In charge of our lives today is essentially a politics of tamed temporality, where the past has been emptied of meaning and weight and the future has been made "perfect."

Thus both the future and the past as realms of open possibility have been inscribed into the political and technological operations that police them, "police" used here as a verb in the sense that Jacques Rancière uses the noun, to refer not just to the enforcement of law, but to the capture of persons in a social whole with its "matching" of functions and ways of being that present themselves as determinate and devoid of potentiality. The term "police," Rancière tells us, stands for

> a partition of the sensible that is characterized by the absence of void and of supplement: society here is made of groups tied to specific modes of doing, to places in which these occupations are exercised, and to modes of being corresponding to these occupations and these places. In the matching of functions, places and ways of being, there is no place for any void. It is this exclusion of what "is not" that constitutes the police-principle at the core of statist practices.[3]

"Police" refers here to dominant distributions of modes of sensing and thinking that rule out other, potentially contesting modes, and thus establish consensus and hegemony across culture, politics, and the economy. Rancière evokes the apt phrase "cutting up" (*découpage*) of our sensory apparatus—or of the movies running in our brains, as previous chapters might have said—that anticipates the social reality with its division of shares and parties.[4] This encompasses the standardization and regulation of the values according to which things and beings become perceptually categorized and made sense of; the ruling over what can be recognized as real and what not, over what elements can be assigned (affective, perceptual, or other) significance and what elements cannot and hence must be excluded from the given social order.

In Rancière's idiom, the notion of "police" obviously designates much of what "politics" is ordinarily taken to mean, especially when it comes to the theory of power and governmentality as the establishment of an order of bodies that "defines the allocation of ways of doing, ways of being, and ways of seeing, and sees that those bodies are assigned by name to a particular place and task."[5] But Rancière wants to "reserve the term *politics* for an extremely determined activity antagonistic to policing: whatever breaks with the tangible configuration whereby parties and parts or lack of them are defined by a presupposition that, by definition, has no place in that configuration—that of the part of those who have no part."[6] The concept of politics is here dedicated to intervention and interruption, which processes draw on the anthropologically and biologically unlocatable equality of beings.[7] "Politics" is synonymous with "dissensus," meaning the production, from within a reigning and determined regime of seeing and thinking, of modes of sensing and making sense that are heterogeneous and external to it.[8] What is central for Rancière is the aesthetic dimension of political subjectivation, and politics as a site where what had previously been excluded from the dominant perceptual world is rendered as visible and thinkable, where the ways in which the world appears and we appear to ourselves and to others around us are reconfigured. Politics, in this sense, concerns dispute and struggle about what kinds of combinations and "cuts" organize our personal lives and collective being, and involves introducing indeterminacy to the incisions into the surface of our thoughts.

This chapter approaches the topic of bio*political* screens accordingly, from a perspective that emphasizes interventions into and interruptions of the current logics of power and the refigurations of reigning affective-cognitive realities—or the configurations of "a different world-in-common," to quote Rancière.[9] Whereas the previous chapters dealt mostly with the movement of images in what might be called the "space of police," and with screen-based individuation of bodies in relation to contemporary wars and the economy in particular, this chapter will focus on the undoing of dominant patterns of sensibility.

Interruption in the field of political individuation always implies, at some level, a rupture or break in the functioning of our senses. For instance, Rancière describes such a cut in the ordinary fabric of sensibility by quoting a joiner's third-person description of his experience in 1848: "Believing himself at home, he loves the arrangement of a room, so long as he has not finished laying the floor. If the window opens out onto a garden or commands a view of a picturesque horizon, he stops his arms and glides in imagination toward the spacious view to enjoy it better than the [owners] of the neighboring residences."[10] For a brief moment, the strict coordination between the man's eye and hand breaks down, the man's gaze, pulled away from his duty, wanders out the window, and his mind begins its spontaneous play of figuration.

It is precisely such breaks or gaps in contemporary biopolitical dispositions—in the machinations of our lives and their embodied temporal textures—that this chapter addresses. Here we should note how imagination emerges in the above example as a zone of contest for emancipatory purposes, where the given real is reconfigured in productive acts of figuration. Thus the imagination is not a realm of private fantasies or of "nothingness," as Jean-Paul Sartre said, but rather, following Gilbert Simondon, the invention of new modes of reality.[11] It operates as an unruly hinge between the collective and the individual, the material and the mental. It is here that struggles over what kinds of images will manage and organize our lived realities are staged. Hans Belting points out that "public images have always controlled personal imagination; and the personal imagination, in turn, either cooperates with them or resists them."[12] Looking at the normative power of images, we can see how screen-based mediations become isomorphic with private imaginations, but we can also see how, by resisting and breaking this normative power, the imagination acquires and makes sense of objective images and in doing so twists and resamples them, in turn creating new materializations.

Among those acknowledging the productive and radically political role of imagination, Cornelius Castoriadis observes how, by escaping society's established schemata, the imagination can create "the newly thinkable."[13] Free from the constraints of true and false, it can break with prevailing regimes of sense, presenting novel figures of thought, which are at the heart of attempts to challenge the rules, norms, and laws that structure the relation between our bodies and the world we live in. But rather than considering the imagination as springing from the creativity of the individual, as Castoriadis does, we might better approach it in terms of the complex, however inadvertent life of images themselves, attending to how their movements come to organize the "folds and gaps in the fabric of common experience that change the cartography of the perceptible, the thinkable and the feasible," as Rancière puts it in relation to the joiner's experience.[14] Indeed, if W. J. T. Mitchell is right, "images are like … co-evolutionary lifeforms on the order of viruses," whereas the individual who creates or beholds them is "merely a host carrying around a crowd of parasites that are merrily reproducing themselves, and occasionally manifesting themselves in those notable specimens we call 'works of art.'"[15]

For Simondon, the imagination is a preindividual vehicle of ontogenetic processes by which both material and mental images come into being.[16] He sees images as quasi-organisms of their own kind and imagination as one of the "media" in which they move and become transformed. In Simondon's theory, the life of images is a threefold recursive process, which (1) starts from spontaneous growth in a state of free potential, then develops (2) into perceptual patterns that structure experience and serve adaptation to the object world and finally (3) into a system of relations, evocations, and mutations that creates analogical models (*analoga*) of the world and that allows reflection. Thus the imagination is anything but purely subjective.

As dynamic genetic processes, images are fundamentally autonomous and enjoy an agency of their own. The image, Simondon writes, "resists free will, refuses to let itself be directed by the will of the subject, and presents itself according to its own proper forces, inhabiting consciousness like an intruder who comes to upset the order of a house he was not invited to."[17] There is a latent and emergent potentiality to the image, a constitutive metastability that allows spontaneous mutations. This metastability is critical to invention, which, for Simondon, means not creation ex nihilo but rather modification of the arrangements of images whereby we live. When multiplying, spreading, and reproducing, images can undo and reinvent themselves, move from one state of development to another, and in doing so change the ways in which the objective, the subjective, and the social are coupled together.[18]

Simondon also hints at the political nature of both mental and material images as they form the core of the world's realization. Rather than being symmetrical with the facticity of the present objective reality, images possess an underlying force of plasticity and proneness to transformation; they touch upon future potentialities in molding, independent of our consciousness, what *can* be. In this sense, they are able to challenge the self-evidency of the given real, which is to say, they can undo and then rearticulate our sense of reality—the divisions between visible and invisible, babble and meaning—that guides our actions and thoughts. They can stage and display (to quote Rancière) "a conflict between sense and sense,"[19] and thereby effect cuts into the common fabric of sensibility that bring heterogeneous, even apparently contradictory elements together, so as to retain attendant tensions between them and consequent indeterminacy.

Within this analysis, the movement of images can involve spontaneous breaks within reigning distributions of sensibility and divisions of time, space, and activity. In this chapter, I thus shift my focus from the pervasive logics of control and capture in today's screen culture to attempts at challenging, questioning, and redesigning the images that dominate the neoliberal brain. Drawing on the assumption that the movement and circulation of images constitute not an integrative totality but an open "system," which is both overdetermined and self-reflexive, I will chart and conceptualize moments of critical mediation by which images today can introduce novelty in repetition, potentiality in structure, and break in process.

The concept that perhaps best captures these metastable movements is montage. Though often considered as fixing the play of signification, montage can also, as Jean-Luc Godard puts it in *Histoire(s) du cinéma,* "bring things together which have never been linked and which did not seem to be able to go together."[20] Through montage, incisions into and intervals between images can emerge that decontextualize, inject indefiniteness into, and bring forward novel figurations in perception and thinking. In this sense, whether linear or nonlinear, within one screen or between several screens, montage determines not only the value of images, but, more fundamentally, how they come into contact with and so transform each other, questioning and renegotiating the boundaries of entities and processes that seem more or less self-evident. As such, spatiotemporal intervals, interruptions, associations, and dissociations in the movement of images on the screen's surface serve as materializations of the flights and aberrations of imagination, indeed, as cuts wherein the images we live by can reinvent themselves.[21]

In other words, montage can unleash the political potential of images. Such is the effect of the interval between two screens in Harun Farocki's *Immersion,* which, as noted in chapter 3, intervenes into the action-based imagery used to capture the brain's affective memory circuits in the military context, intercepting their operative logic and turning it into an object of critical evaluation. Decisive to this spatially oriented montage is that, in it, "one image doesn't take the place of the previous one, but supplements it, re-evaluates it, balances it."[22] Farocki calls this kind of composition where images reflect each other "soft montage," whose purpose is to "hold together with invisible forces the things that would otherwise become muddled."[23] The critical momentum of his video installation thus stems not so much from the content of the screens, however intriguing or appalling it may be, as from the two-channel display, which yields the work of imagination shifting between the two screens, and within which our senses can make sense of what is not apparent in a novel way through the activity of images uncertainly evoking and transforming each other.

This chapter explores such self-reflexive acts of image making by inquiring into the possibilities of critical aesthetic and political consciousness, which is shaped by various types of montage that yield both separation and connection. Following Barbara Maria Stafford's observation that the "extensions and contradictions" of video as an utterly malleable time-based medium are "perfectly suited to explore the push and pull of self-awareness," this inquiry involves a sustained critique of the power of the image as image.[24] I will analyze three specific artworks as experimentations on and interventions into the current biopolitical visual economy. Falling within the context of what might be called "projected image art," displayed mainly in galleries and museums, each of these works exemplifies an aspect in the movement of images that allows the viewer to reevaluate and reflect, instead of demanding that she or he immediately reacts; each seeks to critically construct alternative arrangements of the sensible and to yield novel figures of the thinkable.[25] Each of these works thus also demonstrates the political potentialities of aesthetic practice; through different strategies of montage, they articulate "protest against the hitherto existing world," as Georges Bataille observed about "art" and its functions.[26]

I will address operations of montage on the video screen as "protests" that amount to intensive cuts into the composition of neoliberal brainhood, and that show how time-based images can both reveal and mold the ways our mind-brains break down and unify the world in experience. If our mind-bodies, following Belting, constitute "a locus where the images we receive leave behind an invisible trace,"[27] then images can also be considered forces of transformation, even in a material, physiological sense as (potential) fissures in the body's textures. The notions of gap, discontinuity, and interval, as we have seen previously, are also critical to understanding the brain's organization, suggesting how the brain is not predetermined in its makeup but supple, self-organizing, and plastic. Indeed, although biopolitics and the neoliberal economy draw on the cerebral subject's flexibility, so do emancipatory efforts. Catherine Malabou's view of the brain's plasticity both in neuroscience and beyond is helpful here, emphasizing not only the determinacy of continuous adaptations but also regeneration through rupture and resistance, creation through destruction of form. For Malabou, plasticity is an issue of politics in the fundamental sense of self-transformation.[28] If video art, as Rancière argues, can "bring into play the metamorphic, unstable nature of images,"[29] the plasticity of images, their metastability, brings into play the plasticity of our brains; it involves our capacities to transform and "become," indeed, to make sense of ourselves and the world around us differently.

Aniconicity: Disempowering the Image

Trevor Paglen's single-channel video installation *Drone Vision* (2010) cuts into the military imagery of surveillance and killing addressed in chapter 2, images that live and move on the control screens of unmanned aerial vehicles and that establish a specific preemptive visuality in the contemporary wars for world dominance. These are operating parts of what Paul Virilio calls "vision machines," artificial intelligence systems of image recognition, automated to the point of exclusively assigning "the analysis of objective reality to a machine."[30] Virilio sees the development of these devices, spurred by the demands of ever-expanding warfare, as signaling a shift in our visual economies, whereby "instrumental virtual images will be for us the equivalent of what a foreigner's mental pictures already represent: an enigma."[31] The enigmatic surface of the UAV screen is precisely what *Drone Vision* seeks to crack. The piece consists of secret video stream images, which once circulated as encrypted "real-time" data in the global satellite networks of the military-surveillance complex, images taken from a drone deployed somewhere over eastern Europe in 2009.

Despite its covert nature, the drone screen has also come to occupy an iconic position in society's imaginations of itself. It compels the sensibility of a surveillant synoptic eye and a spatiotemporally potent hand that acts at a distance to inscribe the future into the present for the biopolitical management of life. We saw in chapter 2 how such preemptive patterns of affectivity and cognition among players of action-based video games, and of first-person shooter games in particular, have become one of the leading forms of popular sensibility. But more noticeably, it is the new social media that have provided a platform for the evolution of actual drone imagery within today's visual economy, where military modes of perception migrate from the battlefield to everyday screens. In 2008, the U.S. Department of Defense decided to place selected footage from Predator and Reaper drone missions on YouTube in an attempt to give permanency to this imagery in our collective imaginations (figure 4.1). Ranging from wide shots to graphic close-ups, these short clips edited from countless hours of raw footage show insurgents being "eliminated" by drone missiles—clips absorbed by today's "prosumers," as one sometimes calls contemporary consumers who participate in the production of online consumption, if only to act as nodes of circulation. The drone videos went

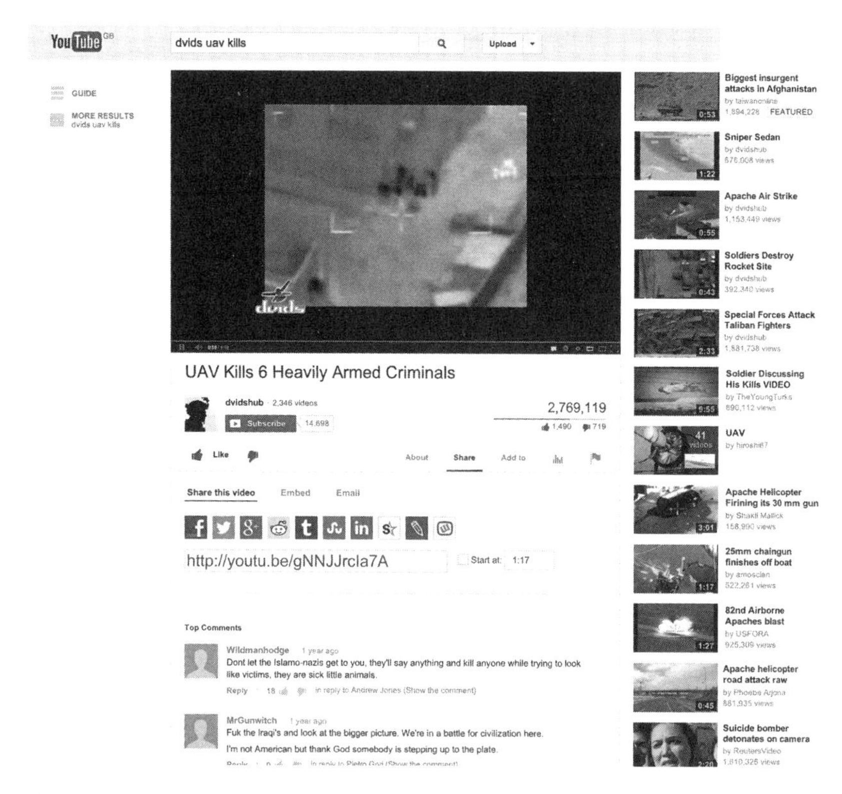

Figure 4.1
Screen grab from UAV mission footage (Baghdad, 2009) on YouTube, published by the U.S. Department of Defense.

"viral," attracting millions of hits, and were promptly dubbed "drone porn" by the mainstream media.

The reference to pornography is telling, emphasizing how these emotionally detached acts of simulation contain a violent, potentially sexual impulse of possession and destruction. Anonymous and fuzzy dark shapes moving on the screen are shadows of individuals quantified as code and threats, but otherwise valueless and expendable in the camera's crosshairs. The human figures rendered on the drone's display represent what Giorgio Agamben calls "bare life" (*la nuda vita*), that is, life reduced to its natural, biological dimension and excluded from the political community of equal and free men and women.[32] The shady silhouettes on drone control screens do not speak, being mere instrumentalities in the hegemon's pursuit of self-protection.[33] They lead a life that involves politics only in their capacity as enemies to be killed.[34] We can recognize them only insofar as they play a part in the necropolitical work of death, or global "war on terror," by means of which neoliberal government today institutes itself.

Against this backdrop, these figures can be seen as examples of what Mitchell calls "biopictures." Products of the union of contemporary forms of power over living beings and digital technology, which provides instantaneous reproduction and circulation, biopictures are for Mitchell metaphors and graphic symbols that currently crystallize how neoliberal societies imagine themselves and others. The essential content of these images, which range from decapitation videos posted online by insurgents to leaked photographs of torture at Abu Ghraib, is "the reduction of the human body to bare life and brutal death."[35] A crucial part of the visual and other forms by which we make sense of our surroundings is the felt reality of immediate threat and reciprocal violence. The production and purpose of such images can be compared to the body's production of antibodies by "mirroring" the antigens of invading microorganisms with the aim of destroying the invaders.[36]

Drone porn obviously has many of the qualities that Mitchell attributes to the current movement of images—notably, mass consumption and the reduction of the other "to a mere image" to be eliminated.[37] Indeed, drone imagery has become iconic of our sociopolitical reality, based as it is on negating alterity. Intrinsic to this negation is the feeling of hate, which psychically circumscribes the biopolitical subject, isolating it from the excluded other. As Sara Ahmed notes, hate "is involved in the very negotiation of boundaries between selves and others, and between communities, where 'others' are brought into the sphere of my or our existence as threat."[38] In this respect, critical to these images is the way they seek to render the everyday as a perpetual war zone, and the vitality of perceptual exploration (recognition, pattern forming) and action (clicking, linking, sharing, and so on) as a simulation of killing. Drone porn thus reiterates and reinforces the militarized immunitary paradigm that shapes contemporary distributions of the sensible "as fighting against, devouring, destroying, attacking, and battling" all "enemies," wherever they may be.[39]

It is also from within this same visual economy that Paglen's *Drone Vision* examines today's visual complex of aerial power and surveillance screens, which aims to turn the globe into an opaque surface of

Figure 4.2
Video feed from a drone deployed over Eastern Europe. Trevor Paglen, *Drone Vision* (2010). Courtesy of Metro Pictures, New York; Altman Siegel, San Francisco; Galerie Thomas Zander, Cologne.

information intelligible only to artificial, controlling brains (figure 4.2). Minimally and, it would seem, haphazardly edited, the work displays fuzzy video footage of the sky and clouds as well as wide-angle synoptic views of hilly and desolate landscapes, crossed by only a few roads. Images become almost abstract variations of shifting shades of gray. The camera's crosshairs and data about altitude, date and time, and so on displayed on the screen's edges nonetheless remind us that these are operational, not aesthetic, images—images that uncover the world as an object of action rather than contemplation. At one point, the footage is interrupted by a shot of a U.S. Air Force wall clock (figure 4.3). Its hands pointing to 2:25, the clock keeps on ticking—tick, tock, tick, tock. Then the camera cuts back to desolate landscapes and clouds. After a few monotonous scenes, the camera surveys a curvy road and, spotting something moving on the road, zooms in on what turns out to be an old tractor pulling a cart. It tracks the vehicle's

Figure 4.3
Close-up of U.S. Air Force wall clock. Trevor Paglen, *Drone Vision* (2010). Courtesy of Metro Pictures, New York; Altman Siegel, San Francisco; Galerie Thomas Zander, Cologne.

movements for a few seconds, then zooms out and continues to survey the area from a distance.

If we consider videos from drone control screens to be "iconic" of the biopolitical imaginary, then we might, with Laura U. Marks, call Paglen's method of hijacking and rearranging this covert footage "aniconic." Focusing on Paglen's photographic documentation of clandestine U.S. military installations, Marks argues that "art is aniconic when the image shows us that what we do not see is more significant than what we do." In aniconic visual works, she explains, "the most important activity takes place at a level prior to the perceptible image. The image that we perceive refers to its underlying cause—in ornament, geometry, pattern, text, and code-generated images."[40] With aniconicity, Marks describes a mode of nonfigurative visual presentation that heralds an awareness of what is beneath images or in between them, an awareness of the constituent forces that bring forth the world of appearances.

Although, in a broader sense, Marks's aniconicity might be said to disregard both the ways in which figurative representations can also elicit such a fundamental "presence of absence" in perception and the figurative nature of aniconic images themselves,[41] I take the notion of aniconicity more narrowly to describe the particular critique of mediation that *Drone Vision* puts forward. As we will see below in greater detail, aniconicity amounts to a mode of visual presentation that tests and probes the limits of appearances, unveiling a void or gap within its own composition. It is worth noting here that the problematic of aniconicity, especially with regard to moral and political debates about iconoclasm, is historically steeped in questions that concern precisely the power and the (in)finitude of images.

At the heart of Byzantine iconoclastic controversies in the eighth and ninth centuries, the dispute about visuality revolved around the possibility of depicting God, considered infinite and indivisible, within a finite figurative composition. An advocate of the iconoclastic position, the emperor Constantine V announced there was no such possibility: material figures were bounded and hence limited in what they could depict. "If the icon draws the figure of the divine, it encloses the infinite within its line, which is impossible," he argued.[42] For their part, the "iconodules" or iconophiles did not recognize such a logical contradiction. Their theories of the image, which, Marie-José Mondzain tells us, were advanced to support clerical authority over profane space and to extend the rule of the Church across the globe, posited no conceptual contradiction between the finite, earthly surfaces of pictures and God's infinite being.[43] Indeed, they argued that the iconic image was fundamentally frameless, unbounded, and infinite by nature, hence capable of expanding the Church's celestial authority indefinitely in space and time.

These debates are not merely historical curiosities. On the contrary, traces of the iconophiles' embrace of "a brilliant light, glory without limit and without borders, cosmic monarchy, ubiquity and perpetuity," as Mondzain describes their veneration of the Christian empire,[44] characterize today's biopolitical visual economy. In fact, the drone as a "vision machine" is a compelling instantiation of the technophilic belief in the infinite powers of the image that animates neoliberalism's quest for global governance. Omer Fast underscores this point in his video installation *Five Thousand Feet Is the Best* (2011), which, like Paglen's *Drone Vision*, takes as its topic instrumentalized and automated killing, although Fast emphasizes the psychological effects of screen-based warfare on those waging it. Based on interviews conducted with an ex–Predator drone operator suffering from posttraumatic stress disorder, *Five Thousand Feet* ends with the operator's voice-over describing an actual incident he was involved in where the U.S. forces preemptively eliminated a group of men suspected of planning a road bomb attack. While the screen displays an aerial shot of nighttime Las Vegas bathed in electric light, we hear the drone operator recount: "Then we do something called the 'light of God'—the marines like to call it the 'light of God'—it's a laser-targeting marker. We just send out a beam of laser and when the troops put on their night-vision goggles, they'll just see this light that looks like it's coming from heaven, pfft, right on the spot. Coming out of nowhere from the sky. It's quite beautiful." Evident in the operator's reminiscences is the imperative to establish unbounded, synoptic control of visibility from the heavens, the management of a visual economy by controlling the vertical axis from a God's-eye viewpoint. With unusual aptness, the U.S. military has given the name Gorgon Stare to a new advanced unmanned aerial vehicle technology currently in development, a "wide-area sensor surveillance system" consisting of nine to twelve visual feeds from a single UAV platform that can cover city-sized areas and be viewed concurrently or separately.[45] Like the mythical Gorgon, the new technology has a gaze that kills.

Returning to *Drone Vision*, Paglen's aniconic method does not amount to simply falsifying the UAV video stream images he hijacks. As in *Five Thousand Feet Is the Best*, which juxtaposes a familiar view of Las Vegas with the observer's imagination of "the light of God," the point here is not whether these images are epistemologically, or even ethically, right or wrong. Rather, it is about producing an alternative kind of understanding of how the images work by making us aware as observers that the images themselves are fundamentally powerless. In this regard, although *Drone Vision* implies that "the point of [technological] power today resides in networks, computers, algorithms, information, and data," all of which underlie the images the video presents us with, it nonetheless suggests that, as conscious observers, we have the power to critique those images, to determine the potentialities and limits of what becomes cognitively apparent and what does not.[46]

Drone Vision transports the ephemeral satellite video feed images into another sensory realm, where they are made to move and live differently, but it does not directly assign them a new, fixed meaning. Instead, Paglen makes us face these undecipherable algorithmic images without attempting to explain how we perceive them. While making us, as observers, aware of the military-technological networks of power within which these videos emerge and circulate, it escapes the critical political aesthetic that insists on clearly drawn cognitive maps for meaning and action. *Drone Vision* undermines what Rancière calls the "mimetic logic of political art, which is based on the axiom that "art compels us to revolt when it shows us revolting things."[47]

Thus, on the one hand, aniconicity in *Drone Vision* circumvents the logic of semblance. *Drone Vision* does not seek to posit a figurative correspondence between the composition of the work and a way of doing and thinking. On the other hand, however, taking into account the video's iconographic context—drone porn on YouTube, video game imagery flashing on console screens, actual video feed images from drone cameras in service to the military-surveillance complex—it leaves another dimension notably invisible. What these banal and covert images working in the current visual economy of militarized sensibility are designed to claim is the *event*, to control the world's occurring and its temporal order. Drone screens strive to preemptively differentiate between the uneventful and the potentially eventful, between normal patterns of life and signs of future threat. Drone porn published by the U.S. Department of Defense capitalizes on political violence and death by turning them into spectacles in the present moment of consciousness, while video games render these spectacles as visceral first-person experiences recursively reappearing on the console screen's action-reaction circuits.

But in *Drone Vision*, video footage is put together in an apparently haphazard manner; indeed, the only "event" is the wall clock that keeps on ticking: tick tock, tick tock. Time is wasted.[48] Instead of feelings of control, hatred, excitement, or fear, it is boredom that shapes the video's affective landscape—boredom in the sense that Martin Heidegger intended it as the experience of the presence of the present, of the now from within which the past has been sealed off and the horizon of the future unbound and, consequently, within which we experience indeterminacy and "self-forming emptiness" rather than being captivated by specific goals for the future.[49]

What is absent in *Drone Vision* is precisely the attempt to seize and claim the event and its meaningfulness that defines the contemporary logics of power and image. It is, first and foremost, this absence that makes the artwork's critique aniconic, an absence that makes us aware of, without directly showing it, a fundamental absence within these images themselves. By constructing a specific abstracted and nonfigurative sensibility of what could be called "uneventfulness," *Drone Vision* seeks to overturn the visual complex that it taps into, to deactualize the power of action-oriented, future-claiming images by suggesting their underlying emptiness: there is no coming event to extinguish, no impending threat to hedge against, nobody to kill. The future is not pregnant of crisis or victory; the present moment is not one of struggle for survival. Images, like reality, unfold just as indifferently as the clock ticks. In this way, *Drone Vision* perceptually challenges the premise, so visible in actual UAV control screens, that everything and everywhere the image intervenes are subsumed under the neoliberal rule; and in challenging, it counters the way necropolitical images that afford "targeted killing" invade prosuming brains and thereby institute authority over the facts of reality on a transnational scale. Indeed, one could say that *Drone Vision* seeks to scramble the "voice" of authority these images emit—a voice echoing that of Nicephorus I, the patriarch of Constantinople and an ardent iconophile: "My authority is not circumscribed. I am the master and the Lord not of this or that people, land, or city, but of angels and of humans and of the earthly, the celestial and the subterranean realms at the same time."[50]

Nicephorus already understood that rule is established by emptying contradictions and differences. Such is precisely the aim of the neoliberal rule's lethal "Gorgon stare." In response, *Drone Vision* seeks to refute the claim that there is no contradiction, to undermine the threat that looking back turns us into stone. The principal operation the video carries out is to strip the image of its agency. If the power of images is bound up in their animation—in the way they lay claim to our affections, imaginations, and actions, making us anxious, fearful, and forgetful, among other things—*Drone Vision*'s aniconic critique succeeds by "deanimating" images, by seizing their movement and keeping them at a standstill in the indifferent present moment. But where does deactualizing the eventfulness and power of images lead us? What are the emancipatory stakes of such an aniconic gesture that disarticulates the image from itself and that abstracts it from whatever consequences it might have? In a sense, the gesture's end is simply to produce and keep on reproducing that very gesture of disarticulation. *Drone Vision* does not try show us what to think or how to behave, but is satisfied instead with this repetitive movement that circles back on itself. But when the event and action—sensation and meaning—are thus uncoupled, what opens up is the randomness and indeterminacy of our reactions.

Drone Vision presents an image of an image: more precisely, it makes us experience the image as an "anti-image." It establishes relationships of differential exchange between images but does not seek balance. It makes preemptive visual configurations reflect and reiterate themselves, creating intervals between images that leave their contents and linking undetermined. In this way, the video effects a cut into the cerebral modulations that dominate the contemporary visual economy, an incision into the current body politic that fundamentally asks our mind-brains to fill in and confabulate.[51] It takes the plasticity of the screen-brain circuit to another level, from adaptation and response to potential transformations of meaning. Paglen's video installation harnesses and modulates what Gerald Edelman calls the brain's "massive recombinatorial and integrative power," evident in its constant production of mental imagery.[52] A key term in describing this power is "reentry," which refers to the recursive exchange of neural signals between neuronal maps that occurs on various levels of brain organization, from local to global brain activity. It explains "how functionally segregated maps in the cerebral cortex may operate coherently together even though there is no superordinate map or logically determined program," in other words, how coherent perceptual scenes can spontaneously emerge in the mind through the binding of different qualities and aspects of experience.[53] Reentry entails a creative synthesis of building relationships between objects and events, such as metaphoric associations at the core of imagination that introduce unforeseen links between disparate entities.[54]

According to Arnold Modell, when spontaneously imagining, the brain creates maps of its own maps.[55] Similarly, in *Drone Vision,* images start to map themselves, making us aware of their workings. To this end, however, the video installation offers no definite gestalt or concept; it makes an incision precisely in the sense that it opens up and wounds. It leaves our mind-brains thus externalized on the screen's surface to vacillate in their uncertain recursive reentrant processes and to combine images by associating, linking, and delinking.

Decoupling image and action, disarticulating the image from whatever claims it might make about the world through the mirroring and reentry of images, means prompting the plastic capacities of our brains to transform and reshape what we see. When the image does not shock, seduce, control, and so on, but is rather undetermined like the flow of clock time, there is a space left open for novel figures of thought to emerge spontaneously. *Drone Vision's* particularly aniconic sensibility of uneventfulness, of the present moment that is devoid of anticipations and retentions, amounts to triggering the observer's spontaneous capacity of generative imagination. This is the first significant aspect to consider when it comes to the possibilities of a critical aesthetic, and also of critical thought, in the contemporary situation.

Analogy: Immunity Reversed

Similar kinds of mirroring, decoupling, and reentry of images through the modulation of the present moment of experience also take place in Chantal Akerman's *From the Other Side* (2002).[56] Although Akerman's work focuses on transnational migration rather than on military vision machines, what is at issue again is a certain kind of self-reflective inquiry into the imagery that shapes and defines the neoliberal brain's mappings of the world. The video installation touches on the plight of illegal Mexican immigrants trying to make the dangerous crossing from Agua Prieta, Sonora, to Douglas, Arizona. It builds on interviews conducted with people on both sides of the border, with Mexicans who recount painful memories of loved ones lost in the Sonoran Desert or who tell of their dreams about the future, and with Americans who fear that swarms of immigrants will take over their land and who criticize the U.S. government's border policy.

From the Other Side bears witness, on the micropolitical level of individual experiences and feelings, to the inclusions and exclusions that define the U.S.-Mexican border, where movements through controlled paths of entrance and exit across the north-south divide are monitored and global distributions of wealth maintained and reinforced. Neoliberal policies of "borderlessness," evident inside today's European Union, for instance, and ideas of networks and connectivity without fixed points apply only to some, just as the global movement of capital benefits merely a fraction of the world's population, while those deprived of resources and excluded from the so-called free flow of bodies, goods, and money are reduced to the status of minimum-wage physical laborers or of "illegal aliens," unauthorized immigrants. In this context, the U.S.-Mexican border is emblematic of the ambivalent processes that shape the contemporary capitalist landscape, where territorial boundaries are enforced even as the freedom of commerce is accentuated. For instance, in 1994, the U.S. government launched its "Operation Gatekeeper," an enhanced boundary enforcement strategy based on "prevention through deterrence," which involved building border walls with the idea of pushing unauthorized immigrants into mountain and desert areas, where they, like true exemplars of *Homo economicus*, would decide that attempting to cross the border was simply not worth the risk.[57]

In the neoliberal context, then, "freedom," to quote Michel Foucault, is "nothing else but the correlative of the deployment of apparatuses of security."[58] Not surprisingly, such apparatuses on the U.S.-Mexican border include not only fences, but also drones, used alongside other kinds of vision technologies such as thermal imaging systems, where they are employed to detect and control the movements of people and to effect immunopolitical closure in the name of protection against invasion.[59] Indeed, there are plans to deploy UAVs over the border "for 24 hours per day and for seven days per week."[60] In a seemingly frictionless manner, the preemptive gaze of drones is thus transported from actual war zones to potential ones. In order to sustain itself, as we have seen in the previous chapters, the neoliberal way of life needs to combat against whatever threatens its expansion. In the name of protecting life, then, biopolitics promotes the work of death, adding to those killed in the neoliberal wars for world dominance those who have died in the harsh conditions of the desert, from thirst, hyperthermia, and fatigue while attempting to join the illicit flow of immigrant labor.[61] In what Ed Cohen calls its "Janus-faced" regime, biopolitics thus engages in the systematic production of death.[62] Indeed, as Roberto Esposito sees it, death becomes "one of the inner folds" of life, "a mode or tonality of its own preservation."[63]

From the Other Side makes an incision into this reality, showing how the biopolitical subject's psyche today suffers from dislocation and from lack of perceptual reintegration. It juxtaposes different kinds of imagery, ranging from a plain, unassuming long shot of an elderly Mexican woman recounting her past and mourning her son and grandson lost in the desert to eerie night vision surveillance footage of captured migrants, shown as fuzzy white figures walking in a row, escorted by policemen, with someone yelling excitedly into the microphone. *From the Other Side* weaves testimonies from both sides of the border into a polyphonic collage of differing perspectives.

The main role in *From the Other Side*, however, is played not by any particular person, group, or surveillance technology, but by the fence the U.S. Department of Homeland Security built on the border in 1994 from discarded metal aircraft landing mats, replaced by a corrugated steel fence in 2011–12.[64] Like an artificial, externalized immune system, the fence identifies foreign bodies seeking to invade the host organism, on the one hand, and defends the organism's integrity, on the other.[65] It represents a material instantiation of, even a monument to, the immunitary logic that gave rise to it: a line of defense that separates inside from outside, self from nonself, and that excludes while including, its main function being to distinguish between what is proper and what is not, as well as to monitor contact or "contagion." Esposito notes how "immunity is a condition of particularity: whether it refers to an individual or a collective, it is always 'proper' in the specific sense of 'belonging to someone' and therefore 'un-common' or 'non-communal.'"[66] But despite the apparent opposition of immunity to the communal, there is a subtle interchange between the two. As Esposito explains:

> What is immunized, in brief, is the same community in a form that both preserves and negates it, or better, preserves it through the negation of its original horizon of sense. From this perspective, one might say that more than the defensive apparatus superimposed on the community, immunization is its internal mechanism [*ingranaggio*]: the fold that in some way separates community from itself, sheltering it from an unbearable excess.[67]

Akerman's *From the Other Side* is a study of the fence as a sheltering fold, both material and psychic, that divides the biopolitical distributions of sensibility from within. It paints a critical image of the fence as a technology of separation by which the psyche closes itself off from its others and defends itself against "unbearable excess." Similarly, to note in passing, the U.S. border security system is also the topic of Paglen's *The Fence* (*Lake Kickapoo, Texas*; 2010), an electromagnetic image of radar surveillance of the entire United States, which tracks any (nonstealth) object flying over the country. The microwave frequencies of the surveillance field, which encloses within itself a hermetic whole, have been changed into frequencies of the visible spectrum, resulting in a picture that resembles an inverted sunset, with hues of yellow in the upper part of the image gradually turning into dark red in the lower part. The basis of the image is similar to that of vision machines carrying out their task of tracking and processing data that elude the human eye and traditional modes of representation. It amounts to a moment of awareness through vague impressions of hues of color by which observers can realize that what they ordinarily take for real in sense perception is pervaded by hidden domains of activity—a redistribution of the sensible that makes the invisible both visible and intelligible.

Akerman's *From the Other Side* also invites observers to question dominant ways of partitioning reality by summoning the self-critical demonstrative powers of the image. On its "fragile surfaces," as Rancière describes the film, it composes "a proposition on what it is that is given to see to us and an interrogation into the power of representation."[68] Yet the aesthetic tactics it employs differ from those in Paglen's *Drone Vision*, revolving around the production of participatory perceptual constellations through analogy rather than through aniconic disarticulation. In lateral long takes and tracking shots, *From the Other Side* studies the fence's patchwork-like structure both by day and by night, alternating shots of urban as well as rural landscapes with interviews on both sides. The rhythm of editing is pointedly slow; the duration of things and events is almost tangible in the video's quiet images, which verge on stillness. The fence on the Arizona-Sonora border, far from being a covert expression of multibillion-dollar technologies and data, is shown as an omnipresent but clumsy and all-too-visible structure. Indeed, its obstructive materiality is precisely its raison d'être. Its imposing presence partitions geopolitical space, marking the boundaries of sovereign territories, of property and law; but, just as important, it partitions embodied and mental space, sensing and making sense.

It is these psychogeographic partitionings that *From the Other Side* seeks to challenge, if not overturn, by demanding a particular kind of cognitive engagement from the observer. In one compelling scene, three Mexicans linger by the fence, while two U.S. Border Patrol agents watch them from the other side (figure 4.4). There certainly are exchanges of looks and perhaps words as well, but, at first glance, it appears that the two types of reality portrayed are fundamentally asymmetrical. The sensibilities do not meet; there is not only a physical but also a mental rift between them. Yet this key scene also demands that we embrace something besides mere separation. Instead of simply accentuating difference, it emphasizes alliance; its

Figure 4.4
Mexicans and U.S. Border Patrol agents by the fence on the U.S.-Mexican border. Chantal Akerman, *From the Other Side* (2002).

composition invites us to perceive both difference and sameness. It evokes a reflective frame of mind that, as Stafford puts it, "searches for some order while recognizing that, at every instant, it needs some similarities-in-difference, some analogues."[69]

Conceptually at least, the scene resembles those visually ambiguous figures that play with the coherence of perception, and that show us plainly how our consciousness cannot hold two different perceptual states at the same time.[70] But this does not mean that our consciousness, with its errant jumps and cuts, or what William James called "perches and flights,"[71] cannot synthesize elements and occasions that, at first sight, seem incoherent and contradictory. There is a particular cognitive power to the portrayal of the fence in this scene in that, by showing separation, it draws connections. It is "analogical" not so much in the technical sense of the term as in its logic of demonstration, which promotes creative thought based on the perceptual weaving and formulation of alliances through difference rather than through reasoning in clear and distinct categories. It invites us to construct pairs of shifting, mirroring patterns in which, as Alfred North Whitehead explains the powers of analogy, "either [pattern] illustrates what in part the other is."[72]

By creating visual ambiguity, the scene amounts to what Stafford might describe as "the aesthetics of the perceptual jump,"[73] referring to how our gaze can wander through and across established divisions and categories. Its long duration gives us the opportunity not to (pro)actively anticipate the next image, but to study how the surface visually patterns itself and to gradually make sense of its vague and subtle impressions. It evokes perception as "being struck that something is, or can be, connected to something else."[74]

Rather than viewing this connection-seeking and contemplative way of perception as an anomaly, we should understand how it underlies any act of thinking that searches for accords and affinities between individualities in its quest for meaning. "The whole understanding of the world," Whitehead writes, "consists in the analysis of process in terms of the identities and diversities of the individuals involved. The peculiarities of the individuals are reflected in the peculiarities of the common process which is their interconnection."[75] Understanding proceeds not simply by recognizing how this or that individual differs from others, but by establishing relations of similitude and equivalence, which relate to the common forms of processes rather than to any fixed and predetermined identity, to "the togetherness of things in occasions of experience."[76] In other words, analogical thinking by its very nature forms patterns in searching for links and resemblances to make sense of what is happening. A key feature of this mode of thought is how it undermines the subject-predicate form of expression, which, Ralph Pred points out, "serves to disembody perception and to erect into syntactic rigidity the disconnection of subject and object."[77] Analogical thinking draws on the mutual interpenetrations and interrelatedness that it brings into appearance. In doing so, Whitehead tells us, it encounters potentiality. As it abstracts similitudes in the actualities of the present, it also affirms the relevance of the present moment to the past and thus measures what could be. "Immediacy," Whitehead writes, "is the realization of the potentialities of the past, and is the storehouse of the potentialities of the future."[78]

It is precisely through such an analogical way of thinking and seeing that *From the Other Side* seeks to acknowledge the reality of the situation on the Sonora-Arizona border, promoting the immanence of perception and thought able to embrace the "togetherness of things." Seeking to conceptualize alternative models of consciousness to modernity's preoccupation with categorical difference and negative dialectics, Stafford turns to analogy both as a primordial visual capacity that brings what is divided and separated into unison and as "a key feature of discernment" that helps us form ideas—mental scenes—from elusive and vague sensory cues.[79] Analogy is a way of mental imaging or mapping that cross-references between between distant and near, self and other, proper and improper. Analogical thought discovers what Stafford calls "appropriate affinities" between things and events. It creatively weaves together individuated and apparently incommensurable phenomena and "regroups them into new coordinations," testifying to the plastic powers of our mind-brains to integrate the unlabeled universe by crossing over distances.[80]

From the Other Side gives this type of analogical consciousness its potentially political relevance by building unseen and discomforting conjunctions. There is another moment when it particularly invites such cross-referential and heterogeneous thinking, which seeks to regroup the visible into new coordinations and to remap the maps we ordinarily make of the situations we live in or are thrown into. Roughly halfway through the single-channel version of the artwork, there is a moment of transition when we are gradually taken across the border: a prolonged, quiet, and uneventful shot of the fence from the Mexican side is followed by an equally prolonged and quiet shot taken from the U.S. side, showing a sign that announces: "Stop the crime wave! Our property and environment is being trashed by the invaders!" (figures 4.5 and 4.6). The sign's message anticipates the thoughts of a couple interviewed later in the film, who own a ranch in the borderlands and who give voice to the workings of the post-9/11 imagination in this remote region. Taking up his partner's worry that the flow of Mexican immigrants could take over and "do a lot of damage," the man explains: "One of our biggest fears actually with the Mexico people coming in, and I know there hasn't been very many cases, but the disease, above anything else, okay? Smallpox and stuff like this, which hasn't—but who's to say it won't—you see what I mean, you know?" And the woman continues: "And there's not enough vaccine for everybody ..."

The immunopolitical overtones of the couple's concerns are obvious, echoing the mainstream media's portrayal of unauthorized immigration as a dangerous breach of national security. They imply that trespassing on property amounts to an assault on the body's sovereignty; the human

Figure 4.5
The fence in the Sonoran Desert. Chantal Akerman, *From the Other Side* (2002).

Figure 4.6
A sign on the U.S.-Mexican border. Chantal Akerman, *From the Other Side* (2002).

organism itself is considered a form of property and the individual person an agent having the rights of self-ownership and self-defense. Ed Cohen notes that this kind of "possessive individual" emerged in the writings of John Locke and Thomas Hobbes, to become an integral part of modern forms of government and capitalist social and economic relations. "To live as body-possessing legal subjects," he argues, "we must first radically abstract ourselves from the lifeworld within which we exist and define ourselves as distinct from the material contexts that make our lives viable."[81] Abstracting ourselves within clearly demarcated perimeters means violently carving imaginary domains of sovereignty out of the material universe, domains predicated on the illusion of self-possession and self-sustainability.

On the other hand, incisions into the dominant conditions of sensibility such as *From the Other Side* makes can breach this cognitive code of immunization. Paradigmatic of this kind of critical gesture in the video's 180-degree cut in the moment of transition, a cut that takes us from the Mexican to the U.S. side of the border (figures 4.5 and 4.6). Whereas the fence has until now, in shots taken from the Mexican side, been consistently situated to the right of the mise-en-scène, we are suddenly facing it from another angle, and the positioning of the sign on the left side of the fence in particular renders our geographical orientation ambiguous. In the thin moment of this spatial trick, it is unclear exactly who or what is meant by "Our Property and Environment."[82] In this sudden shift in perspective, an intuition emerges of boundaries that have become obscure: our spatial disorientation causes the meaning of the word "Our" to vacillate uncertainly between "us" and "them," "host" and "invader." The cut seeks to establish a notion of common process, of commensurability between the two sides. In this fleeting instant, the reality that images convey appears as unlabeled and unstructured, and we need to adapt to it anew by creating mappings and groupings that can address this changing situation, where things and events are cross-referenced in unordinary and unforeseen ways. *From the Other Side* thus touches off the powers of analogy in the minds of its observers by inculcating new patterns and connections, which, rather than comfortably reiterating established categories, have no solid grounding.

The video attempts to overturn the Janus-faced logic of biopolitical immunization that takes place through the often violent negation of the other. It compels us to decipher a shared common pattern between alternative perceptual interpretations. We cannot determine what is the same and what is different. Distinctions between self and nonself, inside and outside, or figure and ground no longer make straightforward sense. This converges with how Esposito describes immunity in its affirmative and positive sense: it conceives of the nonself in terms other than preventive dissolution. Drawing on certain recent developments in immunology, Esposito writes:

> If the external antigen is "seen" from the inside as an antibody, just as, from another perspective, the antibody assumes the function of the antigen, what occurs in this fashion, rather than a confrontation between two different positions, is a comparison; or better, a continuous exchange, between an internalized outside and an externalized inside. In this way, far from being the result of an exclusion—or even a selection—of the differences, it becomes their own result.[83]

In this "perspectival" view, the equilibrium of the immune system and the differentiations between inside and outside it implies are merely temporary and contingent results of continuous encounters and interchanges between elements. At moments of exchange, the outside becomes internalized, and the inside externalized. At the heart of the immune system, according to Esposito, lies "the experience of its own original alteration. Before any other transformation, each body is already exposed to the need for its own exposure."[84] In this analysis, the immune system can define itself not by closing itself off, but only through its fundamental openness.

So powerfully do the images of *From the Other Side* weave together disparate phenomena that both differentiations and identities become relative and even redundant. The political significance of the analogical mode of thought lies in its visual deciphering of reversible correspondences, rather than in its identification of what lies outside as a risk or threat—indeed, it acknowledges how the inside and the outside actually breach each another. The cuts and compositions that shape the movement of images in this video show that life's continuity can be affirmed in ways fundamentally different from militarized acts of immunization. In the dominant visual economy, where screen-based mediations hold the power of defensive mediation, *From the Other Side* shows how images can also operate as "anti-immunizing" forces that externalize our fundamental openness to alterity. Like antigens, they can compel the body to change its composition, at least by cognitively assuming analogous shifts and transitions. It is in this encounter with the infectious mimicry of things and beings that the biopolitical subject's immunopolitical constitution starts to come apart.

Anachronism: Colonial Ghosts

Our exploration of the aesthetico-political potential of contemporary video has taken us from aniconic tactics that self-reflexively divest images of their modulatory powers to analogical montage that, drawing on our mind-brains' recombinatorial ways of visual sense making, undermines the dominant affective-cognitive models of subjectivation. At issue in both kinds of critical incisions is how to effect ruptures—breaks or gaps—in the current redistribution of the ways the sensible order is organized, in the reediting of the cuts that shape our existence and its temporal textures in particular. Whereas aniconicity in Paglen's *Drone Vision* achieves discontinuity by freezing the movement of images and holding them at a standstill, to make us aware of their fundamental powerlessness, analogical montage in *From the Other Side* achieves discontinuity by juxtaposing seemingly disparate elements, to make us aware of the exchanges and interpenetrations that boundaries and separations obscure. Both approaches, however, work against and instigate breaks in the present or, more precisely, in the power invested in images to police the present. Both are characterized by untimeliness and anachronicity in that, even as they address what is happening in the present, they also seek to dislocate the present and subordinate it to a function different from the one ordinarily assigned it. Christine Ross detects in contemporary moving image art a general tendency to explore perceptual limitedness through the suspension of time, which is "both experienced and disclosed but also potentially unlocked and released to activate a temporal passage outside the parameters of progress, teleology and linear succession."[85] Likewise, in Paglen's and Akerman's works, the present moment is held in suspense and cracked open in its potentiality through aesthetic devices that disturb perception, exposing it to unforeseen combinations.

In theorizing about ruptures in ordinary conceptions of time and the predefined roles and functions of things and beings, Gilles Deleuze quotes Friedrich Nietzsche's definition of the "untimely": the "acting counter to our time and thereby acting on our time and, let us hope, for the benefit of a time to come."[86] For Deleuze, every present state of affairs holds the potential of "counteractualization," with a past and a future that cannot be deduced from the now but that can be probed as the alternative to something yet to come, particularly in artistic creations.[87] Viewed in this sense, images can counteractualize themselves as materializations of the present moment's determinacy—of, say, the inevitable military or financial catastrophe that is always just around the corner in today's preemptive politics. A key feature to consider here is that images, though embedded in their sociohistorical context, also bear within themselves traces from the past and anticipations of an unruly and unexpected future consisting of concealed unconscious tracks that run against prevailing models of sense making. Ghostly "actors" that can leap through epochs and interrupt the present with their untimely apparitions, images "carry a temporal form within themselves," Belting tells us, "but they are also … as 'anachronistic,' as outside time as we are ourselves."[88]

The image's complex temporality emerged as an epistemological and ontological concern already in the early twentieth century—particularly in the works of Walter Benjamin and of Aby Warburg—with the advent of motion pictures, which became a potent metaphor for resuscitating the life of things past on the cinema screen's illuminated surface. Benjamin wrote how, with cinema, "a truly new region of consciousness" emerged that discovered "the dynamite of tenths of a second" and so exploded "this old world of incarceration leading us into adventurous journeys among the scattered ruins."[89] Cinema's ability to link and delink images—to make unfold "all the forms of perception, the tempos and rhythms, which lie preformed in today's machines"[90]—heralded, in Benjamin's eyes, a potentially emancipatory moment of awareness that embraced the past as a recurring force in the present, and thus as a dynamic means of encountering the now in a new light. This type of awareness is enlivened by what Benjamin called "dialectical images," "wherein what has been comes together in a flash with the now to form a constellation"[91]—a sudden revelation of what has been in the now. These images embody a historical consciousness that works through juxtapositions and evocations between figures to establish extratemporal correspondences between different sheets of time and to demonstrate the contingency of the present as merely one of many possible results. "In other words," Benjamin wrote, "image is dialectics at a standstill. For while the relation of the present to the past is purely temporal, the relation of what-has-been to the now is dialectical: not temporal in nature but figural [*bildlich*]."[92]

A similar kind of suspension of time, of a differential movement of the past in the present, is manifest in Warburg's anthropological conceptualization of images, in which cinema again figures as a key epistemic model. As most clearly evident in his *Mnemosyne Atlas* project begun in 1924—collages of visual and textual material created according to a common "idea"—art historian Warburg sought to analyze images as parts of larger constellations made up of heterogeneous rhythms, whereby traces (pictorial motifs, figures) from the past outlive their original moment of construction and recur in the present, instigating anachronistic correspondences and linkages. By putting images together in a manner akin to filmic editing, one could understand the cross-temporal undercurrent of images in the human psyche. Warburg's underlying assumption was that each image is overcharged with temporal energy, with the ability to survive (*Nachleben*), which facilitates latent alliances of images across historical periods even if they have been obscured by changing sociocultural circumstances.[93] According to Georges Didi-Huberman, Warburg saw images as also inherently traumatic, or "symptomatic," by nature, as incorporations of a past that the mind in many ways hopes to have forgotten but that stubbornly resists oblivion and persists as unrecognized and unconscious forces in the affective and cognitive patterns through which we make sense of the world.[94] Hence the atlas's role as a map helping us to orient ourselves against what Giorgio Agamben called the "schizophrenia" of our imagination.[95]

To bring these considerations to bear on the ways images can manifest their anachronistic powers within the contemporary context, let us take a last example, Steve McQueen's single-channel video installation *Gravesend* (2007), which is about the mining of columbite-tantalite (coltan) in the Democratic Republic of Congo. McQueen's installation takes us from the immunopolitics of current military-surveillance screens used in war zones and on the U.S.-Mexican border to the technomaterial underpinnings of contemporary visual economies. The mineral that *Gravesend* focuses on, colloquially called "coltan," is used in producing electronic devices such as DVD players, game consoles, cell phones, iPads, liquid crystal display screens, and digital cameras. It is particularly important to today's capacitor industry, being partly responsible for the increasing miniaturization of the "smart" devices we so readily consume and fetishize.[96]

Screen technologies feed on scarce natural resources, among them coltan; indeed, without these, the circulation of images and imaginations on which biopolitical power and the neoliberal economy are based would not be possible. In this respect, the Democratic Republic of Congo, where civil wars and other, more "minor scale" armed conflicts have been fought in search of this mineral over the last twenty years, is emblematic of today's neocolonial reality. Its weak state infrastructure facilitates the largely illicit mining of the mineral (from pits controlled by armed groups, for instance), which through the hands of various parties finds its way to processing plants in Europe, Asia, and North America, and finally to the circuit boards of electronic and digital devices sold by international brand name corporations such as Apple, Canon, Dell, Nokia, Samsung, and Sony Ericsson.[97] The movements and end uses of the mineral thus exemplify how advanced industrialized economies are connected to one of the poorest countries on earth, and how the accumulation of capital in global circuits of production and consumption is still based on the exploitation of physical labor and scarce natural resources.[98] Thus the biopolitics of screens does not merely concern the ways prosuming brains animate and are animated by images circulating in global digital networks; it is undergirded by the appropriation, molding, and exploitation of minerals and working bodies. The movement and evolution of images in today's world is inextricably bound up in the ways the vitality of the earth's crust and of those who labor upon it is turned into property and a source of profit.

Gravesend taps into this darker side of today's visual economy, exploring linkages between technological advancement and the seemingly remote exploitation of natural resources amid war and lawlessness. The installation opens with precision camerawork surveying the efficient movements of automated machines in an English processing plant where columbite-tantalite is refined. Shots of this plant and its faceless workers are soon intercut with footage of the surface of the earth and male bodies shoveling ore in a jungle somewhere in the Congo (figure 4.7). The sounds of the pneumatic devices in the English plant are juxtaposed with the silence of the Congo images. Then, a double exposure between the bodies and the dark silhouettes of factory chimney stacks against the yellow and red hues of a sunset over an industrial port in Gravesend, Kent, takes us back to England (figure 4.8). A factory machine appears, intercut with toiling laborers in the Congo, their hands hammering the mineral from rocks shown in close-ups.

Figure 4.7
Digging for coltan in the Democratic Republic of Congo. Steve McQueen, *Gravesend* (2007). Image © Steve McQueen. Courtesy of Thomas Dane Gallery.

Figure 4.8
Sunset over an industrial port in Gravesend, Kent, England. Steve McQueen, *Graves-end* (2007). Image © Steve McQueen. Courtesy of Thomas Dane Gallery.

Gravesend is structured around such repetitive juxtapositions in which industrial machines evoke human gestures, laboring bodies are cross-referenced with an industrial port. Its various double exposures are pregnant with a past that is not directly shown but only suggested. The estuary in Gravesend at dusk is also where Joseph Conrad's *Heart of Darkness* (1899) begins, the anonymous narrator recounting his encounter with Charles Marlow, who reminisces about his search for Kurtz on a boat traveling up the River Congo in the Congo Free State, ruled by Leopold II of Belgium. "The day was ending in a serenity of still and exquisite brilliance," the narrator says. "The water shone pacifically; the sky, without a speck, was a benign immensity of unstained light; the very mist on the Essex marshes was like a gauzy and radiant fabric, hung from the wooded rises inland, and draping the low shores in diaphanous folds."[99] The double exposure in *Gravesend* does not simply elicit a perceptual transfer between two different locations in the global now, from the harsh conditions of the coltan mines in the Congo to the calm, postcard-like view of the port in England, but also suggests movements between two different temporal registers, creating a feedback loop between images from the colonial past and those circulating in the neoliberal present.

Marlow's account of his journey involves the imperial imagination of conquest that fueled industrial and consumer capitalism in the late nineteenth and early twentieth centuries. The extraction of precious natural resources, especially india rubber—used in such products as the pneumatic bicycle tire invented in the 1890s, hoses, tubes, washers, wiring insulation, and later the automobile[100]—was the main motivation for the conquest of the Congo. Congo Free State was very much a private enterprise of King Leopold II's, where the sovereign rule of the state, a form of politico-juridical rationality, mixed lethally with the economic imperative to maximize profit from the colony's natural resources and native labor force. In the Congo, what Foucault described as "the controlled insertion of bodies into the machinery of production and the adjustment of the phenomena of population to economic processes" indispensable to the development of capitalism, turned into a notoriously deadly enterprise.[101] The organized use of violence (killing, mutilation, unlawful detention) was the main strategy employed in the exploitation of nature and physical labor, both by government officials and the concession companies that operated in parts of the country. The whole "Free State" was put under a state of exception, where the rule of law was suspended and instrumentalized as a strategy in the project of capital accumulation.[102]

Roger Casement, an Irishman working as British consul to the Congo Free State, noted in his governmental report how armed men employed by concession companies had "engaged in military operations on a somewhat extensive scale."[103] Brutal and arbitrary violence was also routinely exercised by the Force Publique, native troops commanded by European officers who were tasked with enforcing the state's rubber quotas. Casement cites a 1899 diary entry, in which a chief state prosecutor (aptly named "Roy" [Roi]) explains what these troops did:

> M. Roy said, "Each time the corporal goes out to get rubber, cartridges are given to him. He must bring back all not used; and for every one used, he must bring back a right hand." M. Roy told me that sometimes they shot a cartridge at an animal in hunting; then they cut off a hand from a living man. As to the extent to which this is carried on, he informed me that in six months they, the State, on the Momboyo River, had used 6,000 cartridges, which means that 6,000 people are killed or mutilated.[104]

Testimonies of this kind, poignantly present in the historical imaginary of colonialism, evoke the close-ups of the diggers gathering the black mineral from rocks cracked open with an iron rod in *Gravesend*. As a collection of ghostly memories from the colonial era, Casement's report is rife with examples of extrajudicial killings and the systematic exploitation of slave labor. This past, *Gravesend* elusively suggests, recurs in the mining sites of present-day Congo, where labor is cheap and child labor common, and where prisoners are made to work in the pits. Systematic killings by armed groups are everyday occurrences, as is sexual violence against women.[105] Production and "antiproduction," life and death, supplement and complement each other in the vicious circles of capitalist imagery.

But the ways *Gravesend* effects its critique are quite subtle. The violence against the miners is not directly shown, and its genealogy is merely alluded to with ambiguous visual cues. As T. J. Demos notes, "the film's 'documentation' is far from traditional; rather, McQueen's figures are unidentified, mere shadows, and fragmented shapes, which dismantles the epistemological presumptions of traditional documentary modes of exposure and journalistic reportage."[106] Furthermore, *Gravesend* undermines any phenomenological truth claim that images often make about present or past facts. In *Gravesend*, shot mostly on 35 mm film, a short animation scene disturbs the unfolding of photorealistic visuals toward the end of the video: a black, river-like, flowing shape, accompanied by cacophonous sounds from radio and television transmissions. It is as though the noise of the real-time communications we make with our electronic and digital devices emerged from the flow, which we associate at once with the flow of the black mineral in our devices, the flow of the River Congo, deeply seated in the Western colonial imagination, and the aberrant flow of time—in particular, the persistence of the past in our perceptions and thoughts.

Gravesend refuses to distinguish between memory and imagination, documentary and fiction. The past recurs on its surfaces not as an index of its obsoleteness, but as a disturbing force that affects how we are able to inhabit and make sense of the present. The texture of the real becomes susceptible to emergent, unruly patterns, which compel our imaginations to wander across temporal layers. In particular, the double exposure between the Thames estuary in Gravesend now and then—between the apparent (perception) and the invisible (memory)—makes colonial ghosts intrude into and haunt our senses. This short moment of perceptual dislocation can thus be considered a potential break, a rupture, which yields new figures of the thinkable by means of the juxtaposition and evocation of images. The felt materiality of screen technologies and the present moment of their experience becomes a matter of reinterpretation through figural correspondences, which makes us aware of the laboring hands and scarce raw materials that underpin our high-technology culture and of the weight of the past that each of our electronic devices carries within itself.

In this sense, the double exposure converges with what Benjamin wrote about the dialectical image as an arresting cut in our thinking, a cut that uproots prevalent paradigms of understanding and divests the now of its habitual recognizability. "To thinking belongs the movement as well as the arrest of thoughts," he explained. "Where thinking comes to a standstill in a constellation saturated with tensions—there the dialectical image appears. It is the caesura in the movement of thoughts. ... It is to be found, in a word, where the tension between dialectical opposites is greatest."[107] Benjamin spoke of such sudden moments in terms of the "interpenetration of images," whereby time turns upon itself.[108] The dialectical image appears like a "flash" in which what has been suddenly emerges in the now.[109] It amounts to a momentary halt in a movement or process; as

Didi-Huberman observes, it effects a counterrhythm in the ordinary course of events.[110]

Such a counterrhythm is what *Gravesend* brings forth in its composition, which creates tensions and interpenetrations between the bodies laboring in today's coltan mines and the bodies of those killed in the colonial conquest of the same region of Africa. Indeed, as Demos notes, "by depicting laboring bodies in the Congo, *Gravesend* mounts a political contestation by rendering visible those typically excluded from globalization's imaginary."[111] It achieves the repartitioning of this imaginary through extratemporal layering, which draws on the ability of our analogical imaginations to bring heterogeneous, even opposing elements together into a constellation—laboring hands with severed ones, india rubber with coltan, the past Thames estuary with the present one. A particular kind of reentry of images is at work here, this time in terms of the spontaneous emergence of anachronistic combinations and reflections that map the biopolitical present with respect to its temporal excess.

The critical incision *Gravesend* makes into the biopolitical regime of sensibility draws on how the felt reality both within and without our bodies, once externalized and modulated on the screen, can change our awareness of the technological mediations shaping the ways we sense the world. The visible is juxtaposed with and reflected in vague, perhaps already forgotten traces of the past; this produces something new, something emergent that exceeds, or counteractualizes, the present state of affairs. In doing so, it invokes potentiality in thought. In cracking open the present moment, the past becomes a force of novelty and frees the present from being the condition of futurity. At the same time, the past becomes the power by which critical awareness, as in a double exposure, grasps an image of something beyond what is apparent. With its elusive figural associations and frail imaginary threads, *Gravesend* compels us to reevaluate and reinterpret the given real, causing the future to refract in the openness and unknowability of the present.

Aniconic mirrorings that divest military imagery of its claimed powers, analogical modes of thought that overturn the immunitary logic of biopolitics, anachronistic montages that summon the colonial past so as to generate new figures of the thinkable—these are merely a few of the possible critical tactics in contemporary screen culture. But these few demonstrate tendencies and directions in the life of images that effectively challenge prevailing ways of sensing and making sense and their attendant models of individuation. This chapter has sought to show how images can counteractualize the exchanges and mediations of affective and cognitive dispositions prevalent in today's visual economy—and the posttraumatic logic that defines them. The works discussed put forward modulations of our times that differ markedly from those we encountered in the previous chapters. Thus, they tell us, the past is not a private horror movie to be erased by technological means; the future is not the realm of anticipated catastrophe the financial-military apparatus seeks to turn it into; and the present is not an impoverished now between a forgotten past and a securitized future. Instead, pierced by the past, which introduces contingency and novelty, and by the future, which carries transformation and alteration into it, the present can be seen as emergent, open to potentiality.

Such modulations of the temporal fabric of our existence can become the seeds of critical political consciousness. They point toward a realm of the political where the demands of the finance economy do not dominate, where biopolitics does not control the potentials of our lives, but where the elements and processes of the biopolitical system may begin to bifurcate and become "subject to drifting."[112] Rather than speculate on the contents of this consciousness, however, the works discussed simply stand for its possibility. And, rather than rooting their observers within an already apportioned or anticipated alternative perceptual world, they generate affective and cognitive indeterminacy as well as aesthetic indifference. Crucially, these represent the first workings of imagination—of the aberrant, inadvertent movements of images that animate our gestures and thoughts, whether brutal or discreet, submissive or critical, shallow or shrewd.

Critical thinking starts in the kinds of gaps that each of the analyzed works produces in the dominant ways of sensing and making sense. It is fueled by disidentification, which is precisely what aesthetic experimentations can accomplish. We should be careful not to assume any direct connection between aesthetic experience and political subjectivation, between a work's composition and embodied political reality. On the contrary, if Rancière is right, no work of art manages "to sidestep the incalculable tension between political dissensuality and aesthetic indifference."[113]

But these tensions—and the associations and dissociations that various montages of images encompass—are what we have in common and can share. They are where possibility lurks. They hold the seeds of imagination, where the world must first be staged before it can be realized. It is in the reentrant movement of images that we can reconsider and rearticulate the times of our lives, the past becoming a force that lets us realize the present in its unpredictability and affirm the future in a way that defies what is expected of it.

Epilogue

Melanie Gilligan's video *Popular Unrest* (2010) pictures a future world governed by global capitalism—an apparatus of profitability that has grown beyond anyone's control. The source of the apparatus' life and power are our bodies and minds, the "sum total," the video tells us, "of all interactions between everyone on earth doing exactly what they please every day." Lurking everywhere at every moment, the apparatus subjects every aspect of our lives—how much time we spend at work, what we consume, our physical fitness, our sexual habits, and much more—to constant monitoring and calculation. It scans our brains in order to abstract and control our imaginations and dreams. It measures our behavior to profit from feelings of closeness and intimacy. Finally, it kills its subjects in endless self-perpetuating wars, turning a politics of nurturing life into a politics of disseminating death.

Made after the crash of 2007–08, *Popular Unrest* proposes an allegory of the present moment by envisioning a possible future. In this future, nothing has changed since the financial meltdown; the apparatus that turns our lives and every corner of the planet into exchange value keeps on heading, step by step, toward the complete destruction of itself and its subjects. The video seeks to reveal how the present is apportioned and ruled by casting it as an alternative future. Drawing on the kinds of popular images that largely define our everyday life worlds—television commercials professing to promote our health and fitness, computer-generated animations functioning as avatars of ourselves, TV dramas filling our moments of boredom, neuroscientific visualizations scanning our psyches—it seeks to overturn the functions and roles of these images and imaginations. Crucially, *Popular Unrest* shows the images not as facts of the now, but as signs of the future, a possible world that closely resembles ours. The critical momentum of the video lies in its casting what we recognize to be our present reality as something that is only possible, thus injecting possibility into the facticity of the here and now. In short, *Popular Unrest* "virtualizes" the events and actions that shape the present into potential events and actions, one possible set of such events and actions among many others.

Hopefully similarly virtualizing in its effects, *Biopolitcal Screens* has provided a series of figurations of how screen-based mediations work in the current world. It has explored the movement of images as part of the biopolitical apparatus in charge of our lives today—a "blind and mute" system, as Deleuze characterized it, that makes us speak of and see ourselves, perceive the world and other around us, and act in particular ways. In this respect, the book has sought to relate current screens and the kinds of images animated on them to the fabrication of the "neoliberal brain," a key anthropological figure the apparatus has manufactured for its own purposes.

We have seen how, in the context of video game and virtual reality technology, an unprecedented regime of popular "imageness" has emerged, one that represents a new aspect in visual culture, at least when it comes to embodiment and engagement. At issue are behavioristic images, which curate our perceptions and memories and teach affective and cognitive adaptation to a world of struggle, risk, and survival. These images are the key to understanding how power works in contemporary societies. They are meant to provide relief from the traumatic pasts that the biopolitical apparatus generates. But above all, they crystallize in their aesthetic the logics of anticipation and preemption that define biopolitics today, ranging from the neuroscientific episteme that formulates the truths about who we are to the finance economy and the current wars waged in pursuit of capital accumulation. In the view of biopolitics, the unknowability and contingency of the future have already been weighed and played out in the present; the unexpected has been turned into an impoverished "will have been."

Seen from this perspective, the domination of our lives hinges on erased pasts and securitized futures. But time is a dialectic force that cannot be so easily tamed. Within the present moment of experience, ruptures or tears in the ruling distributions of sensing and making sense can spontaneously occur, produced by the imagination in its role of bringing together and sampling images. When removed from their original contexts and brought into unruly constellations, images come to reflect back on their own making and activity, and thus to undo and redo themselves. We have seen this take place in artistic interventions into the perceptual arrangements of the military-security complex (Paglen), the cognitive logic of immunization in neoliberalism (Akerman), and the technomaterial underpinnings of the current screen culture (McQueen). These works make critical cuts into and rearrangements of the movies running in our brains. They compel unexpected affiliations between things and beings and give rise to new figures of the thinkable—figures that cut across established categories and bind the future to the present in its openness. In this way, they bring forth the "emergent present," a moment of imagination and thinking that can picture what is not yet but could be.

If every image is ontogenic by nature, bringing forth an embodied reality, then imagination signals the power of images to mirror or countermimic their own composition and thus generate something new and unexpected, something that was not already. As such, imagination can also be seen as the definitive source and power of critique. And if ours is indeed a disillusioned world populated by atomistic individuals, or "neoliberal brains," whose past is a recurrent nightmare of catastrophe and whose future has been deprived of its promise (other than the deathliness of militarization and financialization), we have an acute need for acts of imagination that can configure alternative temporalities, in particular, future possibilities open to alterity. Every image holds the seeds of this aberrant force of time. By means of devices such as montage, we can unleash this force. What we need are montages that critically tap into and reveal the patterns shaping existence even as they invent new ones—and that bring things together.

Notes

Preface

1. For a more detailed discussion of "economy" in this sense, see Marie-José Mondzain, *Image, Icon, Economy: The Byzantine Origins of the Contemporary Imaginary*, trans. Rico Franses (Stanford: Stanford University Press, 2005), 18–66.

2. See Pasi Väliaho, *Mapping the Moving Image: Gesture, Thought and Cinema circa 1900* (Amsterdam: Amsterdam University Press, 2010).

3. Giorgio Agamben, "Difference and Repetition: On Guy Debord's Films," trans. Brian Holmes, in *Art and the Moving Image: A Critical Reader*, ed. Tanya Leighton (London: Tate, 2008), 328–333.

4. David Panagia, *The Political Life of Sensation* (Durham: Duke University Press, 2009), 3.

5. W. J. T. Mitchell, *What Do Pictures Want? The Lives and Loves of Images* (Chicago: University of Chicago Press, 2005), 11.

6. Hans Belting, *An Anthropology of Images: Picture, Medium, Body*, trans. Thomas Dunlap (Princeton: Princeton University Press, 2011), 36.

7. Nicholas Mirzoeff, *The Right to Look: A Counterhistory of Visuality* (Durham: Duke University Press, 2011), 3.

8. Tim Ingold, *Being Alive: Essays on Movement, Knowledge and Description* (London: Routledge, 2011), 3.

9. Michel Foucault, *Security, Territory, Population: Lectures at the Collège de France 1977–1978*, trans. Graham Burchell, ed. Michel Senellart (Basingstoke: Palgrave Macmillan, 2007), 70.

10. Melinda Cooper, *Life as Surplus: Biotechnology and Capitalism in the Neoliberal Era* (Seattle: University of Washington Press, 2008), 19.

11. I use "training" here in Walter Benjamin's sense. See Benjamin, "The Work of Art in the Age of Its Technological Reproducibility: Second Version," trans.

Edmund Jephcott and Harry Zohn, in *Selected Writings*, vol. 3: *1935–1938*, ed. Howard Eiland and Michael W. Jennings (Cambridge, MA: Belknap Press, 2002), 101–133; especially 108.

12. See Jacques Rancière, *Dissensus: On Politics and Aesthetics*, trans. and ed. Steven Corcoran. (London: Continuum, 2010).

13. Gilles Deleuze, *Foucault*, trans. Seán Hand (Minneapolis: University of Minnesota Press, 1988), 34–37.

Chapter 1

1. See Antonio Damasio, *The Feeling of What Happens: Body and Emotion in the Making of Consciousness* (San Diego: Harcourt, 1999), especially 9–11.

2. See Barbara Stafford, *Echo Objects: The Cognitive Work of Images* (Chicago: University of Chicago Press, 2007), 95.

3. See Aby Warburg, *Images from the Region of the Pueblo Indians of North America*, trans. Michael P. Steinberg (Ithaca: Cornell University Press, 1995), 35–38.

4. Aby Warburg, "Memories of a Journey through the Pueblo Region," in Philippe-Alain Michaud, *Aby Warburg and the Image in Motion*, trans. Sophie Hawkes (New York: Zone Books, 2004), 293–330; quotations on 324.

5. Ibid., 325. In his study on imagination and metaphor, Arnold Modell argues that, even if we no longer believe in the kind of "danced causality" that the Hopi ritual plays out, we are still open to the evocative power of images. Laden with fantasies, dreams, emotions, desires, and beliefs, images from paintings, photographs, films, video games and other sources animate the imaginations that make up our lived reality. See Modell, *Imagination and the Meaningful Brain* (Cambridge, MA: MIT Press, 2006), 183–192. According to Warburg, the evocative power of images is based on empathic engagement, which he conceptualized with his notion of "emotive formulas" (*Pathosformeln*), referring to those dynamic forms of movement such as gestures and postures in artistic and other kinds of pictures which reveal the inner emotions of the figures concerned and which animate motor and affective responses in their viewers. On Warburg's concept of emotive formula, see Kurt Forster, "Introduction," in Aby Warburg, *The Renewal of Pagan Antiquity: Contributions to the Cultural History of the European Renaissance*, trans. David Britt, ed. Kurt Forster (Los Angeles: Getty Research Institute, 1999), 1–75; especially 15.

6. See David Freedberg, *The Power of Images: Studies in the History and Theory of Response* (Chicago: University of Chicago Press, 1989), 32.

7. Barack Obama, as quoted in William Branigin, "Obama Will Not Release Bin Laden Photos, White House Says," *Washington Post*, May 4, 2011, http://www

.washingtonpost.com/national/cbs-obama-says-he-wont-release-bin-laden-photos/2011/05/04/AFyB5aoF_story.html?hpid=z1.

8. Freedberg, *The Power of Images*, 32.

9. See, for example, W. J. T. Mitchell, *Cloning Terror: The War of Images, 9/11 to the Present* (Chicago: University of Chicago Press, 2011), 21.

10. Gilbert Simondon, *Imagination et invention: 1965–1966*, ed. Nathalie Simondon (Chatou: Les Editions de la Transparence, 2008), 7, 13, 186.

11. Ibid., 9, 13. Translations from Simondon in this chapter and chapter 4 and from Jean-Luc Godard in chapter 4 are mine. The original French text reads: "Contenant en quelque mésure volonté, appétit et mouvement, elles apparaissent presque comme des organismes secondaires au sein de l'être pensant: parasites ou adjuvanttes, elles sont comme des monades secondaires habitant à certains moments le sujet et le quittant à certains autres."

12. "Every image," Simondon asserts, "is susceptible of being incorporated into a process of recurrence that can be either materializing or idealizing; inserted into fashion, art, monuments, technical objects, the image becomes the source of complex perceptions that generate movement, cognitive representation, affections and emotions." Ibid., 13. The original French text reads: "Toute image est susceptible de s'incorporer à un processus de récurrence matérialisant ou idéalisant; déposée dans la mode, l'art, les monuments, les objets techniques, l'image devient source de perceptions complexes éveillant mouvement, représentation cognitive, affections et émotions."

13. See Belting, *An Anthropology of Images*, 15.

14. Anne Friedberg, *The Virtual Window: From Alberti to Microsoft* (Cambridge, MA: MIT Press, 2006), 5.

15. Belting, *An Anthropology of Images*, 16. The analytical distinction Belting makes between the medium and the image corresponds to my distinction between the screen and the image in this book. "The image always has a mental quality," Belting writes, "the medium always a material one, even if they both form a single entity in our perception. The presence of the image, however, entails a deception, for the image is not present the same way its medium is present. It needs the act of animation by which our imagination draws it from its medium. In the process, the opaque medium becomes the transparent conduit for its image. The ambiguity of presence and absence extends even to the medium in which the image is born, for in reality it is not the medium but the spectator who engenders the image within his or her self." Ibid., 20.

16. Hans Belting, "Image, Medium, Body: A New Approach to Iconology," *Critical Inquiry* 31 (Winter 2005): 302–319; quotation on 306.

17. Mitchell, *What Do Pictures Want?*, 87.

18. See Belting, *An Anthropology of Images*, 15.

19. Ibid., 16.

20. Mondzain, *Image, Icon, Economy*, 22.

21. Ibid., 2–3.

22. Ibid., 151.

23. Ibid., 162.

24. On contemporary imperial visual economies, see Susan Buck-Morss, "Visual Empire," *diacritics* 37, nos. 2–3 (2007): 171–198.

25. See Belting, "Image, Medium, Body," 304. See also Mirzoeff, *The Right to Look*, 58.

26. On the cinema's contribution to modernity's self-perception, see, for example, Stanley Cavell, *The World Viewed: Reflections on the Ontology of Film*, enlarged ed. (Cambridge, MA: Harvard University Press, 1979), especially 16–23; Gilles Deleuze, *Cinema 1: The Movement-Image*, trans. Hugh Tomlinson and Barbara Habberjam (London: Athlone Press, 1986), especially 56–70; see also Väliaho, *Mapping the Moving Image*, especially 109–181.

27. I borrow the notion of "thanatographic" images from John Protevi, who develops it in *Political Affect: Connecting the Social and the Somatic* (Minneapolis: University of Minnesota Press, 2009), 159.

28. According to David Rodowick, for example, the appearance of digital media marks the demise of the metaphysical restlessness and curiosity analog film was supposed to convey, and the desire to view the world gives way to a desire to control and manipulate it. "In the highly mutable communities forged by computer-mediated communications," Rodowick writes, "the desire to know the world has lost its provocation and its uncertainty. Rather, one seeks new ways of acknowledging other minds, without knowing whether other selves are behind them." Rodowick, *The Virtual Life of Film* (Cambridge, MA: Harvard University Press, 2007), 175.

29. See Siegfried Kracauer, "The Mass Ornament," in *The Mass Ornament: Weimar Essays*, trans. and ed. Thomas Y. Levin (Cambridge, MA: Harvard University Press, 1995), 75–86.

30. Siegfried Kracauer, "Cult of Distraction: On Berlin's Picture Palaces," in *The Mass Ornament*, 323–328; quotation on 326.

31. Benjamin, "The Work of Art in the Age of Its Technological Reproducibility," 3:101–133; quotation on 3:108.

32. Miriam Bratu Hansen, "Room-for-Play: Benjamin's Gamble with Cinema," *October* 109 (Summer 2004): 3–45; quotation on 43.

33. See Jacques Rancière, *The Politics of Aesthetics*, trans. Gabriel Rockhill (London: Continuum, 2006), 12.

34. On the notion of the "postcinematic," see Steven Shaviro, "Post-Cinematic Affect: On Grace Jones, *Boarding Gate* and *Southland Tales*," *Film Philosophy* 14, no. 1 (2010), http://www.film-philosophy.com/index.php/f-p/article/view/220/173, which charts the novel capacities of digital media to affect us and to make us feel the world in the current neoliberal age. For Shaviro, "postcinematic" refers to "the emergence of a different media regime, and indeed of a different mode of production, than those which dominated the twentieth century. Digital technologies, together with neoliberal economic relations, have given birth to radically new ways of manufacturing and articulating lived experience." Ibid., 2.

35. See Sheldon Wolin, *Democracy Incorporated: Managed Democracy and the Specter of Inverted Totalitarianism* (Princeton: Princeton University Press, 2008).

36. See Nick Dyer-Witheford and Greig de Peuter, *Games of Empire: Global Capitalism and Video Games* (Minneapolis: University of Minnesota Press, 2009), 3–33.

37. Michel Foucault, *"Society Must Be Defended": Lectures at the Collège de France, 1975–1976*, trans. David Macey, ed. Mauro Bertani and Alessandro Fontana (London: Penguin, 2004), 15.

38. See James Der Derian, *Virtuous War: Mapping the Military-Industrial-Media-Entertainment Network*, 2nd ed. (New York: Routledge, 2009), 125–126.

39. Mitchell, *Cloning Terror*, xix.

40. See, for example, Wendy Hui Kyong Chun, *Programmed Visions: Software and Memory* (Cambridge, MA: MIT Press, 2011); Alexander Galloway, *Protocol: How Control Exists after Decentralization* (Cambridge, MA: MIT Press, 2006).

41. Rodowick, *The Virtual Life of Film*, 125.

42. See Mitchell, *What Do Pictures Want?*, 91.

43. Fuller refers to "dynamic systems in which any one part is always multiply connected, acting by virtue of those connections, and always variable, such that it can be regarded as a pattern rather than as an object." Matthew Fuller, *Media Ecologies: Materialist Energies in Art and Technoculture* (Cambridge, MA: MIT Press, 2005), 4.

44. On the concept of the screen, see Charles Acland, "The Crack in the Electric Window," *Cinema Journal* 51, no. 2 (2012): 169–173. On the materiality of contemporary screen technologies, see Sean Cubitt, "Current Screens," in *Imagery in the 21st Century*, ed. Oliver Grau with Thomas Veigl (Cambridge, MA: MIT Press, 2011), 21–35.

45. Jacques Rancière, *The Future of the Image*, trans. Gregory Elliott (London: Verso, 2009), 7.

46. Rancière, *The Politics of Aesthetics*, 12.

47. Gerald M. Edelman and Giulio Tononi, *A Universe of Consciousness: How Matter Becomes Imagination* (London: Penguin, 2000), 44–45.

48. Patricia Pisters, *The Neuro-Image: A Deleuzian Film-Philosophy of Digital Screen Culture* (Stanford: Stanford University Press, 2012), 148. On using neuroscientific concepts to understand the contemporary culture of advertising, for instance, see Warren Neidich, "From Noopower to Neuropower: How Mind Becomes Matter," in *Cognitive Architecture: From Biopolitics to Noopolitics; Architecture and Mind in the Age of Communication and Information*, ed. Deborah Hauptmann and Warren Neidich (Rotterdam: 010 Publishers, 2010), 538–581.

49. Pisters, *The Neuro-Image*, 17.

50. On the "cerebral" quality of virtual reality images in new media art, see Mark B. N. Hansen, *New Philosophy for New Media* (Cambridge, MA: MIT Press, 2004), 189–195.

51. On the gestural dynamic of new media, see Brian Rotman, *Becoming beside Ourselves: The Alphabet, Ghosts, and Distributed Human Being* (Durham: Duke University Press, 2008), 41–54.

52. See Gilles Deleuze and Félix Guattari, *Mille plateaux: Capitalisme et schizophrénie 2* (Paris: Les Editions de Minuit, 1980), 545–560.

53. See Jonathan Crary, *Suspensions of Perception: Attention, Spectacle and Modern Culture* (Cambridge, MA: MIT Press, 1999), 31.

54. Ibid., 39.

55. "Governmentality" was the key concept with which Foucault described the neoliberal mode of power, which is primarily concerned not with the sovereign juridical rule of a territory nor with the discipline of bodies and persons, but rather with governing the movements of free, active, and productive individuals, and their relationships with each other and with their material environment. It seeks to shape how people organize their daily lives through habits and customs as well as how they think about themselves and about the others around them; to direct economic relations and the management of resources; to insure individuals and populations against accidents and the perils of the natural environment. It is concerned with a complex of rationalities, bodies, perceptions, material resources, and natural events, in short, with humans and nonhumans in a heterogeneous assemblage. See, for example, Foucault, *Security, Territory, Population*, 96.

56. See Michel Foucault, "The Confessions of the Flesh," in *Power/Knowledge: Selected Interviews and Other Writings, 1972–77*, trans. Colin Gordon et al., ed. Colin Gordon (New York: Pantheon Books, 1980), 194–228; especially 194–195.

57. See Gilles Deleuze, "Qu'est-ce qu'un dispositif?" in *Deux régimes de fous: Textes et entretiens, 1975–1995,* ed. David Lapoujade (Paris: Les Editions de Minuit, 2003), 316–325; especially 320.

58. Giorgio Agamben, "What Is an Apparatus?," in *What Is an Apparatus? and Other Essays,* trans. David Kishik and Stefan Pedatella, ed. Werner Hamacher (Stanford: Stanford University Press, 2009), 1–24; quotation on 14.

59. On "economy" in the history of Christian thought and the relevance of "divine economy" to contemporary biopolitics, see also Giorgio Agamben, *Le règne et la gloire: Homo sacer, II, 2,* trans. Joël Gayraud and Martin Rueff (Paris: Seuil, 2008), 41–91.

60. Agamben, "What Is an Apparatus?," 15.

61. Ibid., 22.

62. Jean-Louis Baudry famously described cinema as a "*dispositif*," referring both to film as a technology that generates a particular kind of viewing position with specific psychic effects and to institutionalized film forms that keep on reproducing this type of spectatorship. See Baudry, "Le dispositif: Approches métapsychologiques de l'impression de réalité," *Communications* 23 (1975): 56–72. For a recent reinterpretation of the concept of *dispositif* in the context of the study of film history, see Frank Kessler, "The Cinema of Attractions as Dispositif," in *The Cinema of Attractions Reloaded,* ed. Wanda Strauven (Amsterdam: Amsterdam University Press, 2009), 57–69. Recently, François Albera and Maria Tortajada have developed the notion of "dispositive," inspired by Foucault's *dispositif,* in relation to the analysis of viewing positions throughout the history of audiovisual media. "Dispositive," for them, addresses the "epistemic schemas" that in given historical and technical arrangements determine the coming together of viewers, machines, and representations. See Albera and Tortajada, eds., *Cinema beyond Film: Media Epistemology in the Modern Era* (Amsterdam: Amsterdam University Press, 2010), especially 12–13. In a more philosophical guise, the concept of *appareil* has resurfaced in Jean-Louis Déotte's work in the field of aesthetics and art history to designate the cultural objects—ranging from architectural styles to techniques of the perspective—that shape how the world becomes visible and sensible at a given social and historical moment. Drawing on Gilbert Simondon's philosophy of technology and culture, Déotte understands that an *appareil* prescribes the ways in which the world can appear and thus orients and captures shared sensibilities, common ways of having sensations and thinking of the world. In distinguishing an *appareil* from a technical object, Déotte argues, that a technical object has a practical function in prolonging action that modifies the natural environment, whereas an *appareil* has as its condition of operation the transformation of the human milieu into a community. *Appareils* produce and disseminate shared modes of sensation and perception and reconfigure the ways in which individuals come together as collectives. Which is to say, they produce the social. See Déotte, "Le milieu des appareils," in *Le milieu des appareils,* ed. Jean-Louis Déotte (Paris: L'Harmattan, 2008), 9–21.

63. One should not confound the concept of apparatus as presented in this book with the concept of technology. Whatever meaning one wishes to assign to "technology"—from rationalized destruction of nature (Martin Heidegger), to fundamental factor in the bodily and cognitive development of *Homo sapiens sapiens* (André Leroi-Gourhan, Bernard Stiegler), to beneficiary in its digital media manifestations of nonhuman animal (insect) social mechanisms and distributed intelligence (Jussi Parikka)—"technology" concerns the more or less complex tools and machines we create and their impact on the arrangement and development of human bodies and cultures as well as natural environments. An apparatus, on the other hand, concerns the government of how we become both individual and social beings, although, of course, it can include technologies as essential elements in our networks. Moreover, an apparatus does not in its operations follow ontological categorizations; its networks can be utterly heterogeneous, bringing together, among other things, the discursive and the nondiscursive, the human and the nonhuman, the living and the nonliving. What elements it brings together and with what kinds of effects depends on the nature of the apparatus and the strategic functions it has in a given social process. On "technology" in the above senses, see Martin Heidegger, "The Question Concerning Technology," in *Basic Writings*, rev. and exp. ed., ed. David Farrell Krell (London: Routledge, 1993), 307–342; André Leroi-Gourhan, *Gesture and Speech*, trans. Anna Bostock Berger (Cambridge, MA: MIT Press, 1993), especially 114–115, 145–146; Bernard Stiegler, *Technics and Time 1: The Fault of Epimetheus*, trans. Richard Beardsworth and George Collins (Stanford: Stanford University Press, 1998), especially 29–81; Jussi Parikka, *Insect Media: An Archaeology of Animals and Technology* (Minneapolis: University of Minnesota Press, 2010), especially 203–206.

64. Jean-Pierre Changeux, *Neuronal Man: The Biology of Mind*, trans. Laurence Garey (Oxford: Oxford University Press, 1985), xvi.

65. Vilayanur S. Ramachandran, "Preface," in *Encyclopedia of the Human Brain*, vol. 1, ed. Vilayanur S. Ramachandran (San Diego: Academic Press, 2002), xxxv.

66. Joelle Abi-Rached and Nikolas Rose, "The Birth of the Neuromolecular Gaze," *History of the Human Sciences* 21, no. 1 (2010): 11–36; quotation on 31. See also Nikolas Rose and Joelle M. Abi-Rached, *Neuro: The New Brain Sciences and the Management of Mind* (Princeton: Princeton University Press, 2013), 25–52.

67. Joseph LeDoux, *Synaptic Self: How Our Brains Become Who We Are* (New York: Viking Penguin, 2002), 324.

68. See Alain Ehrenberg, "Le cerveau 'social': Chimère épistémologique et vérité sociologique," *Esprit*, January 2008, 79–103; especially 84.

69. LeDoux, *The Synaptic Self*, 2.

70. Fernando Vidal, "Brainhood: Anthropological Figure of Modernity," *History of the Human Sciences* 22, no. 1 (2009): 5–36; quotation on 6.

71. Changeux, *Neuronal Man*, 170.

72. The concept of "biopolitics" itself dates back at least to the early twentieth century and the work of Swedish political scientist Rudolf Kjellén, who used the term in describing his vitalistic conception of the state seen as something like a natural organism, rather than as a subject of law. This conjunction of the political and the biological—a view of life as external to politics but at the same time as something that conducts and justifies political action—became prominent in German political philosophy of the 1920s and 1930s. It included biologist Baron Jakob von Uexküll's thesis that the social body is a holistic whole whose integrity and organization need to be protected from parasitical forces. Likewise in England, Morley Roberts used the "biopolitics" concept to understand government as "a tentative and experimental physiological apparatus responding to the internal and external environment in accordance with physical law." Roberts, *Biopolitics: An Essay on the Physiology, Pathology and Politics of Social and Somatic Organisms* (London: Dent, 1938), 206. Although the concept was revisited in French and Anglo-Saxon discourses in the 1960s and 1970s, which saw politics as something that has life (nature, for instance) as its object of regulation and preservation, it was not until Foucault's work that "biopolitics" was deconstructed. On the history of the "biopolitics" concept, see Roberto Esposito, *Bíos: Biopolitics and Philosophy*, trans. Timothy Campbell (Minneapolis: University of Minnesota Press, 2008), 13–44. Already before Kjellén, the German philosopher of technology Ernst Kapp had conceptualized the state as something that reproduces in its organization the physiology of the human body. See Kapp, *Grundlinien einer Philosophie der Technik: Zur Entstehungsgeschichte der Cultur aus neuen Gesichtspunkt* (Braunschweig: George Westermann, 1877).

73. See Esposito, *Bíos*, 28.

74. Michel Foucault, *The Birth of Biopolitics: Lectures at the Collège de France 1978–1979*, trans. Graham Burchell, ed. Michel Senellart (Basingstoke: Palgrave Macmillan, 2010), 317.

75. See Michel Foucault, *The Will to Knowledge*, vol. 1 of *The History of Sexuality*, trans. Robert Hurley (London: Penguin, 1998), 148.

76. Foucault, *Security, Territory, Population*, 21.

77. See Cooper, *Life as Surplus*, 5–7.

78. Ibid., 7.

79. Foucault, *The Birth of Biopolitics*, 317.

80. On market rationality's saturation of the state, politics, and the social under neoliberalism, see Wendy Brown, "American Nightmare: Neoliberalism, Neoconservatism, and De-Democraticization," *Political Theory* 34, no. 6 (2006): 690–714.

81. See Foucault, *The Birth of Biopolitics*, 323.

82. Wendy Brown, "Neo-liberalism and the End of Liberal Democracy," *Theory and Event* 7, no. 1 (2003): para. 123; emphasis in original, http://muse.jhu.edu/login?auth=0&type=summary&url=/journals/theory_and_event/v007/7.1brown.html.

83. Neoliberalism's generalization of these economic ideals renders the democratic ideals of public goods, rights, and debate essentially meaningless. Brown writes: "Having reduced the political substance of democracy to rubble, neoliberalism then snatches the term for its own purposes, with the consequence that 'market democracy'—once a term of derision for right-wing governance by unregulated capital—is now an ordinary descriptor for a form that has precisely nothing to do with the people ruling themselves." Wendy Brown, "'We Are All Democrats Now ...,'" in Giorgio Agamben et al., *Democracy in What State?*, trans. William McCuaig (New York: Columbia University Press, 2011), 44–57; quotation on 48.

84. Cooper, *Life as Surplus*, 9.

85. See Brown "Neo-liberalism and the End of Liberal Democracy," para. 160. See also David Harvey, *A Brief History of Neoliberalism* (Oxford: Oxford University Press, 2005), 64–67.

86. Foucault, *The Birth of Biopolitics*, 242.

87. Ibid., 226.

88. See Brown, "Neo-liberalism and the End of Liberal Democracy," para. 258.

89. See Foucault, *The Birth of Biopolitics*, 66. A further dimension of this type of government through freedom and fear is the pervasive, curiously corrective and coercive phenomenon of indebtedness. Although capital accumulation in today's flexible finance economy of derivatives, securities, debt swaps, and the like takes place through the exploitation of risk (speculation on future capacity to pay back debts), social organization, largely in the name of privatization, has started to follow the asymmetrical power relationship between lender and borrower. The logic of financial debt has expanded over the boundaries of the economy proper and grown into a specific governmental principle that seeks to act on the future actions of individuals by reducing and regularizing the range of their choices about how to shape themselves in everyday life. Debt enables, but in enabling indirectly molds individuals through impersonally embodied future obligations to conform to the neoliberal model of calculating and disaggregated economic actors who exercise their "freedom" within a clearly demarcated and limited field of possibilities. On government through debt, see Maurizio Lazzarato, *La fabrique de l'homme endetté: Essai sur la condition néolibérale* (Paris: Editions Amsterdam, 2011), especially 15–31.

90. Wolin, *Democracy Incorporated*, 196.

91. See Foucault, *The Birth of Biopolitics*, 269–270.

92. Vidal, "Brainhood," 7.

93. Catherine Malabou, *What Should We Do with Our Brain?*, trans. Sebastian Rand (New York: Fordham University Press, 2008), 53.

94. Ibid., 43, 41.

95. See Gerald Edelman, *Second Nature: Brain Science and Human Knowledge* (New Haven: Yale University Press, 2006), 41, 92. See also Nikolas Rose, *The Politics of Life Itself: Biomedicine, Power, and Subjectivity in the Twenty-First Century* (Princeton: Princeton University Press, 2007), 188.

96. See Edelman, *Second Nature*, 55.

97. Malabou, *What Should We Do with Our Brain?*, 13.

98. See Nikolas Rose, "'Screen and Intervene': Governing Risky Brains," *History of the Human Sciences* 23, no. 1 (2010): 79–105.

99. On "brain-enhancement" devices used in brain clinics, see Jonna Brenninkmeijer, "Taking Care of One's Brain: How Manipulating the Brain Changes People's Selves," *History of the Human Sciences* 23, no. 1 (2010): 107–126.

100. On neuroimaging technologies, particularly fMRI, see Peter A. Bandettini, "Functional Magnetic Resonance Imaging," in *Methods in Mind*, ed. Carl Senior, Tamara Russell, and Michael S. Gazzaniga (Cambridge, MA: MIT Press, 2006), 193–235. See also Rose and Abi-Rached, *Neuro*, 65–81.

101. Alain Ehrenberg, "Le sujet cérébral," *Esprit*, November 2004, 154.

102. See Rose and Abi-Rached, *Neuro*, 78.

103. See Adina L. Roskies, "Are Neuroimages like Photographs of the Brain," *Philosophy of Science* 74, no. 5 (2007): 860–872; especially 864.

104. Belting, *An Anthropology of Images*, 19.

105. See Rose and Abi-Rached, *Neuro*, 55, 81.

106. Emily Falk et al., "Predicting Persuasion-Induced Behavior Change from the Brain," *Journal of Neuroscience* 30, no. 25 (June 2010): 8421–8424; quotation on 8421.

107. Chris Frith, *Making Up the Mind: How the Brain Creates Our Mental World* (Oxford: Blackwell, 2007), 68.

108. See, for example, Rodolfo Llinás and Sisir Roy, "The 'Prediction Imperative' as the Basis for Self-Awareness," *Philosophical Transactions of the Royal Society B* 364, no. 1515 (2009): 1301–1307.

109. See Melinda Cooper, "Turbulent Worlds: Financial Markets and Environmental Crisis," *Theory, Culture and Society* 27, nos. 2–3 (2010): 167–190; especially 175.

110. On the logic of finance, see Marieke De Goede, "Beyond Risk: Premediation and the Post-9/11 Security Imagination," *Security Dialogue* 39, nos. 2–3 (2008): 155–176.

111. See Michael Dillon and Julian Reid, *The Liberal Way of War: Killing to Make Life Live* (London: Routledge, 2009), especially 127–128. See also Randy Martin, *An Empire of Indifference: American War and the Financial Logic of Risk Management* (Durham: Duke University Press, 2007), especially 64–96.

112. See Richard Grusin, *Premediation: Affect and Mediality after 9/11* (New York: Palgrave Macmillan, 2010), especially 4.

113. See Brian Massumi, "The Future Birth of the Affective Fact: The Political Ontology of Threat," in *The Affect Theory Reader*, ed. Melissa Gregg and Gregory J. Seigworth (Durham: Duke University Press, 2010), 52–70.

Chapter 2

1. Cooper filmed his video using the Interrotron technique, developed by Errol Morris, which shows subjects looking right into the camera lens.

2. On the notion of the gaze in the Western strategies of representation since the Renaissance, see Hans Belting, *Florence and Baghdad: Renaissance Art and Arab Science*, trans. Deborah Lucas Schneider (Cambridge, MA: Belknap Press, 2011), 84–89.

3. Freedberg, *The Power of Images*, 325.

4. Oliver Grau, *Virtual Art: From Illusion to Immersion*, trans. Gloria Custance (Cambridge, MA: MIT Press, 2003), 13.

5. Alexander Galloway, *Gaming: Essays on Algorithmic Culture* (Minneapolis: University of Minnesota Press, 2006), 4.

6. Ibid., 2–3.

7. Ibid., 4.

8. Claus Pias, "The Game Player's Duty: The User as the Gestalt of the Ports," in *Media Archaeology: Approaches, Applications, and Implications*, ed. Erkki Huhtamo and Jussi Parikka (Berkeley and Los Angeles: University of California Press, 2011), 164–183; quotation on 173.

9. On rhythmicity as used here, see Ingold, *Being Alive*, 60.

10. See Graeme Kirkpatrick, *Aesthetic Theory and the Video Game* (Manchester: Manchester University Press, 2011), 151.

11. "What the cockfight says," Geertz writes, "it says in a vocabulary of sentiment—the thrill of risk, the despair of loss, the pleasure of triumph. Yet what it says is not

merely that risk is exciting, loss depressing, or triumph gratifying, banal tautologies of affect, but that it is of these emotions, thus exemplified, that society is built and individuals put together. Attending cockfights and participating in them is, for the Balinese, a kind of sentimental education. What he learns there is what his culture's ethos and his private sensibility (or, anyway, certain aspects of them) look like when spelled out externally in a collective text." Cliffold Geertz, "Deep Play: Notes on the Balinese Cockfight," *Daedalus* 134, no. 4 (Fall 2005): 56–86; quotation on 83.

12. Ian G. R. Shaw and Barney Warf, "Worlds of Affect: Virtual Geographies of Video Games," *Environment and Planning A* 41, no. 6 (2009): 1332–1343; quotation on 1341.

13. See, for example, Rancière, *Dissensus*, 139.

14. Keith Stuart and Mark Sweney, "Modern Warfare 3 Hits the $1bn Mark in Record Time," *Guardian*, December 13, 2011, www.theguardian.com/technology/2011/dec/12/modern-warfare-3-breaks-1bn-barrier.

15. See Giorgio Agamben, *The Signature of All Things: On Method*, trans. Luca D'Isanto with Kevin Attell (New York: Zone Books, 2009), 15.

16. See Josh Smicker, "Future Combat, Combating Futures: Temporalities of War Video Games and the Performance of Proleptic Histories," in *Joystick Soldiers: The Politics of Play in Military Video Games*, ed. Nina B. Huntemann and Matthew Thomas Payne (New York: Routledge, 2010), 106–121.

17. For an ethological approach to video games and media technology more generally, drawing on the early twentieth-century work of Jakob von Uexküll and Roger Caillois, see Parikka, *Insect Media*, 57–111.

18. Galloway, *Gaming*, 63.

19. Alva Noë, *Action in Perception* (Cambridge, MA: MIT Press, 2006), 228.

20. Ibid., 20.

21. Gibson goes on to explain: "Vision is *kinesthetic* in that it registers movements of the body just as much as does the muscle-joint-skin system and the inner ear system. Vision picks up both movements of the whole body relative to the ground and movement of a member of the body relative to the whole." James J. Gibson, *The Ecological Approach to Visual Perception* (Hillsdale, NJ: Erlbaum, 1986), 183.

22. Ibid., 283.

23. Barbara Maria Stafford, "Crystal and Smoke: Putting Image Back in Mind," in *A Field Guide to a New Meta-Field: Bridging the Humanities-Neuroscience Divide*, ed. Barbara Maria Stafford (Chicago: University of Chicago Press, 2011), 1–63; quotation on 44.

24. Gibson, *The Ecological Approach to Visual Perception*, 17.

25. See Alain Berthoz, *The Brain's Sense of Movement*, trans. Giselle Weiss (Cambridge, MA: MIT Press, 2000), 9. Berthoz's work in neuroscience develops Gibson's theory of perception.

26. Daniel Stern, *Forms of Vitality: Exploring Dynamic Experience in Psychology, the Arts, Psychotherapy, and Development* (Oxford: Oxford University Press, 2010), 7–8, 83, 88.

27. Ibid., 9.

28. For a similar argument employing Stern's concept of vitality affect in the analysis of screen-based mediations, see Grusin, *Premediation*, 95–96. On affect attunement and video games, see also James Ash, "Technologies of Captivation: Videogames and the Attunement of Affect," *Body and Society* 19, no. 1 (2013): 27–51.

29. Stern, *Forms of Vitality*, 59.

30. Donald Pfaff, *Brain Arousal and Information Theory: Neural and Genetic Mechanisms* (Cambridge, MA: Harvard University Press, 2006), 1.

31. Stern, *Forms of Vitality*, 58.

32. See Pfaff, *Brain Arousal and Information Theory*, 19.

33. See Stern, *Forms of Vitality*, 61.

34. Deleuze, *Foucault*, 34.

35. On the concept of the cerebral subject, see Ehrenberg, "Le sujet cérébral," 130–155. See also Vidal, "Brainhood," 5–36.

36. See Fumiko Hoeft et al., "Gender Differences in the Mesocorticolimbic System during Computer Game-Play," *Journal of Psychiatric Research* 42 (2008): 253–258. See also M. J. Koepp et al., "Evidence for Striatal Dopamine Release During a Video Game," *Nature* 393 (1998): 266–268; Doug Hyun Han et al., "Dopamine Genes and Reward Dependence in Adolescents with Excessive Internet Video Game Play," *Journal of Addiction Medicine* 1, no. 3 (2007): 133–138; Doug Hyun Han et al., "Brain Activity and Desire for Internet Video Game Play," *Comprehensive Psychiatry* 52 (2011): 88–95. It is often argued that video games are very much structured around the notion of reward, which can range from earning simple points upon completing a task, such as killing an adversary in *Modern Warfare 3*, to gaining increased capacities, spatial awareness, or access for one's avatar upon completing a set of tasks. See, for example, Gordon Calleja, *In-Game: From Immersion to Incorporation* (Cambridge, MA: MIT Press, 2011), 147–165.

37. Antonio Damasio, *Self Comes to Mind: Constructing the Conscious Brain* (London: Vintage, 2012), 46–60. On arousal systems in relation to reward and punishment, see, for example, Pfaff, *Brain Arousal and Information Theory*, 53–54.

38. In their fMRI-based study of affective modulation, Christian Montag and colleagues observed differences in neural activity in the lateral prefrontal cortex, thought to be involved in integrating cognition and emotion, between first-person shooter gamers and nongamers when they encountered troubling imagery such as pictures of disasters and accidents, disfigured faces, and scenes where humans are attacked. Whereas a protective mechanism against experiencing negative emotions, with the prefrontal cortex down-regulating limbic brain activity, was triggered in the nongamers, the same was not observed in experienced gamers. Montag et al., "Does Excessive Play of Violent First-Person-Shooter-Video-Games Dampen Brain Activity in Response to Emotional Stimuli?," *Biological Psychology* 89, no. 1 (2012): 107–111.

39. Vilayanur S. Ramachandran and Sandra Blakeslee, *Phantoms in the Brain: Human Nature and the Architecture of the Mind* (London: Harper Perennial, 2005), 83–84.

40. Edelman, *Second Nature*, 92.

41. See also Frith, *Making Up the Mind*, 68.

42. See Michael Dillon and Luis Lobo-Guerrero, "The Biopolitical Imaginary of Species-being," *Theory, Culture and Society* 26, no. 1 (2009): 1–23; quotation on 14 (emphasis in original).

43. Thomas Malaby, "Beyond Play: A New Approach to Games," *Games and Culture* 2, no. 2 (2007): 95–113; quotation on 106.

44. See Malabou, *What Should We Do with Our Brain?*, 39.

45. Changeux, *Neuronal Man*, 127.

46. Edelman, *Second Nature*, 57, 65.

47. György Buzsáki, *Rhythms of the Brain* (Oxford: Oxford University Press, 2006).

48. François Jacob, as quoted in Buzsáki, *Rhythms of the Brain*, 8.

49. See, for example, Berthoz, *The Brain's Sense of Movement*, 5–6, 22.

50. Rodolfo Llinás, *I of the Vortex: From Neurons to Self* (Cambridge, MA: MIT Press, 2001), 151. See also Llinás and Roy, "The 'Prediction Imperative' as the Basis of Self-Awareness," 1301–1307.

51. Berthoz, *The Brain's Sense of Movement*, 1.

52. Ibid., 6.

53. I have borrowed the notion of motor cognition from neuroscientist Marc Jeannerod, who defines this action-oriented cognitive mode as, above all, unconscious and lacking in conceptual content (which is to say, when relating to things and events with an action as our goal, we do not name or consciously recognize them). Consciousness is just there, Jeannerod claims, to give a subjective impression of

coherence and continuity for actions based on discontinuous events. Furthermore, what is specific to motor cognition in relation to other types of mental events is that it represents future rather than present occurrences. Motor cognition is prescriptive by nature, predicting the world as it will appear once an action is executed, and thus also proactive, anticipating the outcome of an action rather than describing the world as it is in the here and now. See Jeannerod, *Motor Cognition: What Actions Tell the Self* (Oxford: Oxford University Press, 2006), 1–3, 49, 58.

54. Foucault, *The Will to Knowledge*, 139.

55. Ibid.

56. Neidich, "From Noopower to Neuropower," 538–581; quotation on 539; emphasis in original.

57. Ibid., 539.

58. Ibid., 550.

59. I am drawing here on Barbara Stafford's neuroscientifically inspired view of binding in visual studies. See Stafford, *Echo Objects*, 65–73.

60. Christian Jacob, *The Sovereign Map: Theoretical Approaches in Cartography throughout History*, trans. Tom Conley (Chicago: University of Chicago Press, 2006), 99.

61. See, for example, Gerald Edelman, *Bright Air, Brilliant Fire: On the Matter of the Mind* (New York: Basic Books, 1992), 16–30; Damasio, *Self Comes to Mind*, 63–65.

62. Damasio, *Self Comes to Mind*, 18.

63. Ibid., 65–66.

64. Frith, *Making up the Mind*, 98.

65. Damasio, *Self Comes to Mind*, 71.

66. Edelman, *Bright Air, Brilliant Fire*, 87.

67. Edelman and Tononi, *A Universe of Consciousness*, 88; emphasis in original.

68. On the modifiability of value systems in humans, see Edelman, *Second Nature*, 94–95.

69. Dyer-Witheford and de Peuter, *Games of Empire*, 93.

70. Foucault, *The Birth of Biopolitics*, 259–270.

71. Ibid., 270.

72. Foucault, *"Society Must Be Defended,"* 246.

73. Oliver Burkeman, "Obama Administration Says Goodbye to 'War on Terror,'" *Guardian*, March 25, 2009, http://www.theguardian.com/world/2009/mar/25/obama-war-terror-overseas-contingency-operations.

74. Daniel S. Roper, "Global Counterinsurgency: Strategic Clarity for the Long War," *Parameters* 38, no. 3 (Autumn 2008): 98–108; quotation on 101.

75. Martin, *An Empire of Indifference*, 18.

76. Joseph Vogl, "Taming Time: Media of Financialization," trans. Christopher Reid, *Grey Room*, no. 46 (Winter 2012): 72–83. See also Elena Esposito, *The Future of Futures: The Time of Money in Financing and Society* (Cheltenham: Edwar Elgar, 2011).

77. Martin, *An Empire of Indifference*, 3.

78. Brian Massumi, "National Enterprise Economy: Steps Toward an Ecology of Powers," *Theory, Culture and Society* 26, no. 6 (2009): 153–185; quotation on 167.

79. Massumi, "The Future Birth of the Affective Fact," 52–70; quotation on 54; emphasis in original.

80. See Joseph LeDoux, *The Emotional Brain: The Mysterious Underpinnings of Emotional Life* (London: Phoenix, 1999), 238.

81. See Andrea Hinds et al., "The Psychology of Potential Threat: Properties of the Security Motivation System," *Biological Psychology* 85, no. 2 (2010): 331–337.

82. See Grusin, *Premediation*, 122–142.

83. LeDoux, *The Emotional Brain*, 128–129.

84. Foucault, *The Birth of Biopolitics*, 66.

85. Esposito, *Bíos*, 45–77.

86. Tim Lenoir, "All but War Is Simulation: The Military-Entertainment Complex," *Configurations* 8, no. 3 (2000): 289–335.

87. See Elizabeth Losh, "A Battle for Hearts and Minds: The Design Politics of ELECT BiLAT," in Huntemann and Payne, *Joystick Soldiers*, 160–177.

88. Patrick Crogan, *Gameplay Mode: War, Simulation, and Technoculture* (Minneapolis: University of Minnesota Press, 2011), 87–109; quotation on 106.

89. Mirzoeff, *The Right to Look*, 280.

90. Carl von Clausewitz, *On War*, trans. Michael Howard and Peter Paret (Oxford: Oxford University Press, 2007), 60.

91. Brian Massumi, "Potential Politics and the Primacy of Preemption," *Theory and Event* 10, no. 2 (2007); emphasis in original, http://muse.jhu.edu/login?auth=0&type=summary&url=/journals/theory_and_event/v010/10.2massumi.html.

92. COIN was preceded by the Shock and Awe doctrine, also known as "Rapid Dominance," a preemptive strategy developed in the mid-1990s and employed in

the 2003 invasion of Iraq. Shock and Awe emphasized, in the words of its developers, Harlan Ullman and James Wade Jr., the "ability to 'own' the dimension of time" and to "move quickly before an adversary can react." Ullman and Wade, *Shock and Awe: Achieving Rapid Dominance* (Washington, DC: National Defense University, 1996), xxv, xxvii, http://www.dodccrp.org/files/Ullman_Shock.pdf. The aim of the doctrine is to force behavioral change by modulating the cognitive underpinnings of action, by controlling what the enemy perceives and does not perceive, knows and does not know. "The image here is the hostage rescue team employing stun grenades to incapacitate an adversary, but on a far larger scale. The stun grenade produces blinding light and deafening noise. The result shocks and confuses the adversary and makes him senseless." Ibid., 28. On the preemptive logic of Shock and Awe, see also Brian Massumi, "Perception Attack: Brief on War Time," *Theory and Event* 13, no. 3 (2010), http://muse.jhu.edu/journals/theory_and_event/summary/v013/13.3.massumi.html.

93. See U.S. Department of the Army, *Counterinsurgency*, Field Manual no. 3-24; Marine Corps Warfighting Publication no. 3-33.5 (Washington, DC: Headquarters, Department of the Army, 2006), http://www.fas.org/irp/doddir/army/fm3-24.pdf.

94. David Kilcullen, *Counterinsurgency* (Oxford: Oxford University Press, 2010), 2.

95. Ibid., 20.

96. Ibid., 194–197, 214–215.

97. See Mirzoeff, *The Right to Look*, 280–282. See also Ben Anderson, "Population and Affective Perception: Biopolitics and Anticipatory Action in U.S. Counterinsurgency Doctrine," *Antipode* 43, no. 2 (2011): 205–236.

98. U.S. Department of the Army, *Counterinsurgency*, 1–23.

99. William Caldwell and Mark Hagerott, "Curing Afghanistan," *Foreign Policy*, April 7, 2004, http://www.foreignpolicy.com/articles/2010/04/07/curing_afghanistan.

100. Jonathan Crary, *24/7: Late Capitalism and the Ends of Sleep* (London: Verso, 2013), 33. See also Mirzoeff, *The Right to Look*, 295. On the paradox of how targeted assassinations carried out with drones by the Israeli armed forces in Palestine actually perpetuate the conflicts they were meant to preempt, see Eyal Weizman, "Thanato-Tactics," in *Beyond Biopolitics: Essays on the Governance of Life and Death*, ed. Patricia Ticineto Clough and Craig Willse (Durham: Duke University Press, 2011), 177–210.

101. Mirzoeff, *The Right to Look*, 303.

102. Pat Biltgen and Robert Tomes, "Rebalancing ISR," *Geospatial Intelligence Forum* 8, no. 6 (2010), http://www.kmimediagroup.com/old/mgt-home/271-gif-2010-volume-8-issue-6-september/3338-rebalancing-isr.html.

103. See Derek Gregory, "From a View to Kill: Drones and Late Modern Warfare," *Theory, Culture and Society* 28, nos. 7–8 (2011): 188–215.

104. Achille Mbembe, "Necropolitics," trans. Libby Meintjes, *Public Culture* 15, no. 1 (2003): 11–40. See also Mirzoeff, *The Right to Look*, 298–307.

105. My description of the Predator drone incident is based on the account by David S. Cloud, which draws on official transcripts of radio transmissions, chat logs, and intercom conversations, in "Anatomy of an Afghan War Tragedy," *Los Angeles Times* April 10, 2011, http://articles.latimes.com/2011/apr/10/world/la-fg-afghanistan-drone-20110410. See also Gregory, "From a View to Kill," 201–203.

106. Gregory, "From a View to Kill," 203.

107. Ibid., 202–203.

108. See Ramachandran, *Phantoms in the Brain*, 67–68. See also Berthoz, *The Brain's Sense of Movement*, 253.

109. Massumi, "The Future Birth of the Affective Fact," 63–65.

110. Damasio, *Self Comes to Mind*, 175.

111. LeDoux, *The Emotional Brain*, 128–129, 170.

112. Hinds et al., "The Psychology of Potential Threat"; Erik Woody and Henry Szechtman, "Adaptation to Potential Threat: The Evolution, Neurobiology, and Psychopathology of the Security Motivation System," *Neuroscience and Biobehavioral Reviews* 35, no. 4 (2011): 1019–1033.

113. Woody and Szechtman, "Adaptation to Potential Threat," 1020.

114. Hinds et al., "The Psychology of Potential Threat," 331–332, 335–336.

115. The full quotation reads: "Facing clear evidence of peril, we cannot wait for the final proof—the smoking gun—that could come in the form of a mushroom cloud." George W. Bush, "President Bush Outlines Iraqi Threat," October 7, 2002. http://georgewbush-whitehouse.archives.gov/news/releases/2002/10/20021007-8.html.

116. See Massumi, "National Enterprise Economy." See also Mirzoeff, *The Right to Look*, 307; Cooper, *Life as Surplus*, 98.

117. Mirzoeff, *The Right to Look*, 21.

118. Massumi, "National Enterprise Emergency," 168.

119. I have borrowed the notion of political physiology from John Protevi, who uses it to emphasize the extent to which the social and the somatic are interlinked, and the ways in which the social is organized through the production and regulation of biological and physiological flows. See Protevi, *Political Affect*, 45–46.

120. Dyer-Witheford and de Peuter, *Games of Empire*, 106, 116.

121. Cooper, "Turbulent Worlds," 167–190; quotation on 180–181.

122. Randy Martin, "From the Race War to the War on Terror," in Clough and Willse, *Beyond Biopolitics*, 258–274; see especially 260–261.

123. Cooper, "Turbulent Worlds," 179.

124. Ibid., 178.

125. Vogl, "Taming Time," 77.

126. Cooper, "Turbulent Worlds," 178–179.

127. For an overview of counterplay, see Tom Apperley, *Gaming Rhythms: Play and Counterplay from the Situated to the Global* (Amsterdam: Institute of Network Cultures, 2010), 132–144.

128. See http://www.delappe.net/project/dead-in-iraq/.

129. Brian Sutton-Smith, *The Ambiguity of Play* (Cambridge, MA: Harvard University Press, 2001), 225–226.

Chapter 3

1. See Harun Farocki, "Cross Influence/Soft Montage," trans. Cynthia Beatt, in *Harun Farocki: Against What? Against Whom?*, ed. Antje Ehmann and Kodwo Eshun (London: Koenig Books, 2009), 70–74. See also Harun Farocki, "Influences transversales," trans. Pierre Rusch, *Trafic*, no. 43 (Autumn 2002): 19–24.

2. See Gerhard Richter, "Miniatures: Harun Farocki and the Cinematic Non-Event," *Journal of Visual Culture* 3, no. 3 (2004): 367–371.

3. Protevi, *Political Affect*, 157; emphasis in original.

4. See Allan Young, *The Harmony of Illusions: Inventing Post-Traumatic Stress Disorder* (Princeton: Princeton University Press, 1995), 7.

5. Judith Herman, *Trauma and Recovery: The Aftermath of Violence—From Domestic Abuse to Political Terror* (New York: Basic Books, 1997), 34.

6. Albert Rizzo, as quoted in Usha Sutliff, "VR Will Treat Stress in Iraq War Vets," *USC News*, March 8, 2005, http://www.usc.edu/uscnews/stories/11070.html.

7. Allan Young, "Bodily Memory and Traumatic Memory," in *Tense Past: Cultural Essays in Trauma and Memory*, ed. Paul Antze and Michael Lambek (New York: Routledge, 1996), 89–102; quotation on 98.

8. See Ruth Leys, *Trauma: A Genealogy* (Chicago: University of Chicago Press, 2000), 231–232. See also Young, *The Harmony of Illusions*, 89–116.

9. See Allan Young, "History, Hystery and Psychiatric Styles of Reasoning," in *Living and Working with the New Medical Technologies: Intersections of Inquiry*, ed. Margaret Lock, Allan Young, and Alberto Camrosio (Cambridge: Cambridge University Press, 2000), 135–164; especially 146.

10. Young, "Bodily Memory and Traumatic Memory," 97.

11. See Bessel van der Kolk and Alexander McFarlane, "The Black Hole of Trauma," in *Traumatic Stress: The Effects of Overwhelming Experience on Mind, Body, and Society*, ed. Bessel van der Kolk, Alexander McFarlane, and Lars Weisaelth (New York: Guilford Press, 1996), 3–23; especially 13.

12. Thomas Parsons and Albert Rizzo, "Affective Outcomes of Virtual Reality Exposure Therapy for Anxiety and Specific Phobias: A Meta-Analysis," *Journal of Behavior Therapy and Experimental Psychiatry* 39 (2008): 250–261; quotation on 251.

13. James Spira et al., "Virtual Reality and Other Experiential Therapies for Combat-Related Posttraumatic Stress Disorder," *Primary Psychiatry* 13, no. 3 (2006): 43–49; quotation on 47.

14. See Dennis Wood, Brenda Wiederhold, and James Spira, "Lessons Learned from 350 Virtual-Reality Sessions with Warriors Diagnosed with Combat-Related Posttraumatic Stress Disorder," *Cyberpsychology, Behavior, and Social Networking* 13, no. 1 (2010): 3–11.

15. Albert Rizzo et al., "A Virtual Reality Exposure Therapy Application for Iraq War Military Personnel with Post Traumatic Stress Disorder: From Training to Toy to Treatment," in *Novel Approaches to the Diagnosis and Treatment of Posttraumatic Stress Disorder*, ed. Michael Roy (Amsterdam: IOS Press, 2006), 235–250; quotation on 246.

16. Maryrose Gerardi et al., "Virtual Reality Exposure Therapy Using a Virtual Iraq: A Case Report," *Journal of Traumatic Stress* 21, no. 2 (2008): 209–213; quotation on 211.

17. Ibid., 211.

18. See, by way of comparison, Jenny Edkins, *Trauma and the Memory of Politics* (Cambridge: Cambridge University Press, 2003), 49–50.

19. Bessel van der Kolk, "The Body Keeps the Score: Approaches to the Psychobiology of Posttraumatic Stress Disorder," in van der Kolk, McFarlane, and Weisaelth, *Traumatic Stress*, 214–241; especially 228–229. See also van der Kolk, "Trauma and Memory," in van der Kolk, McFarlane, and Weisaelth, *Traumatic Stress*, 279–302; especially 280–281.

20. van der Kolk, "Trauma and Memory," 287.

21. Ibid.

22. See Leys, *Trauma*, 249.

23. Bessel van der Kolk, "Clinical Implications of Neuroscience Research in PTSD," *Annals of the New York Academy of Sciences* 1071, no. 1 (2006): 277–293; quotation on 282.

24. Edna Foa and Michel Kozak, "Emotional Processing of Fear: Exposure to Corrective Information," *Psychological Bulletin* 99, no. 1 (1986): 20–35. Thomas Parsons and Albert Rizzo draw conceptually on Foa and Kozak's article in their "Affective Outcomes of Virtual Reality Exposure Therapy."

25. Spira et al., "Virtual Reality and Other Experiential Therapies for Combat-Related Posttraumatic Stress Disorder," 47.

26. See Young, "Bodily Memory and Traumatic Memory," 95.

27. Brenda Wiederhold and Mark Wiederhold, "Lessons Learned from 600 Virtual Reality Sessions," *CyberPsychology and Behavior* 3, no. 3 (2000): 393–400; quotation on 400.

28. See Young, "History, Hystery and Psychiatric Styles of Reasoning," especially 144-151. See also Ian Hacking, *Rewriting the Soul: Multiple Personality and the Sciences of Memory* (Princeton: Princeton University Press, 1995), especially 198–209.

29. See Théodule Ribot, *Diseases of Memory: An Essay in the Positive Psychology*, trans. William Huntington Smith (New York: D. Appleton, 1887), especially 98–116.

30. Crary, *Suspensions of Perception*, 231.

31. See Lisa Blackman, "Reinventing Psychological Matters: The Importance of the Suggestive Realm of Tarde's Ontology," *Economy and Society* 36, no. 4 (2007): 574–596.

32. Foucault, *Security, Territory, Population*, 192–193.

33. See Leys, *Trauma*, 83–119.

34. Sigmund Freud, "Introduction to Psycho-Analysis and the War Neuroses," in *The Standard Edition of the Complete Psychological Works of Sigmund Freud*, vol. 17, trans. and ed. James Strachey, in collaboration with Anna Freud (London: Vintage, 2001), 207–210.

35. Ernst Simmel, Untitled contribution no. 3 to "Symposium Held at the Fifth International Psycho-Analytical Congress in Budapest, September, 1918," in Sandor Ferenczi et al., *Psycho-Analysis and the War Neuroses* (London: International Psycho-Analytical Press, 1921), 30–43; quotation on 34.

36. Ibid., 34.

37. Ibid., 40; emphasis added. The stress Simmel put on affectivity and the prelinguistic in his account of hypnotic therapy was echoed by the British psychologist

William Brown, who also emphasized and promoted the use of hypnosis in the treatment of shell shock patients through emotional catharsis. Critical to the hypnocathartic cure, Brown argued in 1920, was the notion of emotional memory that stores emotions in the mind "like the successive photographic views on a cinematographic ribbon." When these "photographic views" are animated, hypnosis being the principal evocative force in this process, the emotional register of the traumatic event is revived and the subject is to live through the experience again. What Brown thus considered fundamental to therapy was that, in the hypnotic state, the traumatic event was relived in its original affective intensity. Therapy was not based on the patient's cognitive control over the situation but on abreaction that Brown understood as a trance-like "revival of emotions with hallucinatory vividness." William Brown, "The Revival of Emotional Memories and Its Therapeutic Value, 1," *British Journal of Medical Psychology* 1 (1920): 16–19.

38. Simmel, *Kriegsneurosen und "Psychisches Trauma"* (1920), as quoted in Stefan Andriopoulos, *Possessed: Hypnotic Crimes, Corporate Fiction, and the Invention of Cinema* (Chicago: University of Chicago Press, 2008), 112–113.

39. Hansen, *New Philosophy for New Media*, 167, 190.

40. Ibid., 195.

41. Catherine Malabou stresses how psychoanalytic and neuroscientific understandings of trauma are fundamentally incompatible. They diverge not only on the importance of the sexual etiology of traumatic memories (a crucial point for Freud) but also on whether traumatic events can drastically change and re-create the subject's identity. See Catherine Malabou, *Les nouveaux blessés: De Freud à la neurologie, penser les traumatismes contemporains* (Paris: Bayard, 2007), especially 65–89.

42. van der Kolk, "The Body Keeps the Score," 232–234.

43. Parsons and Rizzo, "Affective Outcomes of Virtual Reality Exposure Therapy," 250.

44. Jaak Panksepp, *Affective Neuroscience: The Foundations of Human and Animal Emotions* (Oxford: Oxford University Press, 1998), 55.

45. Ibid., 42.

46. LeDoux, *The Emotional Brain*, 17.

47. See Malabou, *Les nouveaux blessés*, 20.

48. Panksepp, *Affective Neuroscience*, 207.

49. Damasio, *The Feeling of What Happens*, 54.

50. Antonio Damasio, *Looking for Spinoza: Joy, Sorrow, and the Feeling Brain* (San Diego: Harcourt, 2003), 30–32.

51. Paul MacLean, *The Triune Brain in Evolution: Role in Paleocerebral Functions* (New York: Plenum, 1990), 8–9.

52. Ibid., 17.

53. Elizabeth Wilson, *Psychosomatic: Feminism and the Neurological Body* (Durham: Duke University Press, 2004), 86.

54. LeDoux, *The Emotional Brain*, 174.

55. Ibid.

56. Ibid.

57. Panksepp, *Affective Neuroscience*, 75, 123; emphasis in original.

58. Ibid., 207.

59. LeDoux, *The Emotional Brain*, 256–257.

60. See Rodolfo Llinás, *I of the Vortex: From Neurons to Self* (Cambridge, MA: MIT Press, 2002), 7.

61. On the embodied affective texture of the filmic image, see, for example, Vivian Sobchack, *Carnal Thoughts: Embodiment and Moving Image Culture* (Berkeley and Los Angeles: University of California Press, 2004), especially 53–84.

62. Protevi, *Political Affect*, 115–129.

63. Foucault, *Security, Territory, Population*, 75.

64. Stafford, *Echo Objects*, 203.

65. Llinás, *I of the Vortex*, 133.

66. Ibid., 39–40.

67. Mark Muckenfuss, "Military Studies Virtual Reality as Therapy for Post Traumatic Stress Disorder," *Press-Enterprise*, May 9, 2008, http://www.virtuallybetter.com/wp-content/uploads/2012/05/Virtual-reality-article-Johnston.pdf.

68. See Brenda Wiederhold and Mark Wiederhold, "Virtual Reality for Posttraumatic Stress Disorder and Stress Inoculation Training," *Journal of CyberTherapy and Rehabilitation* 1, no. 1 (2008): 23–35.

69. Protevi, *Political Affect*, 159.

70. Massumi, "National Enterprise Emergency," 153–185; quotation on 156.

71. Parsons and Rizzo, "Affective Outcomes of Virtual Reality Exposure Therapy," 251.

72. Wood, Wiederhold, and Spira, "Lessons Learned from 350 Virtual-Reality Sessions with Warriors Diagnosed with Combat-Related Posttraumatic Stress Disorder," 10.

73. Hansen, *New Philosophy for New Media*, 187–188.

74. Malabou, *What Should We Do with Our Brain?*, 17–31. See also Malabou, *Les nouveaux blessés*, especially 45–53. For a history of the notion of neural plasticity in the neurosciences, see Beatrix Rubin, "Changing Brains: The Emergence of the Field of Adult Neurogenesis," *BioSocieties* 4, no. 4 (2009): 407–424.

75. Malabou, *What Should We Do with Our Brain?*, 4.

76. Ibid., 40–54.

77. Luc Boltanski and Eve Chiapello, *The New Spirit of Capitalism*, trans. Gregory Elliott (London: Verso, 2005), 112; emphases in original.

78. Malabou, *What Should We Do with Our Brain?*, 46.

79. See, for example, Rajnish Rao et al., "PTSD: From Neurons to Networks," in *Post-Traumatic Stress Disorder: Basic Science and Clinical Practice*, ed. Priyattam Shiromani, Terence Keane, and Joseph LeDoux (New York: Humana Press, 2009), 151–184.

80. Malabou, *Les nouveaux blessés*, 48–50, 91–122, 237–267.

81. Ibid., 326–327.

82. Leys, *Trauma*, 271–272.

83. See, for example, Ed Cohen, *A Body Worth Defending: Immunity, Biopolitics, and the Apotheosis of the Modern Body* (Durham: Duke University Press, 2009), 257–264.

84. Esposito, *Bíos*, 9.

85. Ibid., 147–148.

86. On the excessive pursuit of the biopolitical imperative, see Foucault, *"Society Must Be Defended,"* 254.

87. Esposito, *Bíos*, 148.

Chapter 4

1. See Belting, *An Anthropology of Images*, 4–5.

2. Barbara Maria Stafford, *Visual Analogy: Consciousness as the Art of Connecting* (Cambridge, MA: MIT Press, 2001), 140–141.

3. Rancière, *Dissensus*, 36.

4. Jacques Rancière, *The Philosopher and His Poor*, trans. John Drury, Corinne Oster, and Andrew Parker, ed. Andrew Parker (Durham: Duke University Press, 2003), 225.

5. Jacques Rancière, *Disagreement: Politics and Philosophy*, trans. Julie Rose (Minneapolis: University of Minnesota Press, 1999), 29.

6. Ibid., 29–30.

7. Rancière, *Dissensus*, 92.

8. See Rancière, *The Philosopher and His Poor*, 226.

9. Rancière, *Dissensus*, 92. It is worth noting that Rancière describes the notion of biopolitics as laid out by Foucault as "confused" for the reason that, in addressing specific practices of power over life, it considers "politics" in terms of "police" rather than in terms of interruption and "supplement" to the dominant adequations of life (ibid., 93). If, however, politics is a question of struggles about the conditions and possibilities of life, it is not obvious why the notion of biopolitics could not be used to account for the twofold processes of domination and contestation. At least, these two presuppose and mutually constitute each another.

10. Joiner's diary, as quoted in Jacques Rancière, *The Emancipated Spectator*, trans. Gregory Elliott (London: Verso, 2009), 71.

11. Simondon, *Imagination et invention*, 16; see also Jean-Paul Sartre, *L'Imagination* (Paris: P.U.F., 1965).

12. Belting, *An Anthropology of Images*, 15.

13. Cornelius Castoriadis, "Logic, Imagination, Reflection," in *Psychoanalysis in Contexts: Paths between Theory and Modern Culture*, ed. Anthony Elliott and Stephen Frosh (London: Routledge, 1995), 15–35; quotation on 33.

14. Rancière, *The Emancipated Spectator*, 72.

15. Mitchell, *What Do Pictures Want?*, 89.

16. Simondon, *Imagination et invention*, 18–23.

17. Ibid., 7. See note 11 to chapter 1. The original French text reads: "résiste au libre-arbitre, refuse de se laisser diriger par la volonté du sujet et se présente d'elle-même selon ses forces propres, habitant la conscience comme un intrus qui vient déranger l'ordre d'une maison où il n'est pas invité."

18. Ibid., 13, 186.

19. Rancière, *Dissensus*, 139.

20. Jean-Luc Godard, *Histoire(s) du cinéma*, 4B: *Les signes parmis nous* (1998). The original French text reads: "Rapprocher les choses qui n'ont jamais été rapprochées et ne semblaient pas disposées à l'être."

21. Georges Didi-Huberman makes a similar argument in *Images malgré tout* (Paris: Les Editions de Minuit, 2003), 151–152. Sarah Kember and Joanna Zylinska have

recently developed the notion of the cut as an ethical and ontological procedure in *Life after New Media: Mediation as a Vital Process* (Cambridge, MA: MIT Press, 2012), 71–95.

22. Rembert Hüser, "Nine Minutes in the Yard: A Conversation with Harun Farocki," in *Harun Farocki: Working on the Sight-Lines*, ed. Thomas Elsaesser (Amsterdam: Amsterdam University Press, 2004), 297–322; quotation on 302.

23. Farocki, "Cross Influence/Soft Montage," 69–74; quotation on 74.

24. Stafford, *Visual Analogy*, 161. Drawing on the media specifics of the electronic video image, Yvonne Spielmann asserts: "Like every other image from the media, video has, on the level of application, on the one hand, the possibility of transparency, of suppressing visible/audible technique in favor of a perfect simulated/illusory image and, on the other, the possibility of emphasizing the level of presentation in the media and the iconic tension. But it is the peculiarity of video that the second possibility does not represent only a question of usage, but denotes, by contrast, the condition of video's reality itself." Spielmann, *Video: The Reflexive Medium*, trans. Anja Welle and Stan Jones (Cambridge, MA: MIT Press, 2008), 44.

25. On the concept of projected image art, see Tamara Trodd, "Introduction: Theorising the Projected Image," in *Screen/Space: The Projected Image in Contemporary Art*, ed. Tamara Trodd (Manchester: Manchester University Press, 2011), 1–22. In this chapter, I do not consider how the spatial arrangement of images' reception in the gallery or museum space itself introduces an aspect of reflexivity. As Boris Groys puts it, "The whole point of visiting an exhibition of time-based art is to take a look at it and then another look and another look—but not to see it in its entirety. Here one can say that the act of contemplation itself is put in a loop." Groys, "Comrades of Time," *e-flux*, no. 11 (12/2009), http://www.e-flux.com/journal/comrades-of-time/. On this problematic, see also Kate Mondloch, *Screens: Viewing Media Installation Art* (Minneapolis: University of Minnesota Press, 2010), 40–59.

26. Georges Bataille, *Prehistoric Painting: Lascaux or the Birth of Art*, trans. Austryn Wainhouse (Lausanne: Skira, 1955), 27.

27. Belting, *An Anthropology of Images*, 38.

28. See Malabou, *What Should We Do with Our Brain?*, 81–82.

29. Rancière, *The Future of the Image*, 26.

30. Paul Virilio, *The Vision Machine*, trans. Julie Rose (Bloomington: Indiana University Press, 1994), 59.

31. Ibid., 60.

32. Giorgio Agamben, *Homo Sacer: Sovereign Power and Bare Life*, trans. Daniel Heller-Roazen (Stanford: Stanford University Press, 1998), 6–11.

33. On the extralegal dimension of power in the age of war on terror, see Judith Butler, *Precarious Life: The Powers of Mourning and Violence* (London: Verso, 2006), 50–100.

34. Agamben, *Homo Sacer*, 11.

35. Mitchell, *Cloning Terror*, 95.

36. See ibid., 48.

37. Ibid., 99.

38. Sara Ahmed, *The Cultural Politics of Emotion* (Edinburgh: Edinburgh University Press, 2004), 51.

39. Cohen, *A Body Worth Defending*, 260.

40. Laura U. Marks, *Enfoldment and Infinity: An Islamic Genealogy of New Media Art* (Cambridge, MA: MIT Press, 2010), 5.

41. See Freedman's critique of "aniconism" in *The Power of Images*, 54–81.

42. Mondzain, *Image, Icon, Economy*, 71.

43. Ibid., 162.

44. Ibid., 167.

45. See, for example, Ellen Nakashima and Craig Whitlock, "With Air Force's Gorgon Drone 'We Can See Everything,'" *Washington Post*, January 2, 2011, http://www.washingtonpost.com/wp-dyn/content/article/2011/01/01/AR2011010102690.html.

46. Alexander Galloway, "Are Some Things Unrepresentable?," *Theory, Culture and Society* 28, nos. 7–8 (2011): 85–102; quotation on 95.

47. Rancière, *Dissensus*, 135.

48. Groys discusses the importance of a "non-teleological time that does not lead to any result, any endpoint" in contemporary time-based arts in "Comrades of Time."

49. See Martin Heidegger, *The Fundamental Concepts of Metaphysics: World, Finitude, Solitude*, trans. William McNeill and Nicholas Walker (Bloomington: Indiana University Press, 1995), 125–127.

50. Nicephorus I, as quoted in Mondzain, *Image, Icon, Economy*, 167.

51. See Edelman, *Second Nature*, 122.

52. Ibid., 100.

53. Edelman and Tononi, *A Universe of Consciousness*, 106.

54. Edelman, *Second Nature*, 57–58.

55. Modell, *Imagination and the Meaningful Brain*, 33–34.

56. *From the Other Side* exists both as a 15-screen gallery installation version and as a single-channel DVD release. This chapter's analysis is based on the DVD version.

57. Joseph Nevins, *Operation Gatekeeper: The Rise of the "Illegal Alien" and the Making of the U.S.-Mexico Boundary* (New York: Routledge, 2002), 2, 121.

58. Foucault, *Security, Territory, Population*, 48.

59. On illegal immigration and the politics of immunity, see Roberto Esposito, *Immunitas: The Protection and Negation of Life*, trans. Zakiya Hanafi (Cambridge: Polity, 2011), 1–3.

60. Ed Pilkington, "U.S. Immigration Deal Envisages Use of Military Surveillance at Southern Border," *Guardian*, June 25, 2013, http://www.theguardian.com/world/2013/jun/25/us-immigration-amendment-surveillance?INTCMP=SRCH.

61. According to conservative estimates, 4,000 unauthorized immigrants lost their lives in the U.S.-Mexico border region during 1994–2006 while trying to cross. See Joseph Nevins, "Dying for a Cup of Coffee? Migrant Deaths in the U.S.-Mexico Border Region in a Neoliberal Age," *Geopolitics* 12, no. 2 (2007): 228–247.

62. Cohen, *A Body Worth Defending*, 18.

63. Esposito, *Immunitas*, 136.

64. On the fence along the Sonora-Arizona border, see Tom Barry, "A Day on the Border: Big Government, Big Fence," *Counterpunch*, January 11, 2012, http://www.counterpunch.org/2012/01/11/big-government-big-fence/.

65. See Alfred Tauber, *The Immune Self: Theory or Metaphor?* (Cambridge: Cambridge University Press, 1994), 3.

66. Esposito, *Immunitas*, 6.

67. Esposito, *Bíos*, 52.

68. Rancière, *Dissensus*, 149.

69. Stafford, *Visual Analogy*, 132.

70. See Edelman and Tononi, *A Universe of Consciousness*, 25.

71. William James, *The Principles of Psychology*, vol. 1 (New York: Henry Holt, 1910), 243.

72. Alfred North Whitehead, *Adventures of Ideas* (New York: Free Press, 1967), 242.

73. Stafford, *Visual Analogy*, 139.

74. Ibid., 138.

75. Alfred North Whitehead, *Modes of Thought* (New York: Free Press, 1968), 98.

76. Whitehead, *Adventures of Ideas*, 233.

77. Ralph Bred, *Onflow: Dynamics of Consciousness and Experience* (Cambridge, MA: MIT Press, 2005), 280. See also Steven Shaviro, *Without Criteria: Kant, Whitehead, Deleuze, and Aesthetics* (Cambridge, MA: MIT Press, 2009), 21.

78. Whitehead, *Modes of Thought*, 99–100.

79. Stafford, *Visual Analogy*, 28–29.

80. Ibid., 61.

81. Ed Cohen, *A Body Worth Defending*, 88.

82. See Terri Ginsberg, "Bordering on Disaster: Toward an Epistemology of Divided Cinematic Space," *Spectator* 29, no. 1 (Spring 2009): 30–36, cinema.usc.edu/archivedassets/096/15612.pdf.

83. Esposito, *Immunitas*, 174.

84. Ibid.

85. Christine Ross, "The Suspension of History in Contemporary Media Arts," *Intermédialités: Histoire et Théorie des Arts, des Lettres et des Techniques/Intermediality: History and Theory of the Arts, Literature and Technology*, no. 11 (2008): 125–148; quotation on 128.

86. Friedrich Nietzsche, as quoted in Gilles Deleuze, *Difference and Repetition*, trans. Paul Patton (New York: Columbia University Press, 1994), xxi.

87. Gilles Deleuze, *The Logic of Sense*, trans. Mark Lester with Charles Stivale (London: Athlone Press, 1990), 150–151.

88. Belting, *An Anthropology of Images*, 36.

89. Walter Benjamin, "A Discussion of Russian Filmic Art and Collectivist Art in General," in *The Weimar Republic Sourcebook*, ed. Anton Kaes, Martin Jay and Edward Dimendberg (Berkeley and Los Angeles: University of California Press, 1994), 626–627; quotation on 626.

90. Walter Benjamin, *The Arcades Project*, trans. Howard Eiland and Kevin McLaughlin, ed. Rolf Tiedemann (Cambridge, MA: Belknap Press, 1999), 394.

91. Ibid., 463.

92. Ibid.

93. See Georges Didi-Huberman, *L'Image survivante: Histoire de l'art et temps des fantômes selon Aby Warburg* (Paris: Les Editions de Minuit, 2002), 51–53.

94. Ibid., 273–277. See also Georges Didi-Huberman, *Devant le temps: Histoire de l'art et anachronisme des images* (Paris: Les Editions de Minuit, 2000), 39–43.

95. See Giorgio Agamben, "Nymphs," trans. Amanda Minervini, in Khalip and Mitchell, *Releasing the Image*, 79.

96. See Michael Nest, *Coltan* (Cambridge: Polity, 2011), 8–9.

97. Ibid., 53–65.

98. I am alluding to Russian mineralogist Vladimir Vernadsky's characterization of life across divisions between the organic and the inorganic in the late nineteenth and early twentieth centuries. See Lynn Margulis and Dorion Sagan, *What Is Life?* (Berkeley and Los Angeles: University of California Press, 1995), 49.

99. Joseph Conrad, *Heart of Darkness*, in *Heart of Darkness and Other Tales*, ed. Cedric Watts (Oxford: Oxford University Press, 2002), 103–187; quotation on 104.

100. See Séamas Ó Síocháin and Michael O'Sullivan, "General Introduction," in *The Eyes of Another Race: Roger Casement's Congo Report and 1903 Diary*, ed. Séamas Ó Síocháin and Michael O'Sullivan (Dublin: University College Dublin Press, 2003), 4.

101. Foucault, *The Will to Knowledge*, 141.

102. On the suspension of law in the confluence of sovereignty and capitalism, see Butler, *Precarious Life*, 54–55.

103. Roger Casement, "The Congo Report," in *The Eyes of Another Race: Roger Casement's Congo Report and 1903 Diary*, ed. Séamas Ó Síocháin and Michael O'Sullivan (Dublin: University College Dublin Press, 2003), 45–177; quotation on 88.

104. Roger Casement, "The Congo Report," 88.

105. See Nest, *Coltan*, 41, 95–99.

106. T. J. Demos, "Moving Images of Globalization," *Grey Room*, no. 37 (Fall 2009): 6–29; quotation on 10–11.

107. Benjamin, *The Arcades Project*, 475.

108. Ibid. For a more detailed discussion of the "interpenetration of images," see Kevin McLaughlin, "Ur-Ability: Force and Image from Kant to Benjamin," in Khalip and Mitchell, *Releasing the Image*, 204–221, especially 220.

109. Benjamin, *The Arcades Project*, 462.

110. Didi-Huberman, *Devant le temps*, 117.

111. Demos, "Moving Images of Globalization," 10.

112. Deleuze, "Qu'est-ce qu'un dispositif?," 316.

113. Rancière, *Dissensus*, 151.

Bibliography

Abi-Rached, Joelle, and Nikolas Rose. The Birth of the Neuromolecular Gaze. *History of the Human Sciences* 21, no. 1 (2010): 11–36.

Acland, Charles. The Crack in the Electric Window. *Cinema Journal* 51, no. 2 (2012): 169–173.

Agamben, Giorgio. Difference and Repetition: On Guy Debord's Films. Brian Holmes, trans. In *Art and the Moving Image: A Critical Reader*, ed. Tanya Leighton, 328–333. London: Tate, 2008.

Agamben, Giorgio. *Homo Sacer: Sovereign Power and Bare Life*. Daniel Heller-Roazen, trans. Stanford: Stanford University Press, 1998.

Agamben, Giorgio. Nymphs. In *Releasing the Image: From Literature to New Media*, ed. Jacques Khalip and Robert Mitchell, 60–80. Stanford: Stanford University Press, 2011.

Agamben, Giorgio. *Le règne et la gloire: Homo sacer, II, 2*. Joël Gayraud and Martin Rueff, trans. Paris: Seuil, 2008.

Agamben, Giorgio. *The Signature of All Things: On Method*. Luca D'Isanto with Kevin Atteli, trans. New York: Zone Books, 2009.

Agamben, Giorgio. What Is an Apparatus? In *What Is an Apparatus? and Other Essays*, trans. David Kishik and Stefan Pedatella, ed. Werner Hamacher, 1–24. Stanford: Stanford University Press, 2009.

Ahmed, Sara. *The Cultural Politics of Emotion*. Edinburgh: Edinburgh University Press, 2004.

Albera, François, and Maria Tortajada, eds. *Cinema beyond Film: Media Epistemology in the Modern Era*. Amsterdam: Amsterdam University Press, 2010.

Anderson, Ben. Population and Affective Perception: Biopolitics and Anticipatory Action in U.S. Counterinsurgency Doctrine. *Antipode* 43, no. 2 (2011): 205–236.

Andriopoulos, Stefan. *Possessed: Hypnotic Crimes, Corporate Fiction, and the Invention of Cinema*. Chicago: University of Chicago Press, 2008.

Apperley, Tom. *Gaming Rhythms: Play and Counterplay from the Situated to the Global*. Amsterdam: Institute of Network Cultures, 2010.

Ash, James. Technologies of Captivation: Videogames and the Attunement of Affect. *Body and Society* 19, no. 1 (2013): 27–51.

Bandettini, Peter A. Functional Magnetic Resonance Imaging. In *Methods in Mind*, ed. Carl Senior, Tamara Russell, and Michael S. Gazzaniga, 193–225. Cambridge, MA: MIT Press.

Barry, Tom. A Day on the Border: Big Government, Big Fence. *Counterpunch*, January 11, 2012. http://www.counterpunch.org/2012/01/11/big-government-big-fence/.

Bataille, Georges. *Prehistoric Painting: Lascaux or the Birth of Art*. Austryn Wainhouse, trans. Lausanne: Skira, 1955.

Baudry, Jean-Louis. Le dispositif: Approches métapsychologiques de l'impression de réalité. *Communications* 23 (1975): 56–72.

Belting, Hans. *An Anthropology of Images: Picture, Medium, Body*. Thomas Dunlap, trans. Princeton: Princeton University Press, 2011.

Belting, Hans. *Florence and Baghdad: Renaissance Art and Arab Science*. Deborah Lucas Schneider, trans. Cambridge, MA: Belknap Press, 2011.

Belting, Hans. Image, Medium, Body: A New Approach to Iconology. *Critical Inquiry* 31 (Winter 2005): 302–319.

Benjamin, Walter. *The Arcades Project*. Howard Eiland and Kevin McLaughlin, trans. Rolf Tiedemann, ed. Cambridge, MA: Belknap Press, 1999.

Benjamin, Walter. A Discussion of Russian Filmic Art and Collectivist Art in General. In *The Weimar Republic Sourcebook*, ed. Anton Kaes, Martin Jay, and Edward Dimendberg, 626–627. Berkeley and Los Angeles: University of California Press, 1994.

Benjamin, Walter. *Illuminations*. Harry Zorn, trans. Hannah Arendt, ed. London: Pimlico, 1999.

Benjamin, Walter. The Work of Art in the Age of Its Technological Reproducibility: Second Version. Edmund Jephcott and Harry Zohn, trans. In *Selected Writings*, vol. 3: *1935–1938*, ed. Howard Eiland, and Michael W. Jennings, 101–133. Cambridge, MA: Belknap Press, 2002.

Berthoz, Alain. *The Brain's Sense of Movement*. Giselle Weiss, trans. Cambridge, MA: MIT Press, 2000.

Biltgen, Pat, and Robert Tomes. Rebalancing ISR. *Geospatial Intelligence Forum* 8, no. 6 (2010). http://www.kmimediagroup.com/old/mgt-home/271-gif-2010-volume-8-issue-6-september/3338-rebalancing-isr.html

Blackman, Lisa. Reinventing Psychological Matters: The Importance of the Suggestive Realm of Tarde's Ontology. *Economy and Society* 36, no. 4 (2007): 574–596.

Boltanski, Luc, and Eve Chiapello. *The New Spirit of Capitalism*. Gregory Elliott, trans. London: Verso, 2005.

Braidotti, Rosi. *Transpositions: On Nomadic Ethics*. Cambridge: Polity, 2006.

Branigin, William. Obama Will Not Release Bin Laden Photos, White House Says. *Washington Post*, May 4, 2011. http://www.washingtonpost.com/national/cbs-obama-says-he-wont-release-bin-laden-photos/2011/05/04/AFyB5aoF_story.html?hpid=z1.

Bred, Ralph. *Onflow: Dynamics of Consciousness and Experience*. Cambridge, MA: MIT Press, 2005.

Brenninkmeijer, Jonna. Taking Care of One's Brain: How Manipulating the Brain Changes People's Selves. *History of the Human Sciences* 23, no. 1 (2010): 107–126.

Brown, Wendy. American Nightmare: Neoliberalism, Neoconservatism, and De-Democraticization. *Political Theory* 34, no. 6 (2006): 690–714.

Brown, Wendy. Neo-liberalism and the End of Liberal Democracy. *Theory and Event* 7, no. 1 (2003). http://muse.jhu.edu/login?auth=0&type=summary&url=/journals/theory_and_event/v007/7.1brown.html.

Brown, Wendy. We Are All Democrats Now... In Giorgio Agamben et al., *Democracy in What State?*, trans. William McCuaig, 44–57. New York: Columbia University Press, 2011.

Brown, William. The Revival of Emotional Memories and Its Therapeutic Value, 1. *British Journal of Medical Psychology* 1 (1920): 16–19.

Buck-Morss, Susan. Visual Empire. *diacritics* 37, nos. 2–3 (2007): 171–198.

Burkeman, Oliver. Obama Administration Says Goodbye to "War on Terror." *Guardian*, March 25, 2009. www.theguardian.com/world/2009/mar/25/obama-war-terror-overseas-contingency-operations.

Bush, George W. President Bush Outlines Iraqi Threat, October 7, 2002. http://georgewbush-whitehouse.archives.gov/news/releases/2002/10/20021007-8.html.

Butler, Judith. *Precarious Life: The Powers of Mourning and Violence*. London: Verso, 2006.

Buzsáki, György. *Rhythms of the Brain*. Oxford: Oxford University Press, 2006.

Caldwell, William, and Mark Hagerott. Curing Afghanistan. *Foreign Policy*, April 7, 2004. http://www.foreignpolicy.com/articles/2010/04/07/curing_afghanistan

Calleja, Gordon. *In-Game: From Immersion to Incorporation*. Cambridge, MA: MIT Press, 2011.

Casement, Roger. The Congo Report. In *The Eyes of Another Race: Roger Casement's Congo Report and 1903 Diary*, ed. Séamas Ó Siocháin and Michael O'Sullivan, 45–177. Dublin: University College of Dublin Press, 2003.

Castoriadis, Cornelius. Logic, Imagination, Reflection. In *Psychoanalysis in Contexts: Paths between Theory and Modern Culture*, ed. Anthony Elliott and Stephen Frosh, 15–35. London: Routledge, 1995.

Cavell, Stanley. *The World Viewed: Reflections on the Ontology of Film. Enlarged edition*. Cambridge, MA: Harvard University Press, 1979.

Changeux, Jean-Pierre. *Neuronal Man: The Biology of Mind*. Laurence Garey, trans. Oxford: Oxford University Press, 1985.

Chun, Wendy Hui Kyong. *Programmed Visions: Software and Memory*. Cambridge, MA: MIT Press, 2011.

Clausewitz, Carl von. *On War*. Michael Howard and Peter Paret, trans. Oxford: Oxford University Press, 2007.

Cloud, David S. Anatomy of an Afghan War Tragedy. *Los Angeles Times*, April 10, 2011. http://articles.latimes.com/2011/apr/10/world/la-fg-afghanistan-drone-20110410.

Cohen, Ed. *A Body Worth Defending: Immunity, Biopolitics, and the Apotheosis of the Modern Body*. Durham: Duke University Press, 2009.

Conrad, Joseph. *Heart of Darkness and Other Tales*. Cedric Watts, ed. Oxford: Oxford University Press, 2002.

Cooper, Melinda. *Life as Surplus: Biotechnology and Capitalism in the Neoliberal Era*. Seattle: University of Washington Press, 2008.

Cooper, Melinda. Turbulent Worlds: Financial Markets and Environmental Crisis. *Theory, Culture and Society* 27, nos. 2–3 (2010): 167–190.

Crary, Jonathan. *Suspensions of Perception: Attention, Spectacle and Modern Culture*. Cambridge, MA: MIT Press, 1999.

Crary, Jonathan. *24/7: Late Capitalism and the Ends of Sleep*. London: Verso, 2013.

Crogan, Patrick. *Gameplay Mode: War, Simulation, and Technoculture*. Minneapolis: University of Minnesota Press, 2011.

Cubitt, Sean. Current Screens. In *Imagery in the 21st Century*, ed. Oliver Grau with Thomas Veigl, 21–35. Cambridge, MA: MIT Press, 2011.

Damasio, Antonio. *The Feeling of What Happens: Body and Emotion in the Making of Consciousness*. San Diego: Harcourt, 1999.

Damasio, Antonio. *Looking for Spinoza: Joy, Sorrow, and the Feeling Brain*. San Diego: Harcourt, 2003.

Damasio, Antonio. *Self Comes to Mind: Constructing the Conscious Brain*. London: Vintage, 2012.

De Goede, Marieke. Beyond Risk: Premediation and the Post-9/11 Security Imagination. *Security Dialogue* 39, nos. 2–3 (2008): 155–176.

Deleuze, Gilles. *Cinema 1: The Movement-Image*. Hugh Tomlinson and Barbara Habberjam, trans. London: Athlone Press, 1986.

Deleuze, Gilles. *Difference and Repetition*. Paul Patton, trans. New York: Columbia University Press, 1994.

Deleuze, Gilles. *Foucault*. Seán Hand, trans. Minneapolis: University of Minnesota Press, 1988.

Deleuze, Gilles. *The Logic of Sense*. Mark Lester and Charles Stivale, trans. London: Athlone Press, 1990.

Deleuze, Gilles. Qu'est-ce qu'un dispositif? In *Deux régimes de fous: Textes et entretiens, 1975–1995*, ed. David Lapoujade, 316–325. Paris: Les Editions de Minuit, 2003.

Deleuze, Gilles, and Félix Guattari. *Mille plateaux: Capitalisme et schizophrénie 2*. Paris: Les Editions de Minuit, 1980.

Demos, T. J. Moving Images of Globalization. *Grey Room*, no. 37 (Fall 2009): 6–29.

Déotte, Jean-Louis. Le milieu des appareils. In *Le milieu des appareils*, ed. Jean-Louis Déotte, 316–325. Paris: L'Harmattan, 2008.

Der Derian, James. *Virtuous War: Mapping the Military-Industrial-Media-Entertainment Network*. 2nd ed. New York: Routledge, 2009.

Didi-Huberman, Georges. *Devant le temps: Histoire de l'art et anachronisme des images*. Paris: Les Editions de Minuit, 2000.

Didi-Huberman, Georges. *L'Image survivante: Histoire de l'art et temps des fantômes selon Aby Warburg*. Paris: Les Editions de Minuit, 2002.

Didi-Huberman, Georges. *Images malgré tout*. Paris: Les Editions de Minuit, 2003.

Dillon, Michael, and Julian Reid. *The Liberal Way of War: Killing to Make Life Live*. London: Routledge, 2009.

Dillon, Michael, and Luis Lobo-Guerrero. The Biopolitical Imaginary of Species-being. *Theory, Culture and Society* 26, no. 1 (2009): 1–23.

Doane, Mary Ann. *The Emergence of Cinematic Time: Modernity, Contingency, the Archive*. Cambridge, MA: Harvard University Press, 2002.

Drummond, Katie. No Fear: Memory Adjustment Pills Get Pentagon Push. *Wired*, December 16, 2011. http://www.wired.com/dangerroom/2011/12/fear-erasing-drugs/.

Dyer-Witheford, Nick, and Greig de Peuter. *Games of Empire: Global Capitalism and Video Games*. Minneapolis: University of Minnesota Press, 2009.

Edelman, Gerald. *Bright Air, Brilliant Fire: On the Matter of the Mind*. New York: Basic Books, 1992.

Edelman, Gerald. *Second Nature: Brain Science and Human Knowledge*. New Haven: Yale University Press, 2006.

Edelman, Gerald, and Giulio Tononi. *A Universe of Consciousness: How Matter Becomes Imagination*. London: Penguin Books, 2000.

Edkins, Jenny. *Trauma and the Memory of Politics*. Cambridge: Cambridge University Press, 2003.

Ehrenberg, Alain. Le cerveau “social”: Chimère épistémologique et vérité sociologique. *Esprit*, January 2008, 79–103.

Ehrenberg, Alain. Le sujet cérébral. *Esprit*, November 2004, 130–155.

Esposito, Elena. *The Future of Futures: The Time of Money in Financing and Society*. Cheltenham: Edwar Elgar, 2011.

Esposito, Roberto. *Bíos: Biopolitics and Philosophy*. Timothy Campbell, trans. Minneapolis: University of Minnesota Press, 2008.

Esposito, Roberto. *Immunitas: The Protection and Negation of Life*. Zakiya Hanafi, trans. Cambridge: Polity, 2011.

Falk, Emily, et al. Predicting Persuasion-Induced Behavior Change from the Brain. *Journal of Neuroscience* 30, no. 25 (June 2010): 8421–8424.

Farocki, Harun. Cross Influence/Soft Montage. Cynthia Beatt, trans. In *Harun Farocki: Against What? Against Whom?*, ed. Antje Ehmann and Kodwo Eshun, 70–74. London: Koenig Books, 2009.

Farocki, Harun. Influences transversales. Pierre Rusch, trans. *Trafic*, no. 43 (Autumn 2002): 19–24.

Foa, Edna, and Michel Kozak. Emotional Processing of Fear: Exposure to Corrective Information. *Psychological Bulletin* 99, no. 1 (1986): 20–35.

Forster, Kurt. Introduction. In Aby Warburg, *The Renewal of Pagan Antiquity: Contributions to the Cultural History of the European Renaissance*, trans. David Britt, ed. Kurt Forster, 1–75. Los Angeles: Getty Research Institute, 1999.

Foucault, Michel. *The Birth of Biopolitics: Lectures at the Collège de France 1978–1979*. Michel Senellart and Graham Burchell, trans. Michel Senellart, ed. Basingstoke: Palgrave Macmillan, 2010.

Foucault, Michel. The Confessions of the Flesh. In *Power/Knowledge: Selected Interviews and Other Writings, 1972–1977*, trans. Colin Gordon et al., ed. Colin Gordon, 194–228. New York: Pantheon Books, 1980.

Foucault, Michel. *Security, Territory, Population: Lectures at the Collège de France, 1977–1978*. Graham Burchell, trans. Michel Senellart, ed. Basingstoke: Palgrave Macmillan, 2007.

Foucault, Michel. *"Society Must Be Defended": Lectures at the Collège de France, 1975–1976*. David Macey, trans. Mauro Bertani and Alessandro Fontana, eds. London: Penguin, 2004.

Foucault, Michel. *The Will to Knowledge*. Vol. 1 of *The History of Sextuality*. Robert Hurley, trans. London: Penguin, 1998.

Freedberg, David. Empathy, Motion and Emotion. In *Wie sich Gefühle Ausdruck verschaffen: Emotionen in Nachsicht*, ed. Klaus Herding and Antje Krause-Wahl, 17–51. Berlin: Driesen, 2007.

Freedberg, David. *The Power of Images: Studies in the History and Theory of Response*. Chicago: University of Chicago Press, 1989.

Friedberg, Anne. *The Virtual Window: From Alberti to Microsoft*. Cambridge, MA: MIT Press, 2006.

Freud, Sigmund. Introduction to Psycho-Analysis and the War Neuroses. In *The Standard Edition of the Complete Psychological Works of Sigmund Freud*, vol. 17, trans. and ed. James Strachey with Anna Freud, 207–210. London: Vintage, 2001.

Frith, Chris. *Making up the Mind: How the Brain Creates Our Mental World*. Oxford: Blackwell, 2007.

Fuller, Matthew. *Media Ecologies: Materialist Energies in Art and Technoculture*. Cambridge, MA: MIT Press, 2005.

Galloway, Alexander. Are Some Things Unrepresentable? *Theory, Culture and Society* 28, nos. 7–8 (2011): 85–102.

Galloway, Alexander. *Gaming: Essays on Algorithmic Culture*. Minneapolis: University of Minnesota Press, 2006.

Galloway, Alexander. *Protocol: How Control Exists after Decentralization*. Cambridge, MA: MIT Press, 2006.

Geertz, Cliffold. Deep Play: Notes on the Balinese Cockfight. *Daedalus* 134, no. 4 (Fall 2005): 56–86.

Gerardi, Maryrose, et al. Virtual Reality Exposure Therapy Using a Virtual Iraq: A Case Report. *Journal of Traumatic Stress* 21, no. 2 (2008): 209–213.

Gibson, James J. *The Ecological Approach to Visual Perception*. Hillsdale, NJ: Erlbaum, 1986.

Ginsberg, Terri. Bordering on Disaster: Toward an Epistemology of Divided Cinematic Space. *Spectator* 29, no. 1 (Spring 2009): 30–36, cinema.usc.edu/archivedassets/096/15612.pdf.

Grau, Oliver. *Virtual Art: From Illusion to Immersion*. Gloria Custance, trans. Cambridge, MA: MIT Press, 2003.

Gregory, Derek. From a View to Kill: Drones and Late Modern Warfare. *Theory, Culture and Society* 28, nos. 7–8 (2011): 188–215.

Groys, Boris. Comrades of Time. *e-flux*, no. 11 (December 2009). http://www.e-flux.com/journal/comrades-of-time/.

Grusin, Richard. *Premediation: Affect and Mediality after 9/11*. New York: Palgrave Macmillan, 2010.

Hacking, Ian. *Rewriting the Soul: Multiple Personality and the Sciences of Memory*. Princeton: Princeton University Press, 1995.

Han, Doug Hyun, et al. Brain Activity and Desire for Internet Video Game Play. *Comprehensive Psychiatry* 52 (2011): 88–95.

Han, Doug Hyun, et al. Dopamine Genes and Reward Dependence in Adolescents with Excessive Internet Video Game Play. *Journal of Addiction Medicine* 1, no. 3 (2007): 133–138.

Hansen, Mark B. N. *New Philosophy for New Media*. Cambridge, MA: MIT Press, 2004.

Hansen, Miriam Bratu. Room-for-Play: Benjamin's Gamble with Cinema. *October* 109 (Summer 2004): 3–45.

Harvey, David. *A Brief History of Neoliberalism*. Oxford: Oxford University Press, 2005.

Heidegger, Martin. *The Fundamental Concepts of Metaphysics: World, Finitude, Solitude*. William McNeill and Nicholas Walker, trans. Bloomington: Indiana University Press, 1995.

Heidegger, Martin. The Question Concerning Technology. In *Basic Writings*, rev. and exp. ed., ed. David Farrell Krell, 307–342. London: Routledge, 1993.

Herman, Judith. *Trauma and Recovery: The Aftermath of Violence—From Domestic Abuse to Political Terror*. New York: Basic Books, 1997.

Hinds, Andrea, et al. The Psychology of Potential Threat: Properties of the Security Motivation System. *Biological Psychology* 85, no. 2 (2010): 331–337.

Hoeft, Fumiko, et al. Gender Differences in the Mesocorticolimbic System during Computer Game-Play. *Journal of Psychiatric Research* 42 (2008): 253–258.

Hüser, Rembert. Nine Minutes in the Yard: A Conversation with Harun Farocki. In *Harun Farocki: Working on the Sight-Lines*, ed. Thomas Elsaesser, 297–322. Amsterdam: Amsterdam University Press, 2004.

Ingold, Tim. *Being Alive: Essays on Movement, Knowledge and Description*. London: Routledge, 2011.

Jacob, Christian. *The Sovereign Map: Theoretical Approaches in Cartography throughout History*. Tom Conley, trans. Chicago: University of Chicago Press, 2006.

James, William. *The Principles of Psychology*. Vol. 1. New York: Henry Holt, 1910.

Jeannerod, Marc. *Motor Cognition: What Actions Tell the Self*. Oxford: Oxford University Press, 2006.

Kapp, Ernst. *Grundlinien einer Philosophie der Technik: Zur Entstehungsgeschichte der Cultur aus neuen Gesichtspunkt*. Braunschweig: George Westermann, 1877.

Kember, Sarah, and Joanna Zylinska. *Life after New Media: Mediation as a Vital Process*. Cambridge, MA: MIT Press, 2012.

Kessler, Frank. The Cinema of Attractions as Dispositif. In *The Cinema of Attractions Reloaded*, ed. Wanda Strauven, 57–69. Amsterdam: Amsterdam University Press, 2009.

Kilcullen, David. *Counterinsurgency*. Oxford: Oxford University Press, 2010.

Kirkpatrick, Graeme. *Aesthetic Theory and the Video Game*. Manchester: Manchester University Press, 2011.

Koepp, M. J., et al. Evidence for Striatal Dopamine Release during a Video Game. *Nature* 393 (1998): 266–268.

Kracauer, Siegfried. *The Mass Ornament: Weimar Essays*. Thomas Y. Levin, trans. and ed. Cambridge, MA: Harvard University Press, 1995.

Lazzarato, Maurizio. *La fabrique de l'homme endetté: Essai sur la condition néolibérale*. Paris: Editions Amsterdam, 2011.

LeDoux, Joseph. *The Emotional Brain: The Mysterious Underpinnings of Emotional Life.* London: Phoenix, 1999.

LeDoux, Joseph. *Synaptic Self: How Our Brains Become Who We Are.* New York: Viking Penguin, 2002.

Lenoir, Tim. All but War Is Simulation: The Military-Entertainment Complex. *Configurations* 8, no. 3 (2000): 289–335.

Leroi-Gourhan, André. *Gesture and Speech.* Anna Bostock Berger, trans. Cambridge, MA: MIT Press, 1993.

Leys, Ruth. *Trauma: A Genealogy.* Chicago: University of Chicago Press, 2000.

Llinás, Rodolfo. *I of the Vortex: From Neurons to Self.* Cambridge, MA: MIT Press, 2001.

Llinás, Rodolfo, and Sisir Roy. The "Prediction Imperative" as the Basis of Self-Awareness. *Philosophical Transactions of the Royal Society B* 364, no. 1515 (2009): 1301–1307.

Losh, Elizabeth. A Battle for Hearts and Minds: The Design Politics of ELECT BiLAT. In *Joystick Soldiers: The Politics of Play in Military Video Games,* ed. Nina B. Huntemann and Matthew Thomas Payne, 160–177. New York: Routledge, 2010.

MacLean, Paul. *The Triune Brain in Evolution: Role in Paleocerebral Functions.* New York: Plenum, 1990.

Malabou, Catherine. *Les nouveaux blessés: De Freud à la neurologie, penser les traumatismes contemporains.* Paris: Bayard, 2007.

Malabou, Catherine. *What Should We Do with Our Brain?* Sebastian Rand, trans. New York: Fordham University Press, 2008.

Malaby, Thomas. Beyond Play: A New Approach to Games. *Games and Culture* 2, no. 2 (2007): 95–113.

Margulis, Lynn, and Dorion Sagan. *What Is Life?* Berkeley and Los Angeles: University of California Press, 1995.

Marks, Laura U. *Enfoldment and Infinity: An Islamic Genealogy of New Media Art.* Cambridge, MA: MIT Press, 2010.

Martin, Randy. *An Empire of Indifference: American War and the Financial Logic of Risk Management.* Durham: Duke University Press, 2007.

Martin, Randy. From the Race War to the War on Terror. In *Beyond Biopolitics: Essays on the Governance of Life and Death,* ed. Patricia Ticineto Clough and Craig Willse, 258–274. Durham: Duke University Press, 2011.

Massumi, Brian. The Future Birth of the Affective Fact: The Political Ontology of Threat. In *The Affect Theory Reader*, ed. Melissa Gregg and Gregory J. Seigworth, 52–70. Durham: Duke University Press, 2010.

Massumi, Brian. National Enterprise Economy: Steps Toward an Ecology of Powers. *Theory, Culture and Society* 26, no. 6 (2009): 153–185.

Massumi, Brian. Perception Attack: Brief on War Time. *Theory and Event* 13, no. 3 (2010). http://muse.jhu.edu/journals/theory_and_event/summary/v013/13.3.massumi.html.

Massumi, Brian. Potential Politics and the Primacy of Preemption. *Theory and Event* 10, no. 2 (2007). http://muse.jhu.edu/login?auth=0&type=summary&url=/journals/theory_and_event/v010/10.2massumi.html.

Mathiak, Klaus, and René Weber. Toward Brain Correlates of Natural Behavior: fMRI during Violent Video Games. *Human Brain Mapping* 27 (2006): 948–956.

Mbembe, Achille. Necropolitics. Libby Meintjes, trans. *Public Culture* 15, no. 1 (2003): 11–40.

McLaughlin, Kevin. Ur-Ability: Force and Image from Kant to Benjamin. In *Releasing the Image: From Literature to New Media*, ed. Jacques Khalip and Robert Mitchell, 204–221. Stanford: Stanford University Press, 2011.

Mirzoeff, Nicholas. *The Right to Look: A Counterhistory of Visuality*. Durham: Duke University Press, 2011.

Mitchell, W. J. T. *Cloning Terror: The War of Images, 9/11 to the Present*. Chicago: University of Chicago Press, 2011.

Mitchell, W. J. T. *What Do Pictures Want? The Lives and Loves of Images*. Chicago: University of Chicago Press, 2005.

Modell, Arnold H. *Imagination and the Meaningful Brain*. Cambridge, MA: MIT Press, 2006.

Mondloch, Kate. *Screens: Viewing Media Installation Art*. Minneapolis: University of Minnesota Press, 2010.

Mondzain, Marie-José. *Image, Icon, Economy: The Byzantine Origins of the Contemporary Imaginary*. Rico Franses, trans. Stanford: Stanford University Press, 2005.

Montag, Christian, et al. Does Excessive Play of Violent First-Person-Shooter-Video-Games Dampen Brain Activity in Response to Emotional Stimuli? *Biological Psychology* 89, no. 1 (2012): 107–111.

Muckenfuss, Mark. Military Studies Virtual Reality as Therapy for Post Traumatic Stress Disorder. *Press-Enterprise*, May 9, 2008. http://www.virtuallybetter.com/wp-content/uploads/2012/05/Virtual-reality-article-Johnston.pdf.

Nakashima, Ellen, and Craig Whitlock. With Air Force's Gorgon Drone "We Can See Everything." *Washington Post*, January 2, 2011. http://www.washingtonpost.com/wp-dyn/content/article/2011/01/01/AR2011010102690.html.

Neidich, Warren. From Noopower to Neuropower: How Mind Becomes Matter. In *Cognitive Architecture: From Biopolitics to Noopolitics; Architecture and Mind in the Age of Communication and and Information*, ed. Deborah Hauptmann and Warren Neidich, 538–581. Rotterdam: 010 Publishers, 2010.

Nest, Michael. *Coltan*. Cambridge: Polity, 2011.

Nevins, Joseph. Dying for a Cup of Coffee? Migrant Deaths in the U.S.-Mexico Border Region in a Neoliberal Age. *Geopolitics* 12, no. 2 (2007): 228–247.

Nevins, Joseph. *Operation Gatekeeper: The Rise of the "Illegal Alien" and the Making of the U.S.-Mexico Boundary*. New York: Routledge, 2002.

Noë, Alva. *Action in Perception*. Cambridge, MA: MIT Press, 2006.

Ó Síocháin, Séamas, and Michael O'Sullivan. General Introduction. In *The Eyes of Another Race: Roger Casement's Congo Report and 1903 Diary*, ed. Séamas Ó Siocháin and Michael O'Sullivan, 1–44. Dublin: University College of Dublin Press, 2003.

Panagia, David. *The Political Life of Sensation*. Durham: Duke University Press, 2009.

Panksepp, Jaak. *Affective Neuroscience: The Foundations of Human and Animal Emotions*. Oxford: Oxford University Press, 1998.

Parikka, Jussi. *Insect Media: An Archaeology of Animals and Technology*. Minneapolis: University of Minnesota Press, 2010.

Parsons, Thomas, and Albert Rizzo. Affective Outcomes of Virtual Reality Exposure Therapy for Anxiety and Specific Phobias: A Meta-Analysis. *Journal of Behavior Therapy and Experimental Psychiatry* 39 (2008): 250–261.

Pfaff, Donald. *Brain Arousal and Information Theory: Neural and Genetic Mechanisms*. Cambridge, MA: Harvard University Press, 2006.

Pias, Claus. The Game Player's Duty: The User as the Gestalt of the Ports. In *Media Archaeology: Approaches, Applications, and Implications*, ed. Erkki Huhtamo and Jussi Parikka, 164–183. Berkeley and Los Angeles: University of California Press, 2011.

Pilkington, Ed. U.S. Immigration Deal Envisages Use of Military Surveillance at Southern Border. *Guardian*, June 25, 2013. http://www.guardian.co.uk/world/2013/jun/25/us-immigration-amendment-surveillance?INTCMP=SRCH.

Pisters, Patricia. *The Neuro-Image: A Deleuzian Film-Philosophy of Digital Screen Culture*. Stanford: Stanford University Press, 2012.

Protevi, John. *Political Affect: Connecting the Social and the Somatic*. Minneapolis: University of Minnesota Press, 2009.

Ramachandran, Vilayanur S. Preface. In *Encyclopedia of the Human Brain*, vol. 1, ed. Vilayanur S. Ramachandran, xxxv. San Diego: Academic Press, 2002.

Ramachandran, Vilayanur S., and Sandra Blakeslee. *Phantoms in the Brain: Human Nature and the Architecture of the Mind*. London: Harper Perennial, 2005.

Rancière, Jacques. *Disagreement: Politics and Philosophy*. Julie Rose, trans. Minneapolis: University of Minnesota Press, 1999.

Rancière, Jacques. *Dissensus: On Politics and Aesthetics*. Steven Corcoran, trans. and ed. London: Continuum, 2010.

Rancière, Jacques. *The Emancipated Spectator*. Gregory Elliott, trans. London: Verso, 2009.

Rancière, Jacques. *The Future of the Image*. Gregory Elliott, trans. London: Verso, 2009.

Rancière, Jacques. *The Philosopher and His Poor*. John, Drury, Corinne Oster, and Andrew Parker, trans. Andrew Parker, ed. Durham: Duke University Press, 2003.

Rancière, Jacques. *The Politics of Aesthetics*. Gabriel Rockhill, trans. London: Continuum, 2006.

Rao, Rajnish, et al. PTSD: From Neurons to Networks. In *Post-Traumatic Stress Disorder: Basic Science and Clinical Practice*, ed. Priyattam Shiromani, Terence Keane, and Joseph LeDoux, 151–184. New York: Humana Press, 2009.

Ribot, Théodule. *Diseases of Memory: An Essay in Positive Psychology*. William Huntington Smith, trans. New York: D. Appleton, 1887.

Richter, Gerhard. Miniatures: Harun Farocki and the Cinematic Non-Event. *Journal of Visual Culture* 3, no. 3 (2004): 367–371.

Rizzo, Albert, et al. A Virtual Reality Exposure Therapy Application for Iraq War Military Personnel with Post Traumatic Stress Disorder: From Training to Toy to Treatment. In *Novel Approaches to the Diagnosis and Treatment of Posttraumatic Stress Disorder*, ed. Michael Roy, 235–250. Amsterdam: IOS Press, 2006.

Roberts, Morley. *Biopolitics: An Essay on the Physiology, Pathology and Politics of Social and Somatic Organisms*. London: Dent, 1938.

Rodowick, David. *The Virtual Life of Film*. Cambridge, MA: Harvard University Press, 2007.

Roper, Daniel S. Global Counterinsurgency: Strategic Clarity for the Long War. *Parameters* 38, no. 3 (Autumn 2008): 98–108.

Rose, Nikolas. *The Politics of Life Itself: Biomedicine, Power, and Subjectivity in the Twenty-First Century*. Princeton: Princeton University Press, 2007.

Rose, Nikolas. "Screen and Intervene": Governing Risky Brains. *History of the Human Sciences* 23, no. 1 (2010): 79–105.

Rose, Nikolas, and Joelle M. Abi-Rached. *Neuro: The New Brain Sciences and the Management of Mind*. Princeton: Princeton University Press, 2013.

Roskies, Adina L. Are Neuroimages like Photographs of the Brain. *Philosophy of Science* 74, no. 5 (2007): 860–872.

Ross, Christine. The Suspension of History in Contemporary Media Arts. *Intermédialités: Histoire et Théorie des Arts, des Lettres et des Techniques/Intermediality: History and Theory of the Arts, Literature and Technology*, no. 11 (Spring 2008): 125–148.

Rotman, Brian. *Becoming beside Ourselves: The Alphabet, Ghosts, and Distributed Human Being*. Durham: Duke University Press, 2008.

Rubin, Beatrix. Changing Brains: The Emergence of the Field of Adult Neurogenesis. *Biosocieties* 4, no. 4 (2009): 407–424.

Sartre, Jean-Paul. *L'Imagination*. Paris: P.U.F., 1965.

Shaviro, Steven. Post-Cinematic Affect: On Grace Jones, *Boarding Gate* and *Southland Tales*. *Film Philosophy* 14, no. 1 (2010). http://www.film-philosophy.com/index.php/f-p/article/view/220/173.

Shaviro, Steven. *Without Criteria: Kant, Whitehead, Deleuze, and Aesthetics*. Cambridge, MA: MIT Press, 2009.

Shaw, Ian G. R., and Barney Warf. Worlds of Affect: Virtual Geographies of Video Games. *Environment and Planning A* 41, no. 6 (2009): 1332–1343.

Simmel, Ernst. Untitled contribution no. 3 to Symposium Held at the Fifth International Psycho-Analytical Congress in Budapest, September, 1918. In Sándor Ferenczi et al., *Psycho-Analysis and the War Neuroses*, 30–43. London: International Psycho-Analytical Press, 1921.

Simondon, Gilbert. *Imagination et invention: 1965–1966*. Nathalie Simondon, ed. Chatou: Les Editions de la Transparence, 2008.

Smicker, Joseph. Future Combat, Combating Futures: Temporalities of War Video Games and the Performance of Proleptic Histories. In *Joystick Soldiers: The Politics of Play in Military Video Games*, ed. Nina B. Huntemann and Matthew Thomas Payne, 106–121. New York: Routledge, 2010.

Sobchack, Vivian. *Carnal Thoughts: Embodiment and Moving Image Culture*. Berkeley and Los Angeles: University of California Press, 2004.

Spielmann, Yvonne. *Video: The Reflexive Medium*. Robert Welle and Stan Jones, trans. Cambridge, MA: MIT Press, 2008.

Spira, James, et al. Virtual Reality and Other Experiential Therapies for Combat-Related Posttraumatic Stress Disorder. *Primary Psychiatry* 13, no. 3 (2006): 43–49.

Stafford, Barbara Maria. Crystal and Smoke: Putting Image Back in Mind. In *A Field Guide to a New Meta-Field: Bridging the Humanities-Neuroscience Divide*, ed. Barbara Maria Stafford, 1–63. Chicago: University of Chicago Press, 2011.

Stafford, Barbara Maria. *Echo Objects: The Cognitive Work of Images*. Chicago: University of Chicago Press, 2007.

Stafford, Barbara Maria. *Visual Analogy: Consciousness as the Art of Connecting*. Cambridge, MA: MIT Press, 2001.

Stern, Daniel. *Forms of Vitality: Exploring Dynamic Experience in Psychology, the Arts, Psychotherapy, and Development*. Oxford: Oxford University Press, 2010.

Stiegler, Bernard. *Technics and Time 1: The Fault of Epimetheus*. Richard Beardsworth and George Collins, trans. Stanford: Stanford University Press, 1998.

Stuart, Keith, and Mark Sweney. Modern Warfare 3 Hits the $1bn Mark in Record Time. *Guardian*, December 13, 2011. www.theguardian.com/technology/2011/dec/12/modern-warfare-3-breaks-1bn-barrier.

Sutliff, Usha. VR Will Treat Stress in Iraq War Vets. *USC News*, March 8, 2005. http://www.usc.edu/uscnews/stories/11070.html.

Sutton-Smith, Brian. *The Ambiguity of Play*. Cambridge, MA: Harvard University Press, 2001.

Tauber, Alfred. *The Immune Self: Theory or Metaphor?* Cambridge: Cambridge University Press, 1994.

Trodd, Tamara. Introduction: Theorising the Projected Image. In *Screen/Space: The Projected Image in Contemporary Art*, ed. Tamara Trodd, 1–22. Manchester: Manchester University Press, 2011.

Ullman, Harlan, and James Wade Jr. *Shock and Awe: Achieving Rapid Dominance*. Washington, DC: National Defense University, 1996.

U.S. Department of the Army. *Counterinsurgency*, Field Manual no. 3-24; Marine Corps Warfighting Publication no. 3-33.5. Washington, DC: Headquarters, Department of the Army, 2006. www.fas.org/irp/doddir/army/fm3-24.pdf.

Väliaho, Pasi. *Mapping the Moving Image: Gesture, Thought and Cinema circa 1900*. Amsterdam: Amsterdam University Press, 2010.

van der Kolk, Bessel. The Body Keeps the Score: Approaches to the Psychobiology of Postraumatic Stress Disorder. In *Traumatic Stress: The Effects of Overwhelming*

Experience on Mind, Body, and Society, ed. Bessel van der Kolk, Alexander McFarlane, and Lars Weisaelth, 214–241. New York: Guilford Press, 1996.

van der Kolk, Bessel. Clinical Implications of Neuroscience Research in PTSD. *Annals of the New York Academy of Sciences* 1071, no. 1 (2006): 277–293.

van der Kolk, Bessel. Trauma and Memory. In *Traumatic Stress: The Effects of Overwhelming Experience on Mind, Body, and Society*, ed. Bessel van der Kolk, Alexander McFarlane, and Lars Weisaelth, 279–302. New York: Guilford Press, 1996.

van der Kolk, Bessel, and Alexander McFarlane. The Black Hole of Trauma. In *Traumatic Stress: The Effects of Overwhelming Experience on Mind, Body, and Society*, ed. Bessel van der Kolk, Alexander McFarlane, and Lars Weisaelth, 3–23. New York: Guilford Press, 1996.

van der Kolk, Bessel, Alexander McFarlane, and Lars Weisaelth, eds. *Traumatic Stress: The Effects of Overwhelming Experience on Mind, Body, and Society*. New York: Guilford Press, 1996.

Vidal, Fernando. Brainhood: Anthropological Figure of Modernity. *History of the Human Sciences* 22, no. 1 (2009): 5–36.

Virilio, Paul. *The Vision Machine*. Julie Rose, trans. Bloomington: Indiana University Press, 1994.

Vogl, Joseph. Taming Time: Media of Financialization. Christophe Reid, trans. *Grey Room* 46 (Winter 2012): 72–83.

Warburg, Aby. *Images from the Region of the Pueblo Indians of North America*. Michael P. Steinberg, trans. Ithaca: Cornell University Press, 1995.

Warburg, Aby. Memories of a Journey through the Pueblo Region. In Philippe-Alain Michaud, *Aby Warburg and the Image in Motion*, trans. Sophie Hawkes, 293–330. New York: Zone Books, 2004.

Weizman, Eyal. Thanato-Tactics. In *Beyond Biopolitics: Essays on the Governance of Life and Death*, ed. Patricia Ticineto Clough and Craig Willse, 177–210. Durham: Duke University Press, 2011.

Whitehead, Alfred North. *Adventures of Ideas*. New York: Free Press, 1967.

Whitehead, Alfred North. *Modes of Thought*. New York: Free Press, 1968.

Wiederhold, Brenda, and Mark Wiederhold. Lessons Learned from 600 Virtual Reality Sessions. *Cyberpsychology and Behavior* 3, no. 3 (2000): 393–400.

Wiederhold, Brenda, and Mark Wiederhold. Virtual Reality for Posttraumatic Stress Disorder and Stress Inoculation Training. *Journal of CyberTherapy and Rehabilitation* 1, no. 1 (2008): 23–35.

Wilson, Elizabeth. *Psychosomatic: Feminism and the Neurological Body*. Durham: Duke University Press, 2004.

Wolin, Sheldon. *Democracy Incorporated: Managed Democracy and the Specter of Inverted Totalitarianism*. Princeton: Princeton University Press, 2008.

Wood, Dennis, Brenda Wiederhold, and James Spira. Lessons Learned from 350 Virtual-Reality Sessions with Warriors Diagnosed with Combat-Related Posttraumatic Stress Disorder. *Cyberpsychology, Behavior, and Social Networking* 13, no. 1 (2010): 3–11.

Woody, Erik, and Henry Szechtman. Adaptation to Potential Threat: The Evolution, Neurobiology, and Psychopathology of the Security Motivation System. *Neuroscience and Biobehavioral Reviews* 35, no. 4 (2011): 1019–1033.

Young, Allan. Bodily Memory and Traumatic Memory. In *Tense Past: Cultural Essays in Trauma and Memory*, ed. Paul Antze and Michael Lambek, 89–102. New York: Routledge, 1996.

Young, Allan. *The Harmony of Illusions: Inventing Post-Traumatic Stress Disorder*. Princeton: Princeton University Press, 1995.

Young, Allan. History, Hystery and Psychiatric Styles of Reasoning. In *Living and Working with the New Medical Technologies: Intersections of Inquiry*, ed. Margaret Lock, Allan Young, and Alberto Cambrosio, 135–164. Cambridge: Cambridge University Press, 2000.

Index

Note: Page numbers in italics refer to figures.